FOOD LOVERS' SERIES

# FOOD LOVERS'
## GUIDE TO®
# PORTLAND, OREGON

The Best Restaurants, Markets
& Local Culinary Offerings

1st Edition

**Laurie Wolf**

Guilford, Connecticut

Copyright © 2014 by Morris Book Publishing, LLC

Food Lovers' Guide to® is a registered trademark of Morris Book Publishing, LLC

Editor: Amy Lyons
Project Editor: Lauren Brancato
Layout Artist: Mary Ballachino
Text Design: Sheryl Kober
Illustrations by Jill Butler with additional art by Carleen Moira Powell and MaryAnn Dubé
Maps: Trailhead Graphics Inc. © Morris Book Publishing, LLC

ISBN 978-0-7627-9213-9

Printed in the United States of America
10 9 8 7 6 5 4 3 2 1

All the information in this guidebook is subject to change. We recommend that you call ahead to obtain current information before traveling.

I have written a bunch of books now and love writing this part. I have a small family and lots of close friends who feel like family. Everyone will be thanked for their part in keeping me part of their lives and encouraging me to do what it is I do.

I am, however, going to dedicate this book to my sister-in-law and brother: Geri and Fred Goldrich. They live across the country, near the other Portland, and they are always there for me, have been for years, at all hours with words of wisdom, love, and support. Geri is kind, smart, and an easy laugh, and my brother was there with me as we became who we were meant to be, the good and the bad, and the shared history is invaluable and wonderful. Thanks, I needed that.

Also to Portland, for being my perfect home.

# Contents

# Recipes, 181

# Appendices, 227

## Index, 256

# About the Author

**Laurie Wolf** is a food writer and recipe developer, skills she began to develop at the Culinary Institute of America. She has been food editor at two national magazines and has written several cookbooks and craft books. Laurie has been a food stylist and has taught cooking throughout her career. Currently writing stories and recipes for Oregon Public Broadcasting, Laurie is thrilled to be part of the vibrant Portland, Oregon, food scene.

# Acknowledgments

Once again I have so many folks to thank for this totally enjoyable project. My editor Amy Lyons is a pleasure, always upbeat and encouraging, and I love her loving to hear and read about this food fabulous city. And she was amazing around Memorial Day, when I needed her most.

Special thanks to Ellis Mendon, college student and food blogger, who was invaluable with her "Eugene" connection and her deep appreciation and understanding of the Oregon food bounty. To Forrest Parker, who could be a great chef someday, for his help in finding some damn good eats in this town that were on and off the beaten path. I get texts from him about burgers and fries, and he is always right on. He knows his stuff. Always willing to help, Ellis and Forrest were invaluable. To Lucy Parkin, who organized and formatted me way beyond my capabilities with a smile on her face and a couple of bulldogs by her side. My students from my "Food for Thought" class, whom I watched get totally turned on to this whole cooking thing. Taylor Penner-Ash was the best T.A. a food lover/teacher could have; she was a delightful presence in the class, with mad cooking and copying skills! To the staff at Riverdale High School, who welcomed me with advice on how to handle hordes of teenagers and how to get in to see Michael Murray, thank you from the bottom of my heart. Paula, Sue, Sam, Michael, and Betsy, you helped me feel so good being there. Jill, Hilary, and Jody—lots of laughs. Jeff Brown and PB, who gave me some great food and wine tips, and Santha who set the bar quite high before me. Gary and Mark, your humor and conversation were a joy. To Carole and Ed for coming all the way from Chicago just for my book signing and for telling me about Mean Street Pizza.

At long last I would like to give thanks to Rachel Litner from Rachel Litner Associates and Mary Rogers at Cuisinart, who have allowed me the opportunity to use all of the high-quality appliances that Cuisinart has to offer. With over 25 years of recipe testing and development I have had the best to work with, and I am deeply indebted.

To the lovely ladies at *Diane Magazine*, for being such pleasures to work with; Claire, Denise, and Sandy, you are the best. Karen Cicero, who for years has been an incredible source of knowledge and employment. We weathered many storms together. To Ellen and Kayo at OPB for the opportunity.

To Steve Flood and Kate for helping to make our dream come true, and to the Parkins, Pratts, Fuscos, Sanders, Micks, Penner Ashes, Mendons, Nichols, and the "girls"; it is all much more fun when you do it with friends. My version of friends with benefits! To Michele Jordan, who gave me some seriously needed words. And to the Jays, the most perfect dining companions. I always get to finish what Janet orders to eat and drink!

And to my family. To my kids, Nick and Olivia, who have all these years put up with some rather strange goings-on. Ours was not the typical household, and they somehow managed to turn out pretty accomplished and lovely. Love to Mary for joining our clan. To Aunt Mousie and Freddi and David, you are always in my heart. And to Bruce . . . what a long, strange (and mostly wonderful) trip it's been. To Eliot, a recent addition to our "family," you are just the cutest. Aaron and JJ, awesome production.

# Introduction

Although Portland is casual, very casual, this does not mean to suggest that the food here is not to be taken seriously. From the farmers to the servers, food is a passionate business. As a rule, I don't find the food here pretentious or forced, which is refreshing. Many restaurants are packed for breakfast, lunch, and dinner. Given the state of the economy, it seems that eating good, high-quality food is a Portland passion. Some of the very best places in town take no reservations, and rain or shine, there are lines of hungry people waiting to get down to it.

Last summer, I was having a coffee and a piece of something delicious at Crema bakery, in the Eastburn Portland neighborhood. I watched as a man walked out of his very cool apartment building in a tasteful bathrobe and made his way to a grilled cheese cart I will talk about later. He walked over, placed his order, and sipped coffee from his mug from upstairs. He got his bag of goodies and went home. And only I blinked. Though not the norm, this was not that surprising. With a city that holds naked bike rides and the occasional body part competition, little makes a Portlander blink or look  twice. When I see someone in a suit, I think something very serious, possibly a funeral, or a costume party, must be going on.

Food is undoubtedly popular here. Everyone loves to talk about food: where they eat, where they shop, and what they cook. In many markets, be prepared to discuss what you have in mind for the groceries

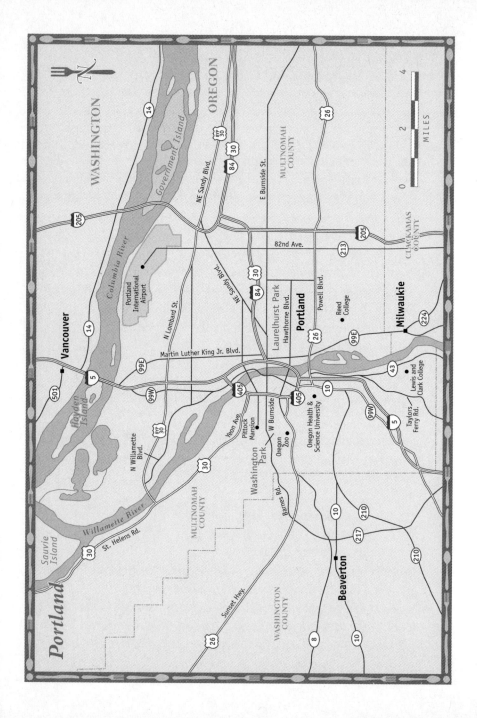

Portland

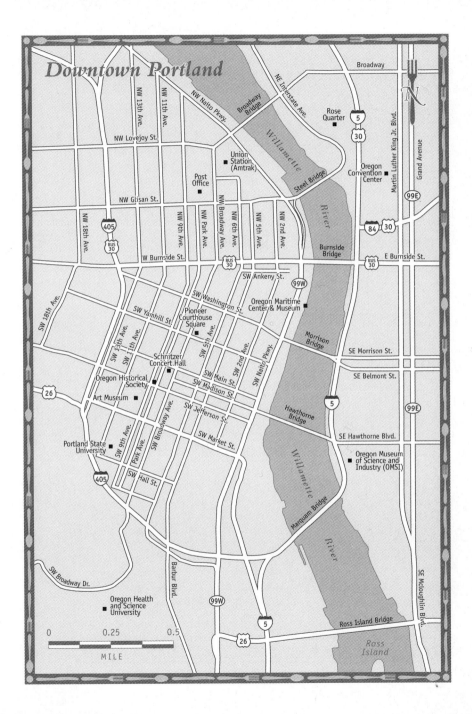

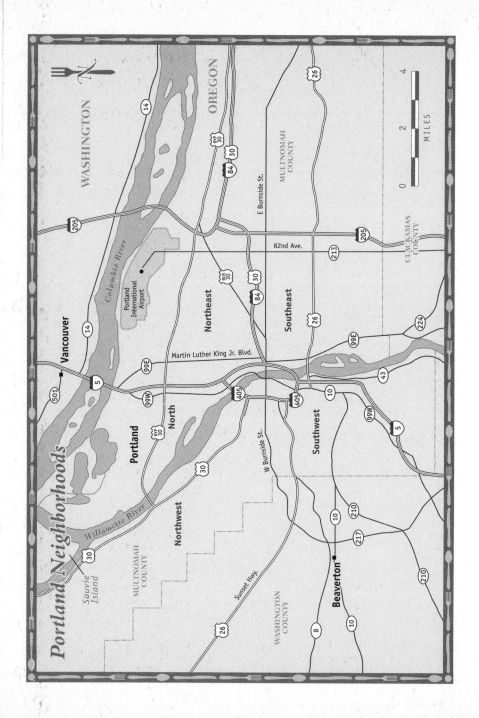

*Portland Neighborhoods*

in your cart. You may very well be asked. I love when people ask me, and have gotten some worthwhile suggestions from people in line or at the register. I have lived in a bunch of cities, but this, aside from NYC, is the best food lover's town. And a coffee- and beer-loving town as well.

As I will mention throughout the book, it rains here a lot. And for sure it can be annoying, even depressing for some. There is, however, a benefit to the plethora of rain. The abundance of fruits and vegetables that grow here is spectacular. When you walk into New Seasons or Barbur World Foods and see fresh olives and dates, or seven kinds of potatoes, it makes the weather seem less bothersome. At least for me. And things start to bloom early. By the end of March there will be camellias in bloom, shortly followed by the lilacs and lots of incredibly beautiful native plants and flowers. On my first trip to Portland, I remember sitting with my friend Janet in the courtyard of her house. I was drinking my first Stumptown coffee and we were eating crumb cake from Baker and Spice. The air smelled like earth. It was sunny one minute and raining the next, but I felt like I was sitting in a place that was good for my soul. And stomach.

I am guessing that it will come as no surprise that people are not coming to Portland in droves because of the weather! There are two seasons here, wet and dry. And although the summers are glorious with low humidity and temperate climate, the gray, rainy winters can be a little tough to take. Soon after arriving here I was told that an old nickname of Portland was "The Gray Lady of the Willamette." That gave me pause. If people have the means, they try to get to some sunshine in the winter months, or they get light boxes, or they do what I do, and when it rains remember that the showers do bring fruit and vegetables that make Portland the phenomenal food city that it is.

When going to one of the super food stores or farmers' markets you can spend hours talking about everyone's plans for the goodies in their recycled bags. When the morels are in season it seems like people camp out the night before to get first dibs. Dungeness crab right from the ocean makes for a great adventure, from the crabbing to the eating. And it is delicious. Several months ago our friends Kristen and Lesley brought us a bucketful. We had crab cakes, crab Louis, and an unbelievable omelet with crab, cream cheese, and scallions.

People go foraging for mushroom varietals and truffles. Both black and white are there for the raking. I feel compelled to say that if you have had a white truffle shaved on your *pici* in Tuscany, you should not get your hopes up. But if you have not had that moment of sheer ecstasy, you will be fine. 'Cuz they are fine. And fun. More fun than fine, to be honest. That said, Jack Czarnowski has created fantastic truffle oil, which is for sale at oregontruffleoil.com. And I will share with my readers some spots to get you some damn good truffle fries.

Portland is the best place I have ever lived. Although there is certainly some truth in the *Portlandia* picture of this town, it is, for me, just about perfect. I can see that this city could drive some people crazy. It would be tough on type-A personalities. PDX (its hip, informal nickname) is far too laid-back and sort of slow moving for someone who thrives on the fast-paced race to climb the ladder. Unless it is a real ladder, and in that case you could see some action. There is a ladder to success here, but I would say that the rungs measure quality of life, not the money in your bank account. It's easy to get stuff done, the day-to-day stuff we all have to do. Going to the DMV, getting cable, getting in to see your doctor—none of that is awful.

At least for me there have been none of those days. If I get grouchy because it has taken me 20 minutes to get home, instead of 10, I remind myself of driving the 40 miles from my office in Manhattan to my house in Westchester, which could occasionally take 2 hours. Don't get me wrong, New York is a great city, but for me Portland is a perfect fit. I feel so lucky to live here.

## Dining around Town

There are over 95 officially named neighborhoods in Portland, each with its own unique character and appeal. I have divided the city into its five distinct geographical locations, not an uncommon way to navigate PDX. The Willamette River runs through Portland, which delineates between the east and west. It's a pretty easy city to get around, and as the population grows, more neighborhoods are developing, and it seems as though new restaurants open daily.

Food carts, coffee shops, and bars are popping up and extending neighborhoods or starting to bring folks in to parts of town that had had no commercial businesses that would attract people from other 'hoods. If you have a car, parking is generally pretty easy, mass transit rocks, and of course bikes are huge. I can remember on one of my first visits to PDX, 7 years ago, having lunch with my bff Janet in the virtually unvisited Alberta neighborhood. We had lunch at the Tin Shed and there were just a couple of shops we visited. Now the street is populated with some of the best shopping and eating in Portland. Go figure! And it's happening in lots of other parts of town. I think it's good and it's bad, but this is neither the time nor the place to get involved in a sociological study. For me, as the city rapidly changes, it remains the perfect city. It fits me like a glove. If only I had put it on sooner.

## How to Use This Book

Since Portland has over 95 "neighborhoods," I think, it's impossible to list each restaurant or cart this way. One person says "Buckman," the other calls it "Belmont." I asked someone where Kenton ended and St. John's began, no clue. For ease and simplicity, I have divided the book into five main chapters covering each of the geographical locations, Northwest, North, Northeast, Southeast, and Southwest, with an extra chapter covering worthy restaurants within 3 hours of Portland. For Portlanders this will be easy, and for food-loving visitors, you will make your way around the city using the most easily navigated descriptions. Everything west is on the business side of the city, where the offices and mainstream cultural happenings are. The east side in large part would be considered more alternative, many areas less expensive and young, though there are some lovely and pricey neighborhoods on the east side as well. And don't get me wrong, the alternative neighborhoods are awesome. If I were younger, I would most certainly live in one. And get some more tattoos!

One thing to keep in mind when using this book is that due to the focus on all things local and seasonal, menus will change, sometimes daily, and you may not be fond of any of the menu items listed available when you visit. There will not be asparagus if it is not in season; it will be beets or peas instead, and it will be fresh. If you want to have wild mushrooms, come during mushroom season, or you will be disappointed. I suggest that if you live in Portland, you keep this book in your car or your bike basket. You never know when you will need a cheap bite to eat or a stellar cup of coffee. Going to a party and need to bring a great selection of cheese? Use the book. Or bring it as a gift. In fact, everyone who reads this book should buy at least 500 copies. In case you lose them or something. Just saying.

Sadly I have noticed that Portland food prices are rising. That happens and I get it; products are top-notch and some restaurants shop at the farmers' market. It's more about new places opening and charging more for the same food. Maybe a little fancier, but essentially the same. There are still lots of amazing, extremely well-priced, and fair places, but I do see a trend to a general price increase in some of the newer places. This is not a city where everyone has deep pockets, but people do love their food. I think that as these new and pricier places open there will be more business for the carts and lower-priced dining.

There are many more restaurants than I have described here. Driving around Portland, I pass places all the time, some new ones, some I may have just never noticed before. Same with bars, coffee shops, and carts. It does seem like there are things opening up daily. And I am sure I have missed some pretty special places. After the book comes out, I will give it a Facebook page. Please write and tell me what I missed, just so I know and for the next edition!

The book has many other chapters, sections, and spotlights. You will find information on local websites, farmers' markets, specialty shops and markets, food-related not-for-profits, food festivals, and a recipe section—a combination of food and drinks from Portland restaurants and bars and some seasonal recipes I have developed for Oregon Public Broadcasting, or OPB—to name a few. Here are some of the categories covered under the main chapters:

### Foodie Faves

These eateries range from hole-in-the-wall joints to the city's best restaurants, places where the food is good and the backstory is often better.

### Specialty Stores, Markets & Producers

Here you'll find our favorite indie food boutiques and coffeehouses, as well as bakeries, ice cream shops, and kitchen stores.

## Price Guide Based on Average Meal

$      You can have a full meal for $10 or less here.

$$      Economical selections from $10 to $25 per person.

$$$      Moderately priced at $25 to $50 per person (a meal equivalent to an appetizer, entree selection, and one alcoholic beverage).

$$$$      Expect to spend $50 to $75 for one appetizer, one entree, and a glass or two of wine.

$$$$$      You will not walk out of this establishment having spent less than $75 to $100 per person; the sky's the limit.

# Getting Around

Rain or even snow, Portlanders hit the roads on their bikes in impressive numbers. I see hills that I think my old car won't go up, and there they go, backpacks, lunch, a water bottle, and a baby or two, perhaps breast feeding, and they are on their way. It's pretty remarkable. Shortly after moving to Portland, we watched a teenage girl, with a very heavy-looking backpack unicycling up a very steep hill. It was awesome. And so Portland.

TriMet provides bus, light rail, and commuter rail service in the Portland metro area. Because Portlanders are so focused on quality of life, including reducing air pollution and easing traffic congestion, the public transportation system makes getting around town quite easy and very reasonable. Many Portlanders live here largely for the casual and relatively easy lifestyle, and decisions are made that often benefit the communities rather than big business or grand profit. In 1974, residents of Southeast Portland rejected a proposed eight-lane freeway that would have destroyed many neighborhoods, and officials decided to put the money toward transit instead. At a time when pavement and parking lots were measures of a city's growth, this was a pioneering decision that marked a new way of thinking about how transportation affects our lives. By the late 1970s the Portland region was embracing the idea of linking land use and transportation to help manage growth and maintain livability. And Portland is a very livable city.

And Portlanders love their city. There is an almost obsessive drive to keep it green, clean, and weird! Just read the bumper sticker on the car in front of you.

# Food Fairs, Festivals & Events

**Bite of Oregon, biteoforegon.com.** The Bite of Oregon is a celebration of the state: its food, its people, and its extraordinary quality of life. It is a giant summer party on the Portland waterfront, and people discover why Portland has earned the reputation as one of the best foodie destinations in the country. I swore I wouldn't say "foodie." Oh well. This event is an opportunity to sample foods from restaurants, carts, wine, and beer, all for a low price. There are food competitions and demos by some well-known chefs around town. The event is held downtown, and it is a great time to party with other food- and drink-loving Oregonians and visitors.

**Bites for Rights, bitesforrights.com.** The 12th annual Bites for Rights event promises to be a good time. For more than 11 years, eateries in PDX and throughout the state have been supporting the work of Basic Rights Oregon through the Bites for Rights fund-raising event. This event is for the LGBT community, which has a strong presence in Portland. For only one fabulous day, equality-loving restaurants, coffee shops, bakeries, and bars donate a percentage of their proceeds to this organization. Bites for Rights has grown in size and scope since its first year. Since its inception, this event has raised almost $200,000 to support the work of Basic Rights Oregon. By dining out on a date in late June, you get to support Oregon's growing movement for equality. Dine out all day long—breakfast, lunch, happy hour, dinner, late-night snack—all purchases will support fairness for LGBT Oregonians.

**Feast, feastportland.com.** Feast is probably the coolest, and most definitely the newest, food and drink festival in the Pacific Northwest, capturing the current energy and enthusiasm driving America's food revolution. It had its opening in 2012

and was a huge success, though kind of pricey. Feast showcases local culinary talent and local ingredients, alongside nationally recognized chefs and others in the biz during a four-day celebration. At the core of the festival is a mission to end childhood hunger in Oregon. It seems so wrong that a state where food is so plentiful also ranks as one of the hungriest in the nation. This is a four-day event that covers the best of the PDX food scene as well as dealing with important social issues. The first year drew an impressive number of people, and it seems to be continuing to draw crowds.

**FredFest, fredfestpdx.com.** What started as a surprise 80th birthday party for well-known beer lover and writer Fred Eckhardt has become a yearly fund-raising event. Fred was a brewer before brewing was cool and popular, and he has written books and lectured on the subject. Guests at the event will sample rare hand-selected beers, as well as food cooked in beer and a birthday cake, complete with a round of "Happy Birthday" just for Fred. Cheeses, chocolate, candy, and even cereal will be offered in abundance so attendees can experience some of Fred's famed beer-and-food pairings. Every year proceeds go to a charity of Fred's choosing. Fred is a good guy.

## Great American Distillers Festival, distillersfestival.com.

This festival is a gathering of small distillers from across the country who come to Oregon, the center of craft distilling, to share their products, their passion, and their expertise in handcrafting spirits. There will be tastings, seminars, a super-fun mixology contest for bartenders, and more! About 50 distillers attend and will be happy to pour and chat. Cocktails will be mixed and "spirits" high.

**Greek Festival, goholytrinity.org/cGreekFest.html.** Immigrants from Greece began arriving in the Northwest in the late 1800s to work

# No, This Doesn't Exist Yet.
# But Don't Rule It Out!

The Great Pacific Northwest Hangover Festival. Once a year, in February, thousands of Portlanders come together and celebrate what would have been the worst hangover of their lives. The entire day before the festival, bars and restaurants allow patrons to come in and drink as much alcohol as they can for only one dollar. They don't have to eat anything and they can stay as long as they like. Each person must be able to prove they have a designated driver, and other than that the sky's the limit. Beers are flowing like water, and the sound of cocktail shakers shaking can be heard throughout the city. Bartenders put on their A game and wait to see if anyone remembers what they drank. At the festival it's a who's who of hangover remedies, from places that serve huge and greasy dripping burgers to people who will walk on your back with hot stones strapped to their feet. There are massage chairs and tables and plenty of herbaceous drinks that are considered cure-alls. Just about every country is represented and it is fascinating to discover ancient hangover techniques from countries you didn't even know existed. The festival is held inside one of the PDX sports arenas, which for obvious reasons has been covered with hemp tarps that will disintegrate into the soil. The event always gets great coverage, and each of the participants is given a box of tissues and a breath mint. It's quite a day!

in fishing, lumber, and the railroad. Settling in Portland, they established their church, Holy Trinity Greek Orthodox in southeast Portland. When the number of churchgoers increased, it was time to find a new spiritual home. Hence, folks decided to help by holding a bazaar with their crafts and traditions. This was the beginning of what is now known as the Annual Greek Festival, one of the largest of its kind. The Greek Festival is a great event with over 15,000 guests and a grand opportunity to participate or just observe Greek customs including dance, music, and most importantly, some amazing food. Each year a portion of festival proceeds are donated to worthy philanthropic organizations in the greater Portland community. The last 2 years the food was some of the best of that cuisine that I have ever had. Unfortunately I have never been to Greece, but I think that I have sampled some authentic and superb culinary offerings at this super fun event.

**Holiday Ale Festival, holidayale.com.** This event features Belgian beers, barley wines, porters, and stouts, all coming together in huge numbers for tastings and demonstrations. Three types of beers are featured here: standard release, holiday, and Sunday brunch beers. Most of the beers are either brewed for the event, or are extremely rare beers that you may never find elsewhere, or vintage beers or beers making their initial debut at the festival. It is a raucous four-day event, and the opportunity to try some of the most hard-to-find libations draw crowds of thirsty beer lovers. And even many who aren't really thirsty at all.

**Northwest Food and Wine Festival, nwfoodandwinefestival .com.** The event features wonderful wines from all over the Northwest and beyond, paired with excellent restaurants in Portland. Every year the event hosts a pâté competition that will feature potential pâté masterpieces from over 25 restaurants paired with wonderful Pinots, excellent Cabs, medium-bodied Merlots, and spectacular Rhone-style wines. There are also plenty of whites to try as well, running the range from sparklings to citrusy Pinot Gris and robust Chardonnays. And don't forget the new rosés. We had a bottle of the delicious Roseo from Penner-Ash Winery last night. The bottle didn't last long!

**Oregon Brewers Festival.** This is a huge event for beer lovers from around the country and beyond. Held on an almost always-sunny July weekend, this is an opportunity to try over 80 craft beers from around the country. Portland and the Pacific Northwest are generously represented. There is food and music and lots of very happy people. Every beer style is represented, and people just go around to different tents and get their beer on. It's a hoot.

**Oregon Cheese Festival,** oregoncheeseguild.org/oregon-cheese-festival. Every March there is an opportunity for folks to meet and taste the best cheeses around. The farmers' market–style festival will include a cheese and winemaker's dinner and lots of opportunities to chat with the purveyors. Visitors will taste sheep, cow, and goat cheese from Oregon creameries including Juniper Grove Farm, Pholia Farm, La Mariposa Creamery, Mama Terra Micro-creamery,  Ochoa Creamery, Tumalo Farms, Tillamook County Creamery, Willa-mette Valley Cheese Co., Fern's Edge Goat Dairy, River's Edge Chevre, Briar Rose Creamery, Oak Leaf Creamery, Portland Creamery, Rogue Creamery, and many others. I know I got a little carried away there with the creamery names, but I find them so lovely and I really love cheese. Oh, well. Local cheeses are getting better and better, and if you are a cheese lover, don't miss this tasty opportunity. I won't.

**Portland Indie Wine Festival.** This festival is in flux at this time; however, Portlanders are hopeful that we will once again be able to attend this terrific event in 2014. Having lost their huge and perfect warehouse location, there is movement to find a new venue. The event typically includes at least 40 wineries and 20 chefs showcasing the best they have. Hopefully this fun experience will once again return to the PDX event scene.

**Wild About Game, nickyusa.com/wag.** As a renowned culinary city, Portland seems slightly meatier (perhaps porkier) than most. The idea of a bunch of chefs hanging out, collaborating, and cooking up ridiculously large amounts of meaty goodness sounds like, you know, the average Tuesday. But on a Sunday in September, a bunch of Portland chefs take a trip to Timberline Lodge for this well-loved event. The competition, developed by local meat purveyor Nicky USA, pits nine local chefs against each other in a "black box" cooking competition using gamier-than-usual ingredients like rabbit, quail, elk, water buffalo, and bison. It's quite an event, and chefs who are often too busy to hang out with other chefs get to party some. And then some more!

## And the Internet Says

These websites focus on the food and bar scene in Portland and greater Oregon. Places open and sadly close and the internet can help you be informed before you head out, or change your plans while you're out and have up-to-the-minute news on who's cooking what and where to get the best new cocktail or seasonal beer. Thank you, Al Gore!

**Barfly, portlandbarfly.com.** This is the site to go for the latest in libation innovation, upcoming events, tastings, and music.

**Chowhound, chowhound.com.** Chowhound is a national site owned by CBS. It's a good way to search out restaurants with reviews from people who have been there, suggestions for ordering, and other tips that will improve your culinary experience.

**Culinate, culinate.com.** Good selection of recipes and articles about the food and farm scene here in PDX. There is a lot of info on the website, and I have found it to be reliable and super informative.

**Edible Portland, edibleportland.com.** Local food is what rules here with lots of info about the goings-on with local food businesses, food producers, and farmers.

**Food Carts Portland, foodcartsportland.com.** Sample menus and up-to-date reviews on this ever-growing phenomenon. Considering there are over 500 hundred carts in Portland, I love having a place to go to get the lowdown on the newest, the spiciest, the earliest, and the greatest.

**Oregon Public Broadcasting, OPB.org.** Interesting articles about the food scene and recipes developed by yours truly and others. Support OPB.

**Under the Table with Jen, underthetablewithjen.com.** Jen has a good sense of humor and in my experience is generally right on with her views and suggestions. Jen reviews local events and keeps you updated with events coming down the pike (no food pun intended).

# Southwest Portland

Southwest Portland is where the business center of town is located. There are also venues for theater, music, museums, and the campus of Portland State University. Many of the spots in this part of town do a more active business at breakfast and lunch; downtown Portland can be pretty quiet in the evening. That said, there are excellent places to dine and drink, not necessarily in that order. Most of the city's hotels are in this part of town as well. The food carts do big business in the downtown area because they are great places to grab lunch and bring it back to the office or sit outside and enjoy life. If it's not pouring.

## Foodie Faves

**Aquariva, River's Edge Hotel & Spa; 0455 SW Hamilton Court, Portland, OR 97239; (503) 802-5850; riversedgehotel.com; Northwest Cuisine; $$$.** I have eaten at this restaurant, ideally positioned at the edge of the South Waterfront District, on a number of occasions. My first visit was just so-so, but recently I have enjoyed some fine meals. It's a lovely quiet spot, the food is good, and I think it's a good choice for a date or special occasion. I enjoyed a sea fennel salad with bacon and a poached duck egg, and the roasted clams were tasty. I am not a pheasant fan, but my friend Carol loved it, and I was very happy with the pork tenderloin that was moist and paired well with the squash pudding. They do an interesting happy hour, and a fine lemon drop.

**Brasserie Montmartre, 626 SW Park Ave., Portland, OR 97205; (503) 236-3036; brasserieportland.com; French; $$.** French food is the reason I got into this crazy business in the first place, having been blown away by an amazing meal at the legendary, no-longer-in-existence restaurant Lutece. I was 12. It is wonderful. And Brasserie Montmartre serves up some of the best in Portland. Located downtown, it gets a busy lunch crowd, busier than dinner when downtown kind of shuts down. The onion soup is perfect, and the wonderful beet salad with arugula, pistachios, and goat cheese is so fresh and good. I love the braised chicken and sausage gumbo, and the scallops were seared caramelized beauties. And it was there that I remembered how good quiche can be, all custardy with a tender, buttery crust. However, the crowning moment was when the fries came. We had two of the five offered, the duck fat fries and the truffle fries. Bruce, who lived the dream of residing in Paris for 5 years, and eating well, said he thought they might be the best fries he has ever had. And they were the perfect fry. With ketchup and aioli. Bliss.

**Chart House, 5700 SW Terwilliger Blvd., Portland, OR 97239; (503) 246-6963; chart-house.com; Seafood; $$$.** Although many are drawn to the Chart House for the spectacular view, last week I had a terrific dinner on a cloudy, no-view night! Chart House is an expensive chain, and I have found that simple is the way to go. The prime rib was just great, and my dear Rose and Terry both enjoyed their perfectly grilled fish. Pan-seared scallops were also good, and the Alaskan king crab was steamed to perfection. Make sure to save room for the chocolate lava cake, and although I have never met one I didn't like, this was pretty fabulous. And when the sun is shining, the view of Mt. Hood is magical.

**Clyde Common,** 1014 SW Stark St., Portland, OR 97205; (503) 228-3333; clydecommon.com; American; $$$. Clyde Common is one of Portland's hot spots. Connected to the ultra-hip Ace Hotel, it is one of the few west-side haunts that draws as many young tattooed hipsters as it does the more expected, not-so-edgy west-side crowd. Both the bar and the dining room are always packed, and the communal tables allow for easy mingling and fun. Clyde Common is a well-located restaurant for attracting both locals and out-of-towners. There is no way someone staying at the Ace can avoid eating a meal or two there, and Portlanders know this is a place to get a great pour and a good meal, and then head over to Powell's or the Living Room Theatre to keep the mood going. The menu is fun, with starters like spiced popcorn and fried chicken wings with pomegranate and orange. Large plates of standout dishes include sturgeon served with Manila clams, fennel, and baby carrots in a prosciutto broth, or grilled steak, Romesco (almond, garlic, and roasted pepper-scented puree) with spring onions and a spicy arugula salad. Seasonal is the name of the game here, the chef working with local farmers and purveyors to keep everything in the community.

**Daily Grill,** 750 SW Alder St., Portland, OR 97205; (503) 294-7001; dailygrill.com; Steak House; $$$. Daily Grill is a high-priced chain in the heart of Portland's business, retail, and cultural district. The restaurant is within walking distance of major retailers and fun boutiques. For some folks travel is stressful, and for people here on business Daily Grill may feel like a comfortable pair of slippers. Again, simple seems the way to go, and their salads and steaks are pretty good. My grilled skirt steak salad was a nice change of pace, and the fish and chips hit the spot. Not everyone wants to try something new and unfamiliar, and the Daily Grill is a safe bet.

**Departures Restaurant,** 525 SW Morrison St., Portland, OR 97204; (503) 802-5370; departureportland.com; Asian; $$$. Located at the top of the fashionable Nines Hotel in downtown Portland, this restaurant has a view that would be reason enough to go for food and drinks. An outside area is just a spectacular place to sit, unwind, and view PDX from above. There is a pretty active bar scene, and it seems to get a somewhat dressier crowd than your average Portland diners. If someone blindfolded me and took me there, I would never guess Portland; it's sleeker and more sophisticated than your typical Rose City spot. That said, there are lots of fun things to drink and yummy food to eat. The food is Asian; they do a fine job with sushi as well as their dim sum and skewered dishes. The place has an electricity that is a welcome change for a once-in-a-while dining experience. Drinks are the classics but with an emphasis on the Asian offerings we Portlanders love. You can experience handcrafted sake from the largest selection in Portland, a signature cocktail crafted with exotic fruits, or a *shochu* fresh from Korea. This is a great spot to take someone who is new in town, just for a drink and the view; on a nice night it rocks.

**Fat City Cafe, 7820 SW Capitol Hwy., Portland, OR 97219; (503) 245-5457; fatcitycafe.net; American; $$.** In a city filled with many distinctly different neighborhoods, there is one part of town that feels like no other. Multnomah Village literally feels like a village within a city. One of the features that sets it apart is that you really can't see anything else when you are there. No tall buildings, no bridges, very little traffic. It is small and charming with a collection of shops that seem to cater to a specific clientele. It's not a common destination for the hatted, tattooed PDX hipster, and it's not a place that typically draws a business crowd. It feels artsy, perhaps like a town on Martha's Vineyard. Fat City Cafe is one of the few true diners in Portland. Because this breakfast and lunch spot is off the beaten path, it is possible to arrive for breakfast or brunch and actually not have to wait in line. The portions are large, and there are many things worth ordering. It is one of those places where we always seem to order something "for the table," which is code or justification for an extra entree. Simple pancakes are perfect, the Frisbee-size freshly baked cinnamon rolls are divine, and the skillet and scrambled egg dishes are all first rate. The staff is friendly, the food comes out quickly, and the coffee is good and constantly being topped off.

**Fulton Pub,** 0618 SW Nebraska St., Portland, OR 97239; (503) 246-9530; mcmenamins.com/fulton; Pub Food; $$. This pub and beer garden makes good cheeseburgers, and the tots are excellent. It's a quiet spot and is friendly and comfortable. No one ever rushes you out, and the vibe is pretty chill and friendly. It's part of the large Mcmenamins chain, and this one is my favorite: The size is perfect, it doesn't get very crowded or loud, and the people who work there are really nice. The location is near the river in the John's Landing neighborhood, and this pub draws a nice and mellow crowd.

**Gilda's,** 1601 SW Morrison St., Portland, OR 97205; (503) 688-5066; gildasitalianrestaurant.com; Italian; $$. I have had mixed experiences at Gilda's over the last few months. My last two dinners were very good, and I am thinking that they have gotten their kitchen act together. A rather small menu, but generally there are many items I want to try. My recent appetizer favorites have been the arancini, (mozzarella-stuffed rice balls) and the meatballs. The wild mushroom risotto was almost perfect, and the chicken saltimbocca was a dish I hadn't had in years, and it was good to eat it again. I loved the lemon olive oil cake, which I had with ice cream and an Illy espresso. Happy.

**Gruner,** 527 SW 12th Ave., Portland, OR 97205; (503) 24 grunerpdx.com; German; $$$. The food at Gruner is German, b\ a lighter hand. There are fresh and creatively prepared greens, an\ entrees are not heavily sauced or covered with sauerkraut. Liptauer cheese, which is a blend of cheeses, capers, paprika, caraway seeds, and mustard, is a light starter and not that easy to find in restaurants. Zabar's in New York has it! The mushroom-stuffed ravioli is made in house, and is earthy and satisfying. Duck schnitzel served with a dilled cucumber salad and a Bing cherry-rhubarb sauce is a clever pairing of ingredients that is just right in both flavor and texture. I love duck just about any way it is served, and this preparation was delectable. See Gruner's recipe for **Liptaeur Cheese** on p. 188.

**Higgins,** 1239 SW Broadway, Portland, OR 97205; (503) 222-9070; higginsportland.com; Northwest; $$$. Greg Higgins, owner and chef of the restaurant that bears his name, has been at the forefront of the Farm to Table movement in Portland way before it became standard operating procedure. Higgins draws a somewhat different demographic than many of the other restaurants that have the same focus and philosophy. There is a huge selection of single malts and terrific beer offerings, and sitting and eating at the bar is great fun, with bartenders who have been there for years and totally know their stuff. As a starter on a recent visit, the asparagus and chèvre bruschetta with roasted garlic and balsamic vinegar was a stunner, and the panzanella salad of roasted beets, spinach with a mint and pea coulis was earthy and fresh, and the hard-shell clams steamed in aji chili and ginger broth with Kolsch beer, leeks, carrots, cilantro, and garlic toast were unique, and no less amazing. Being a sucker for all things pork, I find that the Whole Pig Plate, a posole of Amish butter corn with chorizo, loin, belly, carnitas, and vegetables is an unforgettable experience.

# SMALL FOOD BUSINESSES

**Bob's Red Mill,** *5000 SE International Way, Milwaukie, OR 97222;* *(503) 607-6455; bobsredmill.com.* Becoming familiar with this company has been a joy. The products are great. I do a lot of baking and the ingredients I have used have all been of the highest quality. The flour is fresh and I just seem to get a better end result. Their gluten-free offerings are better than any others I have tried, and they have such a huge selection of whole grains and I know everything will be great. Love the Scottish Oatmeal and the Crunchy Coconut Granola. The company is employee owned, and it's a pleasure to buy their merchandise. Ever been to a grain mill for breakfast? Bob's opens at 6 a.m. just so you can say you have.

**Choi's Kimchee Company,** *PSU Portland Farmer's Market; choiskimchee.com.* Kimchee is a traditional Korean food that is high in vitamins and low in calories. There are many types of kimchee, but mainly it contains cabbage, and the vegetables and seasonings are fermented in a mix of herbs and spices. My favorite is the white radish, which is prepared with cider vinegar, sugar, apple, lemon, sea salt, and red chili pepper. It is spicy and sweet and amazing with Korean fried chicken. In Korea, there is a mad rush for cabbage when it hits the supermarkets. It is sold in huge bags since the fermenting and preparation of kimchee is a joint effort by a group of neighbors. It is a community event and they make enough kimchee to last one whole year.

**Flying Fish Oregon,** *2310 SE Hawthorne Blvd., Portland, OR 97214;* *(503) 260-6552; flyingfishcompany.com.* Flying Fish Oregon sells the best quality fish I have purchased in Portland. They have a sustainable business model, the company is family run, and the prices are quite reasonable. I love to make a seared tuna appetizer and the fish I buy there is fantastic. The black cod I purchased recently was terrific; I cooked it with white miso paste and everyone loved it. I also tried their Alaskan scallops and they were unbelievable. Hard to shop anywhere else. A few years ago I heard from my best friend, OPB Radio, that a market was labeling its fish with the name of the fisherman who caught it. No kidding, scout's honor! Although this sounds like an episode from *Portlandia*, a little absurd, it's one of the things I love about this weird place. BTW, it never caught on, but Johnny K., that was one good rainbow trout you caught. Keep up the good work.

**Genki-Su,** *genkisu.com.* Judy Tan and Takako McNeil make Genki-Su with only natural ingredients and no refined sugar, for a delightful line of drinking vinegars that are refreshing and healthy. When I was a kid, drinking vinegar was a threat if I used a "dirty" word. Not today. Takako grew up in Japan drinking her mother's homemade vinegar from the fruits from her garden. The flavors are unusual and inspired, my current favorite being the Shiso. Shiso is an herb that is a member of the mint family, an extremely important part of Japanese diet and cuisine. This flavor is crisp with a clean taste with subtle hints of basil and mint. I mix the vinegar with sparkling water and it is a perfectly refreshing and delicious drink. Now I can use all the "dirty" words I want.

**Jorinji,** *jorinjisoybeam.com.* Miso is a thick paste made from fermented soybeans and barley or rice malt; it's used in Japanese cooking to make soups or sauces. Miso needs a fermentation process that can take from six months to several years. Earnest and Sumiko Migaki use recipes that have been in their families for years. The products use only the finest ingredients; the miso is not pasteurized and fortunately is available at lots of shops around town. I used their white miso for the amazing black cod I grilled recently, and the results were excellent.

**River Wave Foods,** *riverwavefoods.com.* River Wave Foods is a small company that produces cooking marinades and sauces unique to the Northwest. Their focus is on balancing flavors and producing multicultural, gourmet cooking sauces and tapenade that use only fresh ingredients. My personal favorite is the olive and fig tapenade, and the Argentinean chimichurri sauce. Recently I served the tapenade with a mild goat cheese and a honey drizzle and my guests loved it. The chimichurri sauce is the best I have found that is not homemade.

I marinate skirt steak in this and it is absolutely fantastic. The products are available around town or online.

**Smith Teamakers,** *1626 NW Thurman St., Portland, OR 97209; (503) 719-8752; smithtea.com.* This place is tucked away in Northwest Portland and plays triple duty as the packinghouse, store, and teashop for this excellent line of teas. I am an iced tea addict of sorts, and the black Assam tea over ice with mint and a lemon wedge is next to me all summer long. The shop is small and all teas are available for a brewed pot, or you can order a flight of teas to see what your preferences are. Teas are very different from one another; it's an interesting drinking experience.

**Yume Confections,** *yumeconfections.com.* Gena Renaud is most definitely making the prettiest *wagashi* and *yogashi* in Portland. Her business, Yume Confections, makes handmade Japanese and Asian-inspired sweets, and her stunning edible jewels are showing up all over town. *Wagashi* are traditional Japanese confections that evolved into an art form in the ancient Imperial capital, Kyoto. These confections have been part of the tea ceremony for over 500 years. One of the greatest fascinations in wagashi is their potential for appealing to much more than just the sense of taste. *Wagashi* are an invitation to indulge all five senses and in doing so experience a taste of Japan. Her little works of art are absolutely exquisite, a terrific gift or end to an elegant dinner party. *Wagashi* generally contain red bean, kidney beans, glutinous rice, powdered rice, sweet potatoes, sesame, agar-agar, and sugar. Sounds delicious doesn't it? Surprise, it is! *Wagashi* is high in plant protein. There is almost no animal fat, which makes it a wholesome, healthy product. Natural unrefined sugar is one of the important ingredients in *wagashi*. The confections are not overly sweet, and they are perfect with a cup of tea or warm sake. Bruce likes them with a good single-malt Scotch. *Yogashi* is a western version, due to its use of western ingredients like flour, butter, sugar, and eggs. The inside filling is a traditional white bean paste. Gena's beautiful and tasty desserts are now available on Etsy. That's fun.

**Huber's, 411 SW 3rd Ave., Portland, OR 97204; (503) 228-5686; hubers.com; American; $$.** Huber's opened in 1879 and was initially called "The Bureau Saloon." Purchased in 1891 by Frank Huber, the name was changed and a PDX legend was born. Back in the day, if you bought a drink, you would get a free turkey sandwich and coleslaw. That is how the tradition of Huber's and turkey got its start. Any time of the year you can get a full turkey dinner with all the trimmings. Huber's signature drink, Spanish Coffee, is one of Portland's great culinary traditions. A Spanish Coffee at Huber's consists of 151 proof rum, triple sec, kahlua, coffee, fresh whipped cream, and a touch of nutmeg on top. The drink is made tableside with great flair, and it is warming and delicious.

**Imperial, 410 SW Broadway, Portland, OR 97205; (503) 228-7222; imperialpdx.com; American; $$$.** Vitaly Paley is a Portland food star. He has called Portland his home for years, and he has been involved in many of the great dining spots. Imperial is in a hotel, a lovely hotel named the Lucia, and he is serving food from morning till late at night. At dinner, Imperial serves warm Parker House rolls, which are a great start. Although they cost a dollar, they are very good so we had a couple. We wanted more, but used restraint. The roasted beets and smoked mussels were outstanding, as was the black cod with lentils, pork belly, and a spicy aioli. The steaks have all gotten high marks, and my friend Karen loved the fried rabbit, though Kristen wouldn't touch it. I was crazy about the sticky toffee gingerbread and the Meyer lemon pudding cake. If I were staying at the Lucia, I would be a happy camper.

**Jakes Famous Crawfish, 401 SW 12th Ave., Portland, OR 97205; (503) 226-1419; mccormickandschmicks.com; Seafood; $$$.** Although seafood is not my favorite I have had some very good food at Jakes. Some Portlanders refuse to go, claiming it is only fair and too touristy. It may be a tourist destination, but I think the food is well prepared and the fish is always fresh. They have a huge list of uber-fresh s, and I love the rock shrimp popcorn. Most of the time I order ,eness Crab Louis, for lunch or for dinner, and it is as good as I eaten anywhere. My friend Graeme had the pecan-crusted catfish, ana he said it was excellent. Save room for dessert: They do a light and lovely Key lime pie, which is not that easy to do.

**Little Bird Bistro, 219 SW 6th Ave., Portland, OR 97204; (503) 688-5952; littlebirdbistro.com; French; $$$.** Little Bird draws its crowds from the large concentration of businesses, galleries, and theaters in downtown Portland. The menu is French bistro, and Chef Eric Van Kley is adept at creating exactly what you are longing for in the brasserie repertoire. A couple of starters were particularly delicious. The goat cheese gnocchi were delicate and tasted great with the caramelized onions and walnuts, and we loved the sweetbreads with pickled shallots. The steak frites was perfect and the leek and goat cheese crepe was glorious and perfect for my friend Vicky, a vegetarian. The staff is well trained and friendly. Little Bird has a Parisian feel and a celebratory atmosphere. Oh, and before I forget, what a burger!

**Luc Lac, 835 SW 2nd Ave., Portland, OR 97204; (503) 222-0047; luclackitchen.com; Vietnamese; $$.** My PDX friend Michele works right near this place and loves the food, the generous portions, and the friendly staff. We headed downtown to try it out and she was right on with her suggestion. The salad rolls were fresh and stuffed with all kinds of goodies, and the bowls of pho were huge. We went with three of the Luc Lac specials and were very pleased with each dish. My

favorite was the cubed beef tenderloin, wok seared with Hennessey, beurre de France, garlic, and black peppercorns. They have a fun selection of nonalcoholic drinks. I was crazy about my Vietnamese cafe favorite: avocado, lime, and condensed milk blended together with those bizarre tapioca balls floating around to add texture, flavor, and fun.

**Masu Sushi,** 406 SW 13th Ave., Portland, OR 97205; (503) 221-MASU; masusushi.com; Sushi; $$$. A few of my friends think this is the best sushi in Portland. I have been there several times, and I cannot argue that the fish is super fresh and prepared deftly. The rolls are good—try the volcano roll—and creative. Cooked food is innovative, and on my last visit I thoroughly enjoyed a very unusual duck breast that was presented beautifully. The ramen wasn't as good as I've had elsewhere, but the short ribs were great. I am still trying to decide how I felt about the uni risotto. Bruce is an uni lover and a purist, so he lamented the risotto part. For the most part the staff is friendly and helpful.

**Mother's Bistro,** 212 SW Stark St., Portland, OR 97204; (503) 464-1122; mothersbistro.com; Comfort; $$. Being a New Yorker most of my life, and a mother for half, Mother's has an extra-special place in my heart. And the concept is genuine and sweet. Owner Lisa Schroeder is warm, friendly, and embraces life with a passion you rarely see. She's a pretty special person. And the food is great. Breakfast is outstanding, offering everything you could ever want and done with expertise. And love. The colors of the rooms are as comforting as the food. The cheesy frittata and the salmon hash are my current favorites. Mother's is famous for their crunchy French toast, which is amazing; I always get one of those, or a Belgian waffle, "for the table." For dinner, try the chicken with pillowy dumplings, or maybe the meatloaf. Oh, and the brisket too, you have to have that. And don't forget the best matzo ball soup west of New York. Mother's food is comfort food, with all the love and caring of Mother Lisa. See Mother's Bistro's recipe for **Pear Hazelnut Galette** on p. 193.

**Nel Centro,** 1408 SW 6th Ave., Portland, OR 97201; (503) 484-1099; nelcentro.com; Italian; $$$. The cuisine of Nel Centro is rooted in the Italian and French Riviera. As a fan of some of those regions' specialties, I was overjoyed to find salt cod croquettes and an incredibly rich and tender daube of beef. Ravioli Nicoise, faithful to the region, was authentic and inspiring. Desserts are outstanding, my particular favorites being the blackberry bread pudding with salt-studded caramel ice cream, and the lemon pistachio cake with blueberry compote.

**The Original,** 300 SW 6th Ave., Portland, OR 97204; (503) 546-2666; originaldinerant.com; American; $$. The menu at this well-located spot is mostly of the comfort food category, with offerings like crab cakes, sliders, fried chicken, and breakfast for dinner. The food is good, and the staff is welcoming. Sandwiches are fine and recently I had a very good Reuben, an often-disappointing choice. They do a good Cobb and Caesar salad, and the vegetarian burger was better than average. Their desserts are also in the homey category; I particularly enjoyed a slice of apple pie and Bruce didn't want to share his cheesecake, so it must have been pretty good. And they do Jell-O shots!

**Portland Penny Diner,** 410 SW Broadway, Portland, OR 97205; (503) 228-7222; portlandpennydiner.com; Diner; $$. "Portland is known for our food carts, which evolved from the lunch wagons into the diner," said Chef Vitaly Paley. "I wanted to bring a new type of diner to our city, and Portland Penny Diner will recapture its warmth and comfort while updating and elevating the food and drink. Portland Penny Diner's food is inspired in part by what I ate in diners and greasy spoons while I struggled as a young musician in New York City. Take that and combine it with the bounty of the Pacific Northwest with an updated twist and you have Portland Penny Diner." Portland Penny Diner is a counter-service diner featuring terrific breakfasts to go or stay, and they are inventive, delicious, and fun. The Reuben croissant was very good, although I had my doubts mixing the two, and the toaster tarts are yummy. The daily-made quick breads taste great, as do the large variety of breakfast sandwiches. There are some yummy things to be had at night, to go with a pretty rad cocktail menu. It's part of the Hotel Lucia, so it's always hopping.

**Ración, 1205 SW Washington St., Portland, OR 97205; (971) 276-8008; racionpdx.com; Modern Spanish Tapas; $$$.** Ración provides its guests with 2 beautiful and unique dining options. The restaurant itself is divided into an open kitchen bar, the first of its kind in Portland. This horseshoe-shaped bar wraps around an all-electric kitchen island. There, Chefs Anthony Cafiero and Roscoe Roberson cook and plate each dish from the multicourse tasting menu right before your eyes. Past the open kitchen bar a lounge unfolds under a wall of Douglas fir, where guests can enjoy tapas, cocktails, and wine. South-facing floor-to-ceiling windows along Southwest Washington Street provide an entertaining view and the last rays of the afternoon sun. We loved the halibut cheeks with green apple and black sesame seeds, and for dessert the chocolate ganache with lemon curd and the unusual addition of goat cheese and kumquat actually worked. I admit I was skeptical.

**Raven & Rose, 1331 SW Broadway, Portland, OR 97201; (503) 222-7673; ravenandrosepdx.com; English and Irish; $$.** Raven & Rose offers homey food and fine cocktails in Portland's historic Ladd Carriage House. The dining room is warm and inviting and draws inspiration from the countryside of England and Ireland. The service is both friendly and professional, and we have thoroughly enjoyed several meals there. Most recently the duck braised with semolina noodles was amazing, and we also loved the lamb meatballs with collard greens. Wood-oven-cooked mussels were stellar, and the butterscotch pudding was creamy magnificence.

**Saucebox, 214 SW Broadway, Portland, OR 97209; (503) 241-3393; saucebox.com; Asian Fusion; $$.** This Asian fusion spot has a pretty loyal following, with their tasty appetizers and mostly very good dim sum. The food is occasionally erratic; my recent visits, however, were all quite enjoyable: one lunch, one dinner, and a couple of awesome happy hours. The place is kind of trendy feeling, and they have DJs on occasion, which is not my cup of tea but draws crowds. I had a tender, tasty lemongrass hangar steak and a couple of yummy *hijitos*, a house-infused ginger vodka muddled with mint, ice, lemon-lime, and house-made hibiscus syrup. Very refreshing.

**Tasty n Alder,** **1200–1298 SW Alder St., Portland, OR 97205; (503) 621-9251; tastyntasty.com; American; $$.** Tasty n Alder is the third restaurant opened by John Gorham, whose **Toro Bravo** (p. 92) and **Tasty n Sons** (p. 125) will be discussed in their own neighborhoods. And both are good. The newest member of the restaurant family has a similar style to Tasty n Sons, but the food is different and some of it quite interesting. My first experience with pork skirt steak, which was too salty until you dipped it in the Romesco, then it was divine, sort of like the ugly duckling that became a swan. The baked spinach was creamy goodness with a pork product, and the double grilled rib eye was tender and full of flavor. Having been open only for a couple of weeks and still a "soft" opening, the kitchen and front of the house staff were impressive.

**Urban Farmer,** **525 SW Morrison St., Portland, OR 97204; (503) 222-4900; urbanfarmerportland.com; Steak House; $$$$.** Urban Farmer is not your average steak house. The restaurant in the Nines Hotel offers a range of beef options including grass-fed Oregon beef, pasture-raised, grain-finished beef, as well as corn-fed beef. This rustic-meets-modern northwest spot serves excellent beef, along with some impressive steak house sides and a very impressive wine list. On a

recent visit I started my meal with a caramelized onion soup and Bruce went for the oysters. Karen was fighting him for them, but Bruce prevailed. I tried Graeme's crab cakes, which were excellent, and Karen was happy with her Caesar salad. We all ordered steak, the two favorites being the rare and beautiful Painted Hills Porterhouse and the American Wagyu rib eye. We came close to ordering all the sides, and we liked them all, particularly the creamed spinach, roasted cauliflower, and the grits. Also, the fries were super good. Of course no one had room for dessert, so we ordered only two. The caramel banana pudding was totally delish, as was the mud pie with rocky road ice cream and hot fudge. I couldn't sleep on my stomach all night.

## Specialty Stores, Markets & Producers

**Barbur World Foods, 9845 SW Barbur Blvd., Portland, OR 97219; (503) 244-0670; barburworldfoods.com.** Barbur World Foods is an unpretentious international market that has perhaps the best deli counter in Portland. Owned by John and Mirna Attar, the same folks who have the restaurant **Ya Hala** (p. 69), they have food from more than 50 countries. Interesting products from Turkey, Morocco, and lots from Lebanon, the owner's country of birth. There is also a great selection of the best of Oregon, from salts and hot sauces to bread and lots more. Back to the deli. Ya Hala Chef Mirna Attar supervises the food prep, and the cooked food is great. There is always tender roasted chicken, beef, and lamb along with lots of sides for company. You can order pita bread and it will be baked to order. When I am in a not-cooking mood, I will buy all the meats, some pita, lentils and rice, and their astonishingly garlicky *toom*. Like everything else it is made in-house and it is fantastic. And the prices are unbeatable.

**Blue Star Donuts, 1237 SW Washington St., Portland, OR 97205; (503) 265-8410; bluestardonuts.com.** Blue Star Donuts takes the once simple treat to a rather exotic level. My inclination was to say nay, a downtown venture from Little Big Burger impresarios Micah Camden and Katie Poppe feeling like it's just not something to be toyed with. However, I have not only changed my thinking, I am a regular. The doughnuts are not inexpensive, but they are unusual and taste great. Clearly much care and thought has gone into them, and every bite is a delight. My current faves are the crème brûleé, a brioche-like doughnut filled with a custard with visible specks of vanilla bean and topped with crispy burnt sugar glaze, and the blueberry bourbon basil. Try the dulce de leche hazelnut and the simple glazed—you will be blown away. The doughnuts are kind of expensive at around $2.50 each, but these are not your average doughnuts. I have yet to try the savory doughnuts, like the one served with fried chicken, and rumor has it that it is going to be taken off the menu. Not sure what I think about that combo, though I love fried chicken and waffles.

**Cacao, 414 SW 13th Ave., Portland, OR 97205; (503) 241-0656; 712 SW Salmon St., Portland, OR 97205; (503) 274-9510; cacao drinkchocolate.com.** This gem of a shop has the most amazing hot chocolate. The stores carry a hand-picked selection of chocolate from around the world, including an extensive range of premium solid chocolate bars from small producers, select chocolate from the best local chocolatiers and makers, and their house-made drinking and hot chocolates. Chocolate has become huge, sort of like salt and tea and beer, and it's wonderful to have the friendly shopkeepers to help you get acquainted. There are plenty of samples, and it is fascinating, and delicious, to discover how different chocolates can be. And now that we know how beneficial dark chocolate can be for your health, it is a guilt-free indulgence!

**John's Marketplace, 3535 SW Multnomah Blvd., Portland, OR 97219; (503) 244-2617; johnsmarketplace.com.** Located in the uber-charming Multnomah Village; go here for beer. They have like a thousand, and you can occasionally get the very hard-to-find ones that have people scurrying (well, biking) all over town! It's all about the beer.

# Southeast Portland

This neighborhood, across the river, probably has the highest concentration of interesting and yummy restaurants. Southeast Portland stretches from the industrial warehouses along the Willamette River through historic and funky Hawthorne and Belmont all the way to Gresham, a Portland suburb. Southeast Portland has blue-collar roots and has evolved to encompass a wide mix of backgrounds. Reed College is in this part of Southeast Portland as well as the large concentration of Asian neighborhoods out around 82nd Avenue.

## Foodie Faves

**Accanto,** 2838 SE Belmont St., Portland, OR 97214; (503) 235-4900; accantopdx.com; Italian; $$. A slice of Italian cafe life can be found on the corner of Southeast 28th and Belmont with the opening of Accanto, a casual enoteca with a strong emphasis on local, seasonal ingredients and soulful Italian cooking. Owned by the team re-opening **Genoa** (p. 49), Accanto inhabits a formerly vacant space in the historic Genoa Building. Accanto features many house-made ingredients—from spinach pasta and fresh mozzarella to salumi and grissini. Offering several small dishes for sharing and a handful of entrees, Accanto's menu will change with the seasons. There is a cozy space in the back of the cafe stocked with culinary resources—from magazines and cookbooks, to news about local food and farm organizations. Interested foodies can even browse through the Genoa recipe archives from the past 30 years.

**A Cena**, 7742 SE 13th Ave., Portland, OR 97202; (503) 206-3291; **acenapdx.com; Italian; $$$.** A Cena translates as "come to supper." And we have on several occasions. The restaurant is on the fancy side, and the food is kind of pricey. Emphasis is on fresh ingredients, and there is clearly a lot of love in the planning and preparation. Pastas, breads, and cured meats are handmade, and the wine list is considered to be excellent. I loved my shaved fennel and apple salad, and the white pizza with artichokes and olives was great. It's kind of a fancy vibe, which is not usually my preference, but there is clearly some serious food knowledge going on in there. The best dish of the night, according to me and the rest of our group, was the magnificent *agno-lotti* stuffed with corn, mascarpone cheese, and butter-poached lobster. I ended the meal with an espresso and a chocolate zabaglione cake, which was divine. Bruce had the butterscotch budino, equally brilliant.

**Apizza Scholls**, 4741 SE Hawthorne Blvd., Portland, OR 97215; (503) 233-1286; **apizzascholls.com; Pizza; $$.** Now that Apizza Scholls takes reservations it is easier to get in, but you need to book well in advance, which is kind of a bummer. Who really knows what tomorrow will bring. That said, the pizza is fantastic. Truly. Great toppings, crisp crust, wonderful. Without a doubt, my favorite is the white truffle pizza—melt-in-your-mouth magnificent. I also always order the ama-triciana pizza, which has a light tomato sauce, house-cured bacon, red chili flakes, and red onions. I love these toppings on pasta, and on pizza they shine. They do a few excellent salads, and have decent beer and wine. It's all about the pizza. But then again, isn't life?

**Arleta**, 5513 SE 72nd Ave., Portland, OR 97206; (503) 774-4470; **arletalibrary.com; Comfort; $$.** The biscuits and gravy at this uber-cozy neighborhood spot are pretty amazing. The eggs are done well, and the semolina buttermilk pancakes are fluffy and tender and just about perfect. The coffee cake is among the best I have had, and the bacon is smoky and cut nice and thick, just the way it should be. Every breakfast I have had there has been stellar; we leave full and satisfied. I wish this place was in my 'hood.

**Ate-oh-Ate, 2452 E. Burnside St., Portland, OR 97232; (503) 445-6101; ate-oh-ate.com; Hawaiian; $$.** Chef Ben Dyer was born in Hawaii (808 is the area code), and he knows his way with his native food. The beef short ribs, the island burger, katsu chicken, and the *hekka* were all great, as was a stir-fry with fresh vegetables, a fish cake, and interesting yam noodles. The entrees are served with a very good macaroni salad and rice, and the portions were large but the prices were not. Rumor has it that Chef Ben Bettinger, of **Imperial** (p. 27) and **Portland Penny Diner** (p. 30), stops in every Saturday for a musube: a seaweed, egg, and rice roll with a good-size chunk of grilled out-of-the-can spam. Reluctantly, I tried one. Acquired taste category.

**Ava Genes, 3377 SE Division St., Portland, OR 97202; (971) 229-0571; avagenes.com; Italian; $$$.** I've been to Ava Genes three times now. It has actually gotten better with every visit and is now on the list of places I bring out-of-towners. The staff is professional and super friendly, and they remembered me from my first visit. Possibly because I think I ordered everything on the menu, but maybe because they are just that way. Ava Genes is on the pricey side for Portland, but for a special occasion or people with deep pockets, it could be a frequent stop. I was particularly in love with the warm chicken livers in Marsala and the fresh sheep's cheeses with nettles. The leg of lamb was perfect with lentils and salsa verde, and the steak, served for two or three, was done to perfection. The

panna cotta with pinecone syrup was a sublime way to end the meal. That's right, pinecone syrup.

**Bar Dobre, 3962 SE Hawthorne Blvd., Portland, OR 97214; (503) 477-5266; bardobre.com; Polish; $$.** Hawthorne's much-anticipated Bar Dobre opened to wide praise. I have been three times, and although I want it all again I force myself to get new things. Like Martha Stewart, I love my Polish food, and Bar Dobre does an excellent job preparing what might be close to perfect comfort food. **Mother's Bistro** (p. 29) still holds that number one place in my heart, but this is damn good. I love pierogi and kielbasa, and the fact that there are pizzas on the menu as well threw me off at first, but since they were good, what the heck! There's clearly a person of Italian descent in the kitchen, and every kitchen should have at least one! The atmosphere is friendly and it's a nice place to linger.

**Bertie Lou's, 8051 SE 17th Ave., Portland, OR 97202; (503) 239-1177; Breakfast; $$.** Fortunately for people living in Sellwood, this great breakfast joint is under the radar. There may be a bit of a line, but nothing like what goes on in other equally good places around town. Breakfast portions are huge and very yummy, the coffee is good, and the people are super nice. There are two small rooms, one mostly counter, and sometimes the place can feel a bit tight. However, when you sit down and start the ordering process, all is forgotten and you will love your food.

**Bistro Montage, 301 SE Morrison St., Portland, OR 97214; (503) 234-1324; montageportland.com; Southern; $$.** This super hip spot is under the Morrison Bridge, generally an industrial part of town. It's a very fun spot with good, cheap food. It seems to cater to the younger crowd, no early bird special, and the bar is hopping. The food is Southern, with lots of mac and cheese options and stuff like jambalaya and gumbos. When you are done and have leftovers, which happens often because the portions are huge, they create some magic with your leftovers and aluminum foil. Swans, giraffes, and that kind of thing. It's a great place for a crowd of fun peeps. And an inspiration for future balloon blowers for kid's birthday parties.

**Biwa, 215 SE 9th St., Portland, OR 97214; (503) 239-8830; biwa restaurant.com; Izakaya; $$.** Gabe Rosen, the genteel chef-owner of this laid-back *izakaya*, lets his love of all things Japanese shine in this mellow establishment with earthy tones and lots of wood. You can enjoy all kinds of Japanese food, skewered, stir-fried, steamed, and fermented. Food is taken seriously and is prepared with integrity. The *agedashi* is excellent, *onigiri* the best I have had in Portland, and the selection of sochu and sake top-notch. Biwa stays open late and is just the right kind of food to enjoy into the wee hours. See Chef Rosen's recipes for **Albaore Tataki & Cucumber Sunomono** and **Nabe** on pp. 185 and 186.

**Blossoming Lotus, 1713 NE 15th Ave., Portland, OR 97212; (503) 228-0048; blpdx.com; Vegan; $$.** Blossoming Lotus is possibly the best vegan food in Portland. They do a terrific job, and even non-veganites find the food worthy of repeat visits. The food is seriously seasonal, and not the least bit bland or flat, the frequent flaw in vegan menus. I totally love the mixed greens and romaine, cabbage, carrot, cucumber, raisins, crispy rice stick, fresh herbs, curry peanuts, coconut, and Thai-spiced barbecue soy curls, with sweet ginger dressing and sesame seeds. The phyllo roulade with sweet potato and jerked vegetables is an excellent choice as well.

**Boke Bowl, 1028 SE Water Ave., Portland, OR 97214; (503) 719-5698; bokebowl.com; Asian; $$.** Steamed buns, rice bowls, dumplings, salad, and wet and dry ramen. What the heck is dry ramen, you might ask? I did. Well, it's the crispy noodles that have not been cooked. Most items offered at Boke are inexpensive, and the ingredients are locally sourced and top quality. And for dessert there is a lemongrass ginger soft serve that is really good. And they have **Random Order** (p. 87) fried pie. That is amazing.

**Breakside Brewery, 820 NE Dekum St., Portland, OR 97211; (503) 719-6475; 5821 SE International Way, Milwaukie, OR 97222; (503) 719-6475; breakside.com; Brewpub; $$.** My friends Kristen and Lesley introduced us to their favorite neighborhood brewpub. Most go for the great and constantly changing beers, I go for the house-made stuffed jalapeños and the waffle fries with blue cheese. Breakside serves very good pub food and brews very excellent beers to wash down a few of their fiery offerings. The place is always busy, and when the weather is nice, it's a super-fun place to hang outside. Lots of dogs and bikes and happy people.

**Broder, 2508 SE Clinton St., Portland, OR 97255; (503) 736-3333; broderpdx.com; Swedish; $$.** I fell in love with Broder on my first visit. I was actually there for a photo shoot for *Portland Monthly Magazine* and we were shooting the lamb burger. It was delicious and a pleasure to look at, so it became one of my favorite PDX burgers. The restaurant, which opened in 2007, is in one of my favorite Portland neighborhoods, the Clinton area, which is small and has just the right amount of places to do your shopping and drinking and eating. Part of the charm of Broder, in addition to all the cute Swedish plates and skillets, is the manager of the restaurant, Joe Conklin, who is the sweetest, most adorable guy in Portland. He couldn't be friendlier or more helpful, and everyone who comes in loves him. He can do 50 things at once, all perfectly, with a huge smile on his face. I have not had a lot of experience with food from Sweden, except for the occasional order of Swedish meatballs sitting with a full cart of stuff at Ikea. After my first strictly business visit, I headed there with some friends for brunch. The place is very small, cozy, and charming. The kitchen is tiny, and the selection is fabulous. There are what they call "bords," which are literally wooden boards that hold, for example, brown bread and rye crisp, cured meat, smoked trout, Swedish cheese, a clementine with yogurt, fruit, and roasted apple. It's a great meal. They also do baked scrambles, with gravlax, and wild mushrooms and smoked trout with horseradish cream—also excellent. My favorite dish, and I am certainly not alone in this, is the Aebleskiver, the fluffiest, most extraordinary pancakes served with your choice of two of the following: homemade lemon curd, syrup, lingonberry jam, or house-made applesauce. You can smell them cooking, along with all the other tasty and soul-warming dishes they serve.

**Bunk Bar,** 1028 SE Water Ave., Portland, OR 97214; (503) 894-9708; bunkbar.com; **Bar and Sandwiches; $$.** When you walk into Bunk Bar, you'll think you're in Paris. Paris, Texas, that is. One entire wall is an enormous mural of Harry Dean Stanton from the fabulous movie *Paris, Texas.* Restaurant Owners Tommy Habetz and Nick Mirto are the cutest non-couple duo in town. They are gracious and generous, love good food, and have impressive credentials. They serve some of the best sandwiches in town. The Cubano will knock your rain boots off, as will just about everything you order. They have a couple of spots in town but this one, on Water and Taylor, is my personal fave. There is music, a cool vibe, and a bar that knows how to pour. And these guys are so friendly and nice you may want to stop by just to say hi, and while you are there, split a roasted chicken salad sandwich. You won't be sorry. See Bunk Bar's recipe for **Pork Belly Cubano** on p. 191.

**Castagna,** 1752 SE Hawthorne Blvd., Portland, OR 97214; (503) 231-7373; castagnarestaurant.com; **Northwest Cuisine; $$$$.** Castagna serves probably the most modern and sophisticated food in Portland, one of two places where molecular gastronomy is in full force. Castagna is expensive, and packed, and Chef Justin Woodward is getting raves for his take on this modern food trend. Castagna will be

# CAFE CASTAGNA

**Cafe Castagna,** just next door to the sophisticated Castagna, prepares Pacific Northwest cuisine using local, fresh ingredients in a casual setting. The Cafe offers dinner in a style that is almost the opposite of its sister restaurant. The risotto balls filled with fontina are heavenly, as is the gratin of cauliflower, sunchoke, and turnips. As an entree I like the *zuppa de pesce* and the pork braised with black olives, collard greens, and polenta. In the nice weather there is outdoor seating. My last time there I sat on Hawthorne sipping my coffee and loving my walnut and almond torte, while reaching across the table to take a stab at my husband's chocolate hazelnut mousse.

a totally different dining experience for those unfamiliar with molecular gastronomy. The food is studied, and uses seasonal ingredients in combinations and cooking styles that are not what one expects. Tastes and textures at their most intriguing. For many, this cooking style will be an occasional treat, or experiment, though I do have a friend here in Portland who eats there weekly. What's up with that? To me it is the anti-comfort food. Very interesting and good, just seems as much like science as it does dinner.

**Cheese Bar, 6031 SE Belmont St., Portland, OR 97215; (503) 222-6014; cheese-bar.com; Cheese; $$.** This laid-back shop has a wide variety of cheeses, some hard to find, like burrata and mountina, as well as some more standard favorites at their peak of ripe perfection. There is probably no better place to buy cheese in Portland. Steve Jones knows how to pick his product and is happy to share his knowledge. They have reasonably priced, well-chosen wines by the glass and some excellent beer from small local breweries. The two guys at the

helm, Owner Steve Jones and Chef Tim Daly, run their business in an easy-going and super-friendly style. The grilled mac and cheese, which is amazing, takes an already delicious item to even greater heights, and desserts like bread pudding and fruit crumbles rock. Everyone who comes in, whether they are delivering cheese, beer, or want something to eat, are treated like old friends, and the guys are so helpful, offering tastes and suggestions; the experience is delightful. It is the kind of place that makes you feel so comfortable you end up staying way longer than you need to. Everyone seems to be having a great time. The coconut cauliflower soup is creamy curried deliciousness, and the sandwiches are some of the best in Portland. Daly is a master of ingredient pairings, and it seems like each component gets to shine in its own cheesy, beefy, or porky way.

**Clark Lewis, 1001 SE Water Ave. #160; Portland, OR 97214; (503) 235-2294; clarklewispdx.com; Northwest Cuisine; $$$.** The exposed pipes and garage doors in this otherwise elegant and upscale restaurant are the only indication that this was, at one time, a warehouse. The restaurant is large, and a partial wall of copper and stones divides the bar area from the white-clothed tables and comfy chairs. The bar is a busy scene, and the beer and wine list is impressive and extensive. On a recent visit, the gin and lime gimlet was tart and refreshing. The kitchen is open to the dining area, and there is a wood-burning oven responsible for the expertly presented entrees. Grilled foods are a strong focus here, from a spectacular leg of lamb to the grilled rib eye. It was at Clark Lewis that I first had razor clams. I have been a fan ever since, though they have never lived up to my "first time." The pastas are made in-house, and the combinations reflect the changing seasons and moods of the people behind the stove. The restaurant is elegant and classy, yet remains true to Portland in its

and relaxed atmosphere. Their desserts are a wonderful finale,
eciding is always a tough choice. On my most recent visit, I loved
ck, the tangerine panna cotta, and got to taste Bruce's chocolate
coffee mousse, which was outstanding.

**Compote Cafe and Bakery,** 2032 SE Clinton St., Portland, OR
97202; (503) 234-5689; compotepdx.com; American; $$. I was on
Clinton Street and was feeling a bit peckish. My friend Judy suggested
we try Compote; she had heard good things. I was delighted by the
simply prepared fresh food, particularly loving the gravlax sandwich.
Judy had the latkes and said they were as good as her grandma used to
make, but I doubt her grandmother ever made latkes. You gotta know
Judy to understand. I got a couple of muffins to take with me, and
Olivia gave them a thumbs up.

**Country Cat,** 7937 SE Stark St., Portland, OR 97215; (503) 408-
1414; countrycat.net; American Comfort; $$. The up-and-coming
neighborhood Montavilla is home to some good eating places, and
Country Cat ranks among the best. Chef Adam Sappington and his
wife, Jackie, serve up some of the best brunches, lunches, and dinners in Portland. Adam grew up in central Missouri and spent hours
in the kitchen cooking with his mom and grandma. The love of family
and the love of food brought Adam and Jackie to open Country Cat,
with a menu that dedicates itself to serving hearty comfort food with
strong and gutsy flavors. The corner restaurant
is cozy and friendly, and it is not unusual
to see large families digging into the
Country Cat's Whole Hog plate, consisting of rolled pork belly, a boneless loin
chop, and smoked shoulder with perfect
grits. Another spectacular large plate is
the red wine braised beef on a spring
onion bread salad with bacon vinaigrette.

Although Country Cat is a destination for families, it is also a to go alone, sit with some sort of reading device, and linger over incredible dessert, like the trio of puddings with freshly baked cookies, the perfect way to end a meal. Fried chicken with spoon bread is one of the most popular brunch items. Filling and hearty, the ultimate food to soothe and satisfy, the dish comes with two perfectly fried pieces of chicken and a big piece of spoon bread. It sits on the plate, daring you to eat it all. See Country Cat's recipe for **Butternut Squash & Parsnip Puree** on p. 211.

**Crema, 2728 SE Ankeny St., Portland, OR 97214; (503) 234-0206; cremabakery.com; Bakery/Cafe; $$.** Whether you go for coffee or a sandwich, Crema is a sweet place to be. The staff is super-friendly and the pastries are homey perfection. There are some offerings that are always available, and the specials are not to be missed. Of course, some specials become regular items due to their popularity. Honestly, I have never been disappointed by anything I have ordered there. The manchego and mushroom biscuit is flaky manna from above, and the cream cake is wonderful. Sandwiches are all done with fresh, top-quality ingredients, and the grilled ones are the best. You can sit for hours and watch the interesting crowd gather for their daily dose of Crema goodness. And as per Portland, many people set up laptops and turn Crema into their office. Cookies are chewy and the dog biscuits, according to my dogs, are the best in town. See Crema's recipe for **Crema Cream Cake** on p. 187.

**Cricket Cafe, 3159 SE Belmont St., Portland, OR 97214; (503) 235-9348; cricketcafepdx.com; Comfort; $$.** Cricket Cafe caters to the throngs of people in Portland who love their breakfast. And let me tell you, it is amazing. This bi-level cafe turns out hearty and satisfying breakfasts that will keep you happy till dinner, if you want to go that route—plates of eggs Benedict, chilaquiles hash, biscuits and gravy, and amazing toasted pound cake with espresso icing that will knock your socks off. I have a group of friends who eat there once a week—they are hooked. Bloody Marys are crazy good and the whole experience is a great way to start the day.

**Doug Fir Lounge, 830 SE Burnside St., Portland, OR 97214; (503) 231-9663; dougfirlounge.com; American; $$.** My favorite part  of this very cool-looking place is sitting outside by the fire pits on a dry evening. My least favorite is sitting there in the pouring rain. Just kidding. Of course I don't do that, and the restaurant and bar are perfectly fine and fun places to hang out. The food is good; I like brunch the best, but have never been let down by the wonderful nibbles that go with the well-poured cocktails. They have music often and are part of a cool hotel that is reasonable and I am sure a good way to get a taste of cool Portland. Very good Bloody Marys, spicy and strong.

**East Burn, 1800 SE Burnside St., Portland, OR 97214; (503)-236-2876; theeastburn.com; Bar; $$.** East Burn is about as casual as Portland gets. Well, that is probably not true, but personally I wouldn't want anything more casual. They are a great place to go with a group of fun people. This is not a job interview place unless the job is uber hip and super cool, like director of a naturopathy school, or bartender. They often have live music and are open every night till 2 a.m. There is an ever-changing selection of about 20 draft beers, inventive drinks using locally distilled spirits, and one of those wine machines that keeps each pour as good as the first. The food is good, with the staff occasionally going on field trips to collect some of Oregon's bounty. Not the paper towels though. The food is eclectic, from potato pancakes to steak culottes. I recently had a creamy and yummy lobster mac and cheese, and never pass up the ice cream and cookie sundae, pleasurably rich and decadent. There's great outdoor seating and bar games.

**EC Kitchen, 6335 SE 82nd Ave., Portland, OR 97206; (503) 788-6306; eckitchenllc.com; Chinese; $$.** Finally, good scallion pancakes in Portland. I have been waiting. Love the deep-fried five-spice chicken and the shrimp cake with Chinese sausage. The black pepper beef was as it should be: peppery, tender, and tasty. Interesting tofu desserts finish a satisfying meal. This is the best of Portland's homemade Chinese sausages, Taiwanese sweet sausages, and amazing barbecue pork, beef shanks, preserved duck, and more! They use quality ingredients with no preservatives. Great for take-out too. Although, if you don't live in Portland, it may be cold when you get it home and that's always a bummer.

**Evoe, 3735 Hawthorne Blvd., Portland, OR 97214; (503) 232-1010; pastaworks.com; European; $$.** Eating at Evoe is an adventure in simplicity and brilliance. The restaurant is part of Pasta Works, a terrific gourmet shop on Portland's east side. The dining area is small, with a few tables and some seats at the counter, in front of the tiny, open kitchen. And the kitchen is a mixture of non-state-of-the-art equipment. There is an oven, a couple of griddles, and some cold storage areas. Everything is done to order, and the choices are listed on the blackboard above the cooking area. Chef Kevin Gibson has the cooking cred that puts him up with the best in town. The cooking in France, Italy, and Spain predominantly inspires the menu at Evoe. The sandwiches are outstanding, my personal favorite, at the moment, being the Dansk, made with house-cured gravlax. Another killer dish is the calamari and chickpeas, baked under a spicy aioli, and the Sauvie Island beet salad is the best beet treatment I have had. Being a charter member of the deviled egg fan club, I was momentarily reborn after tasting the stuffed and then griddled version of this dish that I thought could not be improved on. I think I went back, just for the eggs, three times that first week. This place is a monument to food creativity and genius.

**The Farm Cafe, 10 SE 7th Ave., Portland, OR 97214; (503) 736-FARM; thefarmcafepdx.com; Northwest Cuisine; $$.** I like this funky restaurant in an old Victorian house. The food is ingredient driven, with fresh produce at its peak of ripeness and taste. Last visit I thoroughly enjoyed the clams in a white wine sauce, and the beet carpaccio was excellent. For an entree I had the stinging nettle ravioli, and my dining companion had the veggie burger, which she said was the best she had ever had. The trout looked beautiful, seared to perfection, and the people at the next table were loving the gnocchi. Sadly they didn't offer a taste. For dessert we split the apple crisp, and although it was enough, we decided to order the chocolate soufflé with coffee ice cream. Glad we did—it was stellar.

**Fire on the Mountain, 1708 E. Burnside St., Portland, OR 97214, (503) 230-9464; 4225 N. Interstate, Portland, OR 97215, (503) 280-WING; 3443 NE 57th Ave., Portland, OR 97213, (503) 894-8973; portlandwings.com; Wings; $$.** Wings are one of my favorite bar foods. When featured on a menu with cheesesticks and sliders, you never think they will give them the attention they deserve. Fire on the Mountain is all about wings, with a choice of about 12 different sauces, with varying degrees of heat, served with ranch and blue cheese dressing. The fries, both sweet potato and russet, are done crispy but not too, and the onion rings are damn good. There are salads and fried pickles and Oreos at the meal's end. Beers are cold and well chosen, there is iced tea and lemonade, and you get to make your own Arnold Palmer. You place your order and then find a table, which is sometimes a challenge, but totally worth the time. Sometimes they have live music, which is fine but does take up a table or two! Very casual, and if you go with El Hefe on your wings, they will blow your socks off. Pass the Maalox, please.

**Foster Burger, 5339 SE Foster Rd., Portland, OR 97206; (503) 775-2077; fosterburger.com; Burgers; $$.** One of the great Portland burger spots also serves some good poutine. Poutine is a dish from Quebec: fries with cheese curds and gravy, and not for those who never splurge into the decadent realm of dining. There are many types of poutine toppings, including, yes, you guessed it. Bacon. And lots of it. The burgers are thick and juicy and the whole thing is kind of decadent and delicious. The fries with squid ink are unusual and tasty. The milk shakes, what the heck, are also amazing.

**Genies,** 1101 SE Division St., Portland, OR 97202; (503) 445-9777; **geniesdivision.com; Comfort; $$.** Genies' breakfast is the stuff that dreams are made of. First, their Bloody Mary done like 100 ways is a winner. They have so many house infused vodkas if you tried them all you would need an ambulance. The food is great, and the lines out front on brunch days will attest to that. Try the Tasso ham Benedict with thick slices of ham or one of Genies' offerings of scrambles and omelets made with local eggs, or a piled-high order of french toast made with ciabatta bread. French toast with seasonal fruit or the white chocolate chip and toasted hazelnut pancakes are another delectable way to go.

**Genoa,** 2832 SE Belmont St., Portland, OR 97214; (503) 238-1464; **genoarestaurant.com; Italian; $$$$.** Genoa is a production. The meal is set and the dinner is long (it has been trimmed from 7 courses to 5). The food is excellent. The staff is super-professional and attentive to your every need. Ingredients are seasonal and local whenever possible, and expect such delights as braised early morels and a tartare of Oregon bison, pickled green strawberry, cucumber, and black olive. Not an every-night affair but a lovely special occasion experience, Genoa has, from the beginning, sought out the finest, freshest local ingredients. The superb classic cuisine launched the careers of local star chefs, like former co-owner Cathy Whims, John Taboada, Tommy Habetz, and Kevin Gibson: all Portland food stars.

**Ha & Vl,** 2738 SE 82nd Ave., Portland, OR 97266; (503) 772-0103; **Vietnamese; $$.** There was no better person in Portland to go to for Portland Asian food restaurants than Andy Ricker, of Pok Pok fame. Ricker knows his stuff, and he loves Ha & Vl. And so do lots of other people. The house-made noodle soup may be the best I have ever had. There are two soup choices daily, and they are often gone by noon. The turmeric noodles are outstanding, and the broth of the pho bursting with flavor comes to me in my dreams. Very reasonable and very good. If only I could understand the name.

**Jade Teahouse and Patisserie,** 2342 SE Ankeny St., Portland, OR 97202; (503) 236-4998; hjadeportland.com; **Vietnamese; $$.** Located in the Sellwood neighborhood on the east side of the river, Jade is a family-run Vietnamese restaurant that is a home away from home for residents of this cool and quiet part of town. Since it opened in October 2008, the restaurant has become increasingly more popular, and they are in the process of building out and up. Mother/daughter team Lucy and April Eklund are the reason this place is such a jewel. Lucy, who is a grandmother, cooks, bakes, and is responsible for all the food. Daughter April runs the business. The menu is large, there are over 60 loose teas, and some of the best truffle fries in PDX can be found here. The spicy green papaya salad is fiery and sweet, and the homemade rice noodles make for a standout udon soup. Lunchtime is busy, with neighborhood people coming in for one of their fantastic sandwiches on a freshly baked baguette. The fried catfish in a curry sauce pairs beautifully with the spinach and rice. The Vietnamese beef stew with piping hot bread is a perfect dish for bread dunking. For dessert I always have the Thai iced tea with the black rice pudding with coconut milk and green tea. The sesame balls filled with bean paste deliver a burst of chewy sweetness, and they sell out daily. The food at Jade is very reasonably priced, and it is nice to be in a place filled with motherly love.

# Cooking Classes

**Hipcooks,** *3808 N. Williams Ave., Portland, OR 97227; (503) 281-0614; hipcooks.com.* Mostly evening classes or on weekends, the classes are limited in size and they are adults only. All levels are accommodated. There is a set price for each 3-hour class.

**In Good Taste,** *6302 SW Meadows Road, Lake Oswego, OR 97035; (503) 248-2015; ingoodtastestore.com.* Offered in the evenings and on weekends.

**Le Cordon Bleu College of Culinary Arts,** *600 SW 10th Ave., Ste. 500, Portland, OR 97205; (503) 223-2245; chefs.edu/ Portland.* Portland culinary students develop a focused and theoretical foundation and learn essential technical skills that can be applied to the finest European and North American culinary traditions, methods, and industry-current technologies.

**Oregon Culinary Institute,** *1701 SW Jefferson St., Portland, OR 97201; (503) 961-6200; oregonculinaryinstitute.com.* This is THE cooking school in Portland. Many of the city's top chefs have gone to school here and interns from OCI are hired frequently. People speak highly of the classes offered, and the overall curriculum seems focused and well balanced.

**Portland's Culinary Workshop,** *807 N. Russell St., Portland, OR 97227; (503) 512-0447; portlandsculinaryworkshop.com.* From all reports the cooking classes here get high marks; a couple of friends just finished the knife technique class and they claim to now have mad skills. They offer classes weekly and cover the basics, plus.

**Killer Burger,** 8728 SE 17th Ave., Portland, OR 97202; (503) 841-5906; 4644 NE Sandy Blvd., Portland, OR 97213; (971) 544-7521; killerburgerpdx.com; Burgers; $$. These burgers are best with a mess of delicious toppings and cannot be eaten while driving. But boy are they good. All burgers include bacon, which is very Portland. Friends love the burger with peanut butter and pickles, but I usually go for the classic bacon, cheese, lettuce, tomato, smokey house sauce, grilled onion, and pickle. The fries are good, not amazing. They have a veggie burger you  can get without bacon, but no one will talk to you. And a kid size, too. They make their own peanut butter sauce, Swiss blend, bleu cheese blend, and smokey house sauce, and they roast their own chilies.

**Laurelhurst Market,** 3155 SE Burnside St., Portland, OR 97214; (503) 206-3097; laurelhurstmarket.com; Steak House; $$$. People really like Laurelhurst Market. It is always packed with folks at the bar enjoying top-of-the-line cocktail offerings and super-fun food off the standing rail menu. I just loved the fava beans edamame style. It's an interesting place. The butcher shop that is part of the restaurant sells top-quality sausages, pâtés, and rillettes, and it is all done in-house. The food at Laurelhurst is meat centric, although they serve some of the best mussels and clams in town. The spring fritters are outstanding, although I have never met a fritter I didn't like. A chalkboard hanging from the ceiling shows the cuts of beef and what is available on any particular night. The beef is top rate, and there are unusual cuts, teres major for one, that is tender and tasty like a filet mignon but considerably less pricey. The braised pork shank is aromatic and tender. The marrowbones starter is a great use of that now-in-fashion food, with a vinegary dressing of parsley, pickled shallots, and fried capers that cuts the overdose of fat. Desserts are all good, and it's such a nice room that you just want to linger with a cup of coffee and something

tasty and sweet. Oh yes, Bruce reminded me of the giant smoked ice cube they have with certain cocktails and whiskey. Don't even ask how they do it, but they do and it keeps those smoky whiskey drinks, well, smoky!

**Le Pigeon, 738 E. Burnside St., Portland, OR 97214; (503) 546-8796; lepigeon.com; French Inspired; $$$$.** This well-loved Portland restaurant takes reservations, and it's very busy, but always leaves room at the tiny kitchen-fronted counter for walk-ins who start appearing before the 5 p.m. opening time. On a typical evening, there are three chefs working the line. They are a talented bunch who seem to appreciate and take great pride in being part of this extraordinary spot, serious about maintaining its stellar reputation. All ingredients are top quality, coming in fresh from local ranchers and farms daily. Chef Gabriel Rucker is young, heavily tattooed, and he's a huge baseball fan. But seriously, he is generous with his time and knowledge, and well respected in the food community. He always creates a well-balanced and interesting menu, and generally knocks it all out of the park. On a recent visit we dined on fabulously prepared snails served with orzo, cauliflower, and Parmesan. The gnocchi with pheasant and seasonal parsnips was outstanding as well. My main course was a veal marsala, I think better than even the finest Italian restaurants. Bruce went for the burger—awesome. Desserts are noteworthy, and Chef Rucker's signature dish, the *foie gras* ice cream-stuffed profiterole, is famous around town. This was not a dish I ate when I was a child, and something tells me neither did Rucker. However, as a well-fed adult, I have to admit to being impressed by how well these combinations work together. It is a brave and brilliant mind that came up with this bizarre yet delicious offering.

**Levant, 2448 SE Burnside St., Portland, OR 97214; (503) 954-2322; levantpdx.com; French/Arab; $$$.** This French-Arab restaurant opened to excellent reviews, and we went to see what all the fuss is about. Chef-Owner Scott Snyder combines his Jewish family history with his French culinary training and serves a combination of Middle Eastern and North African cuisine with an interesting use of unusual spices and other ingredients. The 50-seat restaurant has an open hearth, and the food is an upscale version of standard Middle Eastern cuisine. On my first visit I was impressed by the powerful combination of flavors and cooking styles, although I am not accustomed to paying high prices for that type of food. My favorite dish was the grilled sweetbreads, and my dining companion loved the fava bean falafel. There is an interesting cocktail menu that emphasizes the unusual spices. They offer mini cocktails, encouraging you to try a medley. When the weather is warm, there will be additional seating outside. One of my favorite PDX places, Alder Bakery, was in that spot last, and I have very happy memories. Hopefully Levant will live up to that level of deliciousness, though in an entirely new guise.

**Lily Day Cafe,** 3524 SE 52nd Ave., Portland, OR 97206; (503) 774-1164; **Bakery and Lunch; $.** When I got the word that Dot's, a bizarre but fun restaurant in the Clinton neighborhood, was under new hands, I kind of panicked. I loved the vibe in that place. As luck would have it, the owners of Dots, sisters Monica and Jennifer Ransdell, opened a new place. Different entirely, but still a good vibe. Phew. They serve all kinds of pastries and wonderful sandwiches for both breakfast and lunch. I don't know about you, but there is something special about a cheesy, warm breakfast sandwich, hopefully with a pork product succulently tucked inside. There is a rockin' drink menu as well, with a very sweet idea for an alcoholic beverage, the "Red-Eye Flight"—vodka on the rocks served with "side shots" of Bloody Mary mix, orange juice, and grapefruit juice. A good way to start a non-workday. Or if you can handle it, a workday, as long as you're not a surgeon or a pilot!

**Luce,** 2138–2140 SE Burnside St., Portland, OR 97214; (503) 236-7195; luceevents.blogspot.com; Italian; $$. Luce is a neighborhood restaurant serving authentic Italian food that captures the flavors of the ingredients in its simple but impeccably prepared dishes. The spaghetti with garlic and hot peppers is as good as that dish gets, and I have enjoyed it all over Italy. The hangar steak with grilled cabbage is superb. Luce is the sibling of the well-loved restaurant **Navarre** (p. 84), and although Luce has not been opened for very long, it is not unusual to wait a bit for a table. Due to its focus on seasonality, the restaurant menu changes frequently. At times that can be a bummer, but I have found that if Luce replaces an item, it is equally as good or better than its predecessor. The chocolate hazelnut cake is amazing, and I would be sad if it wasn't on the menu.

**Mad Greek Deli,** 1740 SE Burnside St., Portland, OR 97229; (503) 645-1650; madgreekdeli.com; Greek; $$. When done well, Greek food is light, fresh, and delicious comfort food. There is a strong Greek community in Portland, and the people I know who are Greek love this place. Start with a plate of Greek fries, covered with Greek seasonings and feta cheese. Fries and feta are a happy couple. The moussaka is good as is the spanakopita. They do an excellent gyro and the falafel is moist (I like to wrap it in my pita bread with some hummus).

**Meat Cheese Bread,** 1406 SE Stark St., Portland, OR 97213; (503) 234-1700; meatcheesebread.com; Sandwiches; $$. There is no question that this small spot makes a great sandwich. Everything is made in-house from the bread to the pickled carrots on the roasted pork loin sandwich. The breakfast burrito is hard to pass up, though on my last visit I opted for the savory bread pudding with fennel, sausage, and cheddar. No regrets. My favorite cold sandwich is the Park Kitchen with flank steak, pickled onions, and blue cheese mayo. For a hot sandwich the green bean with bacon relish, soft boiled egg, Parmesan, and aioli should win an award. And I will present it and then eat the sandwich.

**Michael's Italian Beef & Sausage Co.,** 1111 SE Sandy Blvd., Portland, OR 97214; (503) 230-1899; michaelsitalianbeef .com; **Sausages and Hot Dogs; $$.** Chicago-style subs and hot dogs are nostalgia eats for some, and just plain old awesomeness for others. Meatballs are tender and flavorful, sausage is made there and is done well, and the thinly sliced beef with gravy with peppers or onions, or both, is one great sandwich. Franks are good too.

**Mi Mero Mole,** 5026 SE Division St., Portland, OR 97206; (503) 232-8226; mmmtacospdx.com; **Mexican; $$.** In Mexico, *guisados* are cooked dishes, especially stews and stir-fries, often sold on the streets in Mexico City. The goal at Mi Mero Mole is to serve traditional dishes from Mexico City that folks will love, and offer them at reasonable prices. The street foods from around the world are becoming a big, interesting trend. Tortillas are made fresh using ground *nixtamal* rather than commercial *maseca*. The daily specials and regular menu items are available in tacos, burritos, and quesadillas. The meatballs I had there recently were so good I ordered some for Bruce, and he agreed. Everything served at the restaurant is made in-house, and you can taste the quality and freshness.

**My Brother's Crawfish,** 8220 SE Harrison St., Portland, OR 97216; (503) 774-3786; mybrotherscrawfish.com; **Southern; $$.** My Brother's Crawfish is fun. Two brothers from Vietnam, via Houston, do a terrific take on a selection of Southern-style seafood boils that are full of flavor and spice. Crawfish are flown up twice a week, everything is always fresh, and the boils are cooked to order. While waiting for your entree, enjoy a plate of fried green tomatoes or great Cajun crab cakes. You can't go wrong with anything at this unpretentious place, and wash it all down with an ice-cold Abita beer, from Louisiana. A perfect combo. And for me, the large photo of the Flatiron Building in NYC, my old stomping ground, was nostalgic.

**Nicholas,** 318 SE Grand Ave., Portland, OR 97214; (503) 235-5123; 3223 NE Broadway, Portland, OR 97232; (503) 445-4700; nicholasrestaurant.com; Middle Eastern; $$. Nicholas is my second favorite Middle Eastern restaurant in Portland. From start to finish the food is great. When the platters of hummus and baba ghanoush come to your table, with piping hot bread the size of a pillowcase, expect a feeding frenzy. Grilled eggplant drizzled with olive oil is a thing of beauty, and the kebobs of all types are just right. Service is rushed but friendly, and to-go boxes are offered happily, which is always nice. There are two locations in Portland; the one in north Portland usually does not have a wait.

**Noble Rot,** 1111 E. Burnside St., Portland, OR 97214; (503) 233-1999; noblerotpdx.com; American; $$. Noble Rot is perched atop an award-winning, environmentally forward, LEED-Platinum building (the greenest!). The wine choices are exceptional, and it's easy to familiarize yourself by ordering flights available every day. Noble Rot has a 300-plus bottle list and serves well over 40 wines by the glass. Noble Rot's highly regarded, local, and seasonal menu changes daily, but the regular offerings such as their endive, beet, blue cheese, and hazelnut salad, or creamy onion tart, get lots of warranted attention. Noble Rot has a 3,000-square-foot rooftop garden, which supplies most of the vegetables and herbs during the long, warm summer months. That's pretty amazing, isn't it?

**Nostrana,** 1401 SE Morrison St., Portland, OR 97214; (503) 234-2427; nostrana.com; Italian; $$$. Cathy Whims's restaurant is a lovely place to enjoy an exceptional Italian meal. The restaurant is huge, but nonetheless has a warm almost cozy feel. The bar is beautiful and produces some fine drinks. The pizzas and pastas are top rate, and entrees are excellent. Cathy is warm and lovely, has studied food of all kinds, and has a way of making local and seasonal ingredients shine. And the yogurt panna cotta for dessert is silky and wonderful. Oh yeah, the scissors to cut the pizza are very cool.

**Observatory, 8115 SE Stark St., Portland, OR 97215; (503) 445-6284; theobservatorypdx.com; American; $$.** Montavilla neighborhood is a bit out of the way but it has a very active food scene. Stark Street has fun shopping and a great old-fashioned movie theater, and it has the Observatory. Their veggie burgers are my favorite in town, and the relaxed vibe and good drinks make this a very enjoyable place to get breakfast, lunch, or dinner. The staff is friendly and helpful with your menu choices. My waitress highly recommended the mussels diabla, and they were spicy, super fresh, and plump. Like an old boyfriend I had in high school! The oregano fry bread is perfection served with the basil crème fraîche, and the chicken pâté is a keeper. If meat loaf is your thing, don't pass it up; it's kinda perfect. I would be remiss if I didn't mention both the chocolate torte and the cinnamon sugar bread pudding. Beautiful way to end a meal.

**Ocean City Seafood, 3016 SE 82nd Ave., Portland, OR 97266; (503) 771-2299; oceancityportland.com; Chinese; $$.** I spent the first 6 months in Portland missing my monthly dim sum meals. It was a family tradition. Thankfully we found a few good spots, and Ocean City is my current favorite. I love the whole concept of carts filled with delicious foods actually being wheeled up to me for the taking. Couldn't it always be like that? I love all the dumplings, and the fried chicken wings are amazing. The rice rolls are also as good as NY Chinatown. On weekends there is a wait, but during the week you just walk right in and the carts start rolling. Music to my ears.

**Original Hotcake House, 1102 SE Powell Blvd., Portland, OR 97202; (503) 236-7402; hotcakehouse.com; American; $$.** This is not necessarily the place to bring your mom for Mother's Day, but it is open 24 hours, the food is good, and the prices are low. I have been there twice, both times after midnight, and I love to get steak and eggs or the pancakes. You order cafeteria style so you get to see some things cooking, which helps in the decision-making process. There's an interesting crowd at that time, and it's fun. I pass there all the time on my travels to the east side, and I always want to stop in, but I have decided to save it for midnight and later snacks, keeping my pancake intake a little lower.

**Petite Provence,** 4834 SE Division St., Portland, OR 97206; (503) 233-1121; petiteprovence.com; French; $$. I like to eat here for lunch, the staff is really nice, the salads and sandwiches are always good, and the pastries are pretty amazing. Last visit I had smoked salmon hash, which was so tasty sitting under my two perfectly fried eggs. I was with Madge and Judy, and Judy had the Cobb salad, which she loved, and Madge went for the magnificent Monte Cristo, which she kindly let me share. She's almost ninety and going strong, but her appetite is somewhat smaller than her portions are, so I always sit next to her!

**Pine State Biscuits,** 2204 NE. Alberta St., Portland, OR 97211; (503) 477-6605; pinestatebiscuits.com; Southern; $$. *Esquire* magazine chose Pine State Biscuits' "Reggie Deluxe" as one of the best sandwiches in America. This is the place where folks can enjoy a hearty breakfast or lunch 7 days a week, rain or shine. The Belmont restaurant is small, and I go to the Alberta location because it's bigger and has outside seating. The menu is simple, with a blackboard listing of about a dozen choices. If you are a biscuit purist, Pine State will make you happy. The Stumptown coffee is good, and when you waddle out, you will think you will never eat again. But trust me, you will.

**Pix,** 2225 SE. Burnside St., Portland, OR 97214; (971) 271-7166; pixpatisserie.com; Desserts; $$. I am more a fan of the desserts in the comfort food department, but Pix does what it does very well. The pastries are beautiful, rich, and unusual. I have taken many PDX visitors to Pix upon their request and everyone loves what they order. The macaroons are lovely and the chocolates also a treat.

**Relish Gastropub, 6637 SE Milwaukie Ave., Portland, OR 97202; (503) 208-3442; relishgastropub.com; Gastropub; $$.** Relish Gastropub is a warm food lover's sanctuary, located in the Sellwood-Moreland neighborhood. In the kitchen, Chef Josef Valoff believes in spirited flavors paired with local ingredients, making for some unusual dishes. The food is interesting, not the typical handling of seasonal offerings. The sturgeon and mussel stew, served in a tomato fennel ragout, was a super flavorful dish, tasting fresh and satisfying. The smoked pork shoulder was excellent as well, and they do a very good burger and you can put an egg on it. There are over 20 beers on tap, rotating seasonally. The wine list is well chosen and affordable, with a good selection available by the glass. Cocktails are done well: flavorful, interesting, and potent.

**Roe, 3113 SE Division St., Portland, OR 97202; (503) 232-1566; roe-pdx.com; Seafood; $$$.** This romantic and modern seafood restaurant is discreetly hidden in the back of the boisterous izakaya Wafu restaurant, and is only available by reservation, just three nights per week. Strange, but true. Chef Trent Pierce is considered a seafood master, and Roe has some fine examples of fresh fish at its best in both quality and execution. The cuisine highlights the versatility of seafood through the creative use of ingredients and interesting techniques and presentation. There is an open kitchen located directly in the dining room, and diners get to observe the action in the well-instructed staff. Dishes are accompanied by a rotating beverage selection that is chosen specifically for the week's menu. Pricey and different, this restaurant is an interesting PDX dining experience.

**Roost, 1403 SE Belmont St., Portland, OR 97214; (971) 54** roostpdx.com; American; $$.** For over 2 years now Roost remains the place that never disappoints. I have been there for an amazing number of dinners, New Year's Eve and brunch, birthday dinners and midweek spontaneous dinners, and I always leave thinking that I have had a great meal. In my mind Roost is shockingly underappreciated. And yet it is often super busy in the evening and on weekend mornings. I just have yet to find a flaw. Maybe I am not supposed to say this, but it is by far my favorite restaurant in Portland. Chef-Owner Megan Henzel takes simple ingredients and makes magic. The deep-fried Brussels sprouts with sherry vinegar have been known to make grown women cry, and every way she makes chicken, the bird is elevated to grand proportions. Just last night 6 of us had a dinner there that was total perfection. The braised pork on celery puree was melt-in-your-mouth tender, and the smoked gouda dumplings unbelievable. Henzel knows how to make a salad as interesting and tasty as is possible, and her desserts are fun and totally yummy. Sundae in a tin can, fried custard with a crème Anglaise . . . no need for words. There is a small bar with a good beer and wine selection and the waitstaff, a great crew, makes a good drink. The restaurant is all about good food. No pretense, no BS. Just damn good everything. Bruce, my official proofreader, thinks Roost is as good as it gets in Portland. Honest food, no smoke and mirrors, no *foie gras* and maraschino cherry mixtures. Just great food that makes you wonder why all food doesn't taste this good. Thank you, Megan Henzel. Thank you very much.

**Saburo, 1667 SE Bybee St., Portland, OR 97030; (503) 236-4237;** saburos.com; Sushi; $$.** This is a popular place for Reedies and folks living in Sellwood. The prices are extremely reasonable for fresh and enormous sushi. For those reasons there is almost always a wait, so go early or late if you are not into standing in line. There is some talk about how you aren't supposed to eat such large, at-least-three-bite pieces, but no complaints. It is true that when pieces of sushi can't be popped into your mouth in one bite, it can become a messy proposition, but there are worse things.

**The Sapphire Hotel,** 5008 SE Hawthorne Blvd., Portland, OR 97215; (503) 232-6333; thesapphirehotel.com; Speakeasy; $$. This is kind of a sexy spot that was once a seedy hotel/brothel. There is a candlelit glow and a romantic buzz in the air. The cocktails here are top rate, with a selection of martinis, Manhattans, and all those sophisticated libations we all love. The food is good, and the prices are so reasonable you can forgive the occasional blips of the radar. Love the bacon-wrapped dates and the mussels and clams. The roasted beet burger is a vegetarian's delight, and the beef burger with truffled yam fries are super as well.

**Screen Door,** 2337 SE Burnside St., Portland, OR 97214; (503) 542-0880; screendoorrestaurant.com; Southern; $$. Be prepared to wait a bit at this fun and bustling restaurant, but know that it will be well worth it. Drinks are masterfully prepared, a perfect mint julep is a treat, and the food is fantastic. The fried chicken may be the best in town, and the jambalaya and chicken with waffles at brunch are just right. In addition to the homey and hearty Southern specialties, there are always seasonal fruit and vegetable dishes that can be the perfect balance. You can put together a "Screen Door Plate," choosing just what you are in the mood for. The fried pork chops are so good. Owners David and Nicole Mouton are lovely and kind, busy as they are running a well-loved restaurant and raising a couple of kids. Desserts are great (they used to be just good), and even though the portions are large and you will be stuffed, try something. One plate, four forks. You won't be sorry. See Screen Door's recipe for **Pecan Shortbread** on p. 209.

**Shut Up and Eat,** 3848 SE Gladstone St., Portland, OR 97202; (503) 719-6449; shutupandeatpdx.com; Sandwiches; $$. Shut Up and Eat makes great sandwiches. This Italian-inspired sandwich place started out as a cart, and PDX is happy to have it join the ranks of the "once on wheels to brick and mortar" status. The bread is good hoagie quality, and they do a fine job with seasonal ingredients paired with terrific and well-matched toppings. Excellent meatball sub, Bruce's favorite. He can't resist a meatball hero, as they say on the East Coast. Sandwiches have come a long way, and Shut Up and Eat, despite the possibly disquieting name, is inviting and worth a trip. Or two.

### Simpatica Catering and Dining Hall, 828 SE Ash St., Portland, OR 97214; (503) 235-1600; simpaticapdx.com; Comfort; $$$.
This is a wonderful restaurant with kind of odd hours. On Friday and Saturday Simpatica is a supper club, and on Sunday they serve an amazing brunch, one of the best in town. Simpatica does lots of catering, which I guess explains the shortened restaurant hours. It is always busy, and dinners are by reservation only. The chicken and waffles for brunch are ridiculously good. In fact, everything is amazing. I have been trying to get there with friends from out of town, because the whole scene is quite Portland and gives a real flavor of the food scene in town.

### Stickers Asian Cafe, 6808 SE Milwaukee Ave., Portland, OR 97202; (503) 239-8739; stickersasiancafe.com; Asian; $$.
I walked by Stickers a bunch of times and wondered, but never stopped in. I was visiting with the lovely people at **Savory Spice Shop** (p. 73), and they mentioned that they had just eaten there and that I shouldn't pass it by. I have enjoyed my subsequent meals there. Considering they cover street foods of all of Asia—China, Thai, East Indian, Korean, Malaysian, and Vietnamese—they get it down right. It's a delightful meal, lots of small plates of noodles, curries, dumplings, and satays. They are clearly using fresh ingredients and they never use MSG. Yay!

t. **Jack, 2039 SE Clinton St., Portland, OR 97202; (503) 360 1281; stjackpdx.com; French Bistro; $$.** St. Jack is an authentic-feeling bistro serving the food of the cafes and bistros of Lyon, France. The food is rustic French, and the service is professional and friendly. Our waitress suggested a perfect bottle of wine to accompany an outstanding bowl teeming with plump, super-tasty mussels. Steak tartare was full of spice, and I got some first-timers to try it. And like it. The oxtail bourguignon was divine as was the house-made blood sausage. Pastries at St. Jack are stellar with a fantastic lemon tart and baked to order Madeleine. Lovely feel to the room, nice place to stop for an espresso and a light lunch as well as dinner. And check out the drippy white candles on the copper bar. They are beautiful. Still trying to get the wax off my table from trying this at home. There should have been a sign!

**Sunshine Tavern, 3111 SE Division St., Portland, OR 97202; (503) 688-1750; sunshinepdx.com; Comfort Food; $$.** Sunshine Tavern is aptly named because it feels like an old neighborhood hangout, but with really good food and lots of terrific alcohol, including margaritas from a frozen drink machine. The place is all windows, and like **Lincoln** (p. 120), beautifully designed, with a style mix of sophisticated and funky. A shuffleboard table in the center and a couple of arcade games lend a certain charm, along with the counters at both the bar and in front of the open kitchen. The menu is casual but continues to represent Jenn Louis's flair for ingredient pairing, keeping things fresh, seasonal, and always interesting. The food at Sunshine is more casual than at Lincoln, as it should be; it is a tavern, with great salads, sandwiches, and awesome griddled burgers. The restaurant opens at 5 p.m., and has some great starters such as gravy cheese fries with Italian pork sausage, and creamy and delicious chicken liver mousse with toasted baguette. The candied hazelnuts are a swell little snack, and who doesn't love garlic toast? The terrific pizzas (particularly the roasted asparagus, red onion, garlic, and fontina cheese) and the fried chicken and waffles are just right. Egg dishes, from the brunch menu, include a couple of my favorites in town. Baked eggs with chickpeas, spinach, anchovy, tomatoes, and garlic are served with quintessential hash browns, and the hangtown frittata with fried oysters and pork belly draws me in monthly. The soft-serve ice cream, from their very own machine, is a welcome change of pace, and when it's topped with hazelnut crunch, it is legendary. Ricotta doughnuts sprinkled with ginger sugar are the perfect complement to a superb cup of Ristretto coffee. And not to be missed is the spectacular Murphy's Irish stout float.

**Tannery Bar, 5425 E. Burnside St., Portland, OR 97215; (503) 236-3610; facebook.com/pages/The-Tannery-Bar/164035380404462; Upscale Bar Food; $$.** First of all, I love the name Caleb McBee. When Caleb had the now closed Skin and Bones restaurant, he was an absolute delight, in the kitchen and on the floor. He opened Tannery Bar in the same spot as his restaurant, which is right next to his home. He has an impressive garden that he tends in his overalls, with his sweet smile, long hair, and gauges. I am guessing he is tattooed; I'll check it out next time. The drinks at Tannery are excellent, creative, and potent. The space is cool: farmhouse meets hipster. The food is reasonably priced and is comfort food that is interesting and quite tasty. My last time there was for my friend Dina's birthday, and we enjoyed platters of yummy cheeses, charcuterie, and other house-made delights. And Caleb is so cute, friendly, and totally knows his way around the open kitchen.

**Tanuki, 8029 SE Stark St., Portland, OR 97215; (503) 477-6030; tanukipdx.com; Izakaya; $$.** Tanuki is an izakaya in the up-and-coming Montavilla neighborhood in north Portland. This is drinking food: small bites paired with beer or sake or whatever your pleasure happens to be. It is not for kids, it is crowded, and the music is loud and there are bizarre Japanese movies playing on many TVs. The food can be inconsistent, but when it is good, it is very good. There are snacks, skewers, and large plates, and if you are in the mood to be in a place that is not your typical Portland chill, this is the place. I love the *hotate* (marinated scallops), and the seared wild sockeye salmon and crispy duck skin is just awesome.

**Tapalaya, 28 NE 28th Ave., Portland, OR 97232; (503) 232-6652; tapalaya.com; New Orleans; $$.** I recently covered a Portland Dish Crawl for OPB and happily discovered the wonders of this small plate/tapas-style restaurant. The food is New Orleans, the chef is from New Orleans, and the food is very good. And to be able to get small plates of everything, with a large enough group you could actually order everything on the menu. I would love to be at that meal.

**Tarad, 601 SE Morrison St., Portland, OR 97214; (503) 234-4102; taradpdx.com; Thai; $$.** Tarad serves some tasty eats prepared by talented Chef Ning Purnabimba, who is from Chang Mai, Thailand. Chang Mai is the cultural center of Thailand and known for pretty glorious food. Shelves are stocked with all kinds of goodies, tempting you to try your hand at making some Thai dishes at home. There are even Thai cookbooks with English translations. A counter up front has a limited though satisfying menu of goodies like custardy duck egg dumplings, perfect baos, soup bowls filled with exquisite pork broth and meatballs, and thick, highly spiced stews of pork belly and shoulder. This is a Thai food lover's mini paradise.

**Three Doors Down, 1429 SE 37th Ave., Portland, OR 97214; (503) 236-6886; 3doorsdowncafe.com; Italian; $$.** This restaurant deserves more attention than it gets. Much more. The owners are lovely, the staff knowledgeable, and the food frequently delicious. Appetizers are rustic Italian, with a terrific anchovy crostini and spaghetti squash fritters. Pastas and risottos are first rate, and entrees are hearty and often inspired. I would highly recommend the white chocolate bread pudding with bourbon hard sauce. That alone is worth the experience.

**Toast,** 5222 SE 52nd Ave., Portland, OR 97206; (503) 774-1020; toastpdx.com; American; $$. Hundreds of drawings, by both kids and adults, adorn the walls of this 35-seat (with more outside) restaurant on the edge of the Woodstock neighborhood. It's pretty great-looking, like the coolest wallpaper ever. Tiny antique toasters line a few shelves, and there is a blackboard with the daily specials. The place is hopping with local families, Reedies (the super-smart people who attend Reed College), and others coming from all over town for the glorious breakfast and lunch offerings. There is also dinner served three nights a week. When you first sit down at Toast, tiny and terrific scones are brought to the table, whetting your appetite for more. The house-made granola, called "Hippies Use Front Door," is outstanding, and the curried tofu scramble is a favorite with vegetarians as well as meat eaters. Sandwiches are delish, and only the freshest ingredients are used. Throughout the day farmers are dropping by to deliver just about everything the restaurant serves. No big supply houses, just small farms, as local as possible. On my last visit, gorgeous heirloom tomatoes were being admired by the chef and cooks, right off the back of the farmer's truck. Drinks are creative and fun, both nonalcoholic and the hard stuff. The blood orange mimosa is a refreshing and potent libation, and the Morning Glory, a blend of black currant, lemonade, ginger syrup, and tequila, is too easy to drink. Dinners rock.

**Victory Bar,** 3652 SE Division St., Portland, OR 97202; (503) 236-8755; thevictorybar.com; Comfort; $$. The Victory Bar has special status in Portland. It is one of the "go to" restaurants for many of

Portland's top chefs. The doors open at 5 every night, and the tables and bar get progressively more crowded as the night unfolds. This restaurant has quite a following. Owner Yoni Laos, who now runs the show alone, is making history, winning a "Bar of the Year" award from a PDX newspaper. And Yoni Laos is what the bar is all about. The beer selection is renowned, and the cocktails are creative and delightfully drinkable. Don't miss the Victory Martini—that's an order! The pro-paganda-themed art, including his silk-screened lamps and curtains, reflect Yoni's ongoing love affair with being an artist. Victory Bar is casual, the menu is eclectic, and it is in a part of town that is quickly becoming a foodie destination. Amazing spaetzle many ways, and a lamb sandwich that is meltingly tender and combined with tangy feta, is awesome. It is my kind of place, casual and warm, comfortable and delicious. When my son Nick and his lovely lady friend Mary came into town, at midnight we headed right to Victory Bar to hasten their transition from East Coast to west.

**Waffle Window, 3610 SE Hawthorne Blvd., Portland, OR 97214; (503) 239-4756; wafflewindow.com; Waffles; $.** Portland-style Liege sugar waffles are made to order, and they are served from a service door that was converted to a Dutch door, with wafting waffle smells greeting you as you approach. Premium local and seasonal ingredients set in a fun and whimsical atmosphere. This is an amazing waffle experi-ence, with waffles ranging from the classic with Pearl sugar to a recent addition of a cheese, bacon, and jalapeño variety. The hot apple pie waffle is as good as it sounds, and the whole vibe of this place will draw you back again and again. Oh yeah, the waffle ice cream sandwich.

**Woodsman Tavern, 4537 SE Division St., Portland, OR 97206; (971) 373-8264; woodsmantavern.com; American; $$$.** Food at the Woodsman Tavern is good, kind of pricey, and I have to admit that I have enjoyed my brunches there perhaps more than dinner. And dinner was good. I like the deviled egg and the pickled shrimp, and my latest entree was a perfectly cooked pork chop with peppers and onions. For brunch, just last week, I started with a spicy Bloody Mary and the unbelievably delicious oven pancake with ricotta, apples, and bacon. By the way, apples and bacon are a lovely duo. My husband had crispy fried pork with grits and he was a happy man. The restaurant is great-looking, and the market next door sells the best of specialty foods, including carefully chosen food, flowers, beer, and wine.

**Xico,** 3715 SE Division St., Portland, OR 97202; (503) 548-6343; xicopdx.com; Mexican; $$. Happily, one of Portland's recently opened Mexican restaurants gets better and better. My first couple of visits were kind of underwhelming, but last week I had a meal that knocked my shoes off. The *queso fundido* was terrific, and the house-made corn tortillas were perfect. My vegetarian dining companion liked her tacos, and the chicken mole was complex and worked well blanketing the tender chicken. The lemongrass-stuffed game hens cooked on a charcoal rotisserie smelled divine. And the margarita was tasty and potent. Definitely going back.

**Ya Hala,** 8005 SE Stark St., Portland, OR 97215; (503) 256-4484; yahalarestaurant.com; Lebanese; $$. After receiving 27 points from Zagat and winning Portland Iron Chef at a yearly fundraising competition, Ya Hala is starting to get the attention it most definitely deserves. This restaurant, owned by Mirna and John Attar, serves the most delicious Lebanese food I have eaten. Now I have not been to Lebanon, but I have been around, and this place is outstanding. Mirna Attar is the self-taught chef, and everything she makes, from the pita bread she pops into the oven when you are seated, to the stunning array of desserts is a treat that boggles the palate. The lamb shanks are tender with a deep, complex flavor, and the standard Lebanese fare is anything but ordinary. Her hummus, with the warm bread, is magnificent. When Mirna has a special on the menu, order it; you will not be let down. The servers are often family and friends, and if they aren't they certainly reflect the Attar hospitality. The Attars also own **Barbur World Foods** (p. 33).

## A Cooking Class at Ya Hala

Join Mirna Attar, the chef and owner of the Montavilla neighborhood restaurant **Ya Hala** for a cooking class right here at the end of this book. Check out Appendix D (page 250) for recipes such as Lamb Kabobs, Fatayer, and Moujardi.

# Specialty Stores, Markets & Producers

**Belmont Station,** 4500 SE Stark St., Portland, OR 97215; belmont-station.com. When I heard about this place I wanted to blindfold my friend Graeme and take him there. But he was driving so I decided against it. This is a beer lover's mecca. I'm not much of a beer fan, so it doesn't do much for me, but I see folks in there, spending hours perusing the over 1,200 varieties with looks of joy on their faces. So far they have had anything my husband, Bruce, has hoped for, and lots more. The people who work there are helpful, working with me on preparing some well-appreciated gift baskets for deserving, beer-loving friends.

**Fubonn Shopping Center,** 2850 SE 82nd Ave., Portland, OR 97266; (503) 517-8899; fubonn.com. This is an extraordinary market for all things Asian. Walking the aisles is fascinating: so many unfamiliar products and the prices are way less than what you would pay at many PDX shops. Meat and fish are also reasonably priced, and you will see many cuts and varieties that you won't see elsewhere. In the shopping center are places to get baked goods, bubble tea, and other Asian delights. Before my daughter went to study in Japan we bought her going-away cake from the bakery there. It was light and fruity and said "Sayonara." Yummy cake.

**Laurelhurst Market,** 3155 SE Burnside St., Portland, OR 97214; (503) 206-3099; laurelhurstmarket.com. Before I wax poetic about the quality of the meats and pâtés, I will profess my love for the sandwiches they make there on Fleur De Lis bread, one of the best in Portland. You can take the sandwiches to go or find a seat in the restaurant during off hours. When the restaurant is open you will never find a seat.

The butcher shop provides the highest quality products available in the city, all natural, hormone and antibiotic free. I mean, that whole antibiotic thing is awful. The meats and poultry are all from local ranchers, interesting cuts, well priced. While there, it is hard to pass on one of their sandwiches, all house-cooked and cured meats with nothing but the best produce, bread, and their "special sauce." I go for # 3 every time—what a great sandwich. Everything is made in-house—12 flavors of hand-stuffed sausage, pâtés, and lots of bacon. Of course, it's Portland. The people who work there know their meat, and it's a terrific shopping experience.

**Pastaworks, 3735 SE Hawthorne Blvd., Portland, OR 97214; (503) 232-1010; pastaworks.com.** This market has my favorite cheese selection in town. They are very willing to give samples, and what they have is at the peak of ripeness and a great variety. The whole store is top rate, with a fine butcher shop that makes the best pastrami I have had in Portland. The products they carry are the best of the category, the produce quality is superb, and when something is not in season it will not be there. The wine selection is well thought out, and the fresh pasta and house-made sauces are a perfect simple meal after a busy day. Evoe is part of the shop, and getting a bite to eat before or after shopping is a must.

**Peoples Food Co-op, 3029 SE 21st Ave., Portland, OR 97202; (503) 674-2642; peoples.coop/.** When I want a health food item that is hard to find, I head to Peoples. It's a bit of a throwback and reminds me of my hippie days in delightful Brattleboro, Vermont. They know their stuff here and are super nice and laid-back. Cuz that's how hippies roll.

**Piece of Cake, 8306 SE 17th Ave., Portland, OR 97202; (503) 234-9445; pieceofcakebakery.net; Bakery.** I love all of the cakes and cupcakes at this kind of odd bakery in Portland. They make beautiful cakes for all occasions, and their selection of gluten-free and vegan options is large and the quality is great. They made a cake in the shape of a Ford Raptor pickup truck for a friend's birthday. No, it was neither vegan nor gluten-free. That would have been very funny, a vegan, gluten-free, big, red monster truck. I love the carrot cake and the oatmeal cake, and would never pass up anything chocolate from there. There's a banana chocolate cupcake that I wasn't going to taste; moans from a friend changed my mind, and I have to add yet another thing that I crave and eat too often. It's excellent.

**Savory Spice Shop,** 7857 SE 13th Ave., Portland, OR 97202; (503) 928-3099; savoryspiceshop.com/sellwood. Jim and Anne Brown run this amazing spice shop in the quiet and cool Sellwood neighborhood. They are friendly and unbelievably helpful. They love their store and know their spices. I tried some of their more unusual spices on my last visit and loved the dehydrated corn they were offering for folks while shopping. I did a bit of experimenting with some of their unusual offerings. I am currently writing a spice story for OPB with their help and guidance. They offer samples of everything, and they often have tasty treats to showcase some interesting flavors. They do beautiful gift boxes that are premade or of the spices you choose. I think they have over 400 spices; there have to be a few you don't know but should!

**Sheridan,** 409 SE Martin Luther King Jr. Blvd., Portland, OR 97214; (503) 236-2114; sheridanfruit.com. The bulk section of this large market in the SE industrial neighborhood is impressive. Everything you ever wanted to buy in bulk is there for great prices with friendly service to boot. They make a good sandwich, and their meat counter is well priced with a terrific selection of sausages and meats. Fun place to shop. It's not super fancy, just a supermarket!

**Woodsman Market,** 4537 SE Division St., Portland, OR 97206; (971) 373-8267; thewoodsmantavern.com/market. Located just next door to The Woodsman Tavern, the Woodsman Market is open 7 days a week, 9 a.m. to 7 p.m. They have some well-picked produce and a selection of cheeses and products from local artisans and excellent products from around the globe. The bread they carry is from **Little T Bakery** (p. 238), and they have a small but strong selection of beers and wine. And they make a very good sandwich. The Rocky, I guess that's

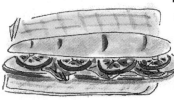 Rocky Balboa, is an excellent rendition of one of the things I miss most in the food department—a true Italian submarine sandwich. Or hoagie, wedge, hero, or grinder. Layered sopressata, capocollo, paper-thin prosciutto, hot peppers, and cheese curds. It's a delicious and

substantial sandwich. The last time I was there they offered a breakfast sandwich with the usual ingredients (bacon, egg, and cheese), and it all was the best of each ingredient. The roll was a great choice, kind of half roll, half English muffin. The market is not cheap, but if you've got it, it's a good place to spend it.

# Northeast Portland

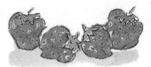

Northeast Portland contains a diverse collection of neighborhoods. For example, while Irvington and the Alameda Ridge feature some of the oldest and most expensive homes in Portland, nearby King is a more working-class neighborhood. Because it is so large, Northeast Portland can essentially be divided ethnically, culturally, and geographically into inner and outer sections. There is some great dining and cool shopping and people watching in this part of town.

## Foodie Faves

**Acadia,** 1303 NE Fremont St., Portland, OR 97212; (503) 249-5001; creolapdx.com; **Creole; $$.** Acadia uses locally grown fruits, vegetables, and meats, as well as exclusively wild-caught seafood from the Gulf Coast and Pacific Northwest. The Louisiana classics are done well; I thoroughly enjoyed the gumbo and the barbecue shrimp. My friend Karen had the jambalaya, and she loved it and took half of it home. She eats like a bird! Graeme had the soft-shell crab and he finished it and had room for a magnificent piece of vanilla custard bread pudding. And I loved my two Sazeracs. Or was it three?

**Autentica,** 5507 NE 30th Ave., Portland, OR 97211; (503) 287-7555; autenticaportland.com; **Mexican; $$.** Dining at Autentica is a treat. Everyone is warm and welcoming, and the place, while not small, still manages to be cozy. Sitting in the back garden, brightly colored and filled with flowers, feels like you have been transported to another place entirely. Oswaldo Bibiano came to Portland in his early 20s after working, from the age of 14, in the kitchens in Acapulco, several hours from his native town of Guerrero. The menu is not typical Mexican fare. Autentica does offer a plate that includes 2 different enchiladas and a chili relleno, but each is prepared so artfully as to give diners the feeling that they are finally experiencing these foods the way they were meant to be. The *queso fundido con chorizo* (Oaxacan melting cheese and chorizo served with fresh corn tortillas) black bean or corn tortilla is beyond magnificent, and the tacos al pastor is without question the best I have ever eaten. The 30-spice chicken mole is absolutely stunning, and the *camarones al autentico mojo de ajo* (deep sea Mexican prawns cooked with garlic sauce) could not be any better. Thursday is posole night, but get there early or you may never get in!

**Aviary,** 1733 NE Alberta St., Portland, OR 97211; (503) 287-2400; aviarypdx.com; French; $$. Aviary is one of those small plates places that seems to get strong reactions, both positive and negative. The prices are pretty reasonable, though the portions are small and to be satisfied you need to order a bunch of stuff. There are three chefs in the kitchen and they are inventive and polished, with impressive resumes. There is an intensity to the food, with some standouts like braised pork belly with mustard greens and ginger caramel, a beautifully prepared Japanese eggplant, and the famous, or infamous, crispy pig ear. They also do a good steak smoked over Douglas fir. Happy hour is a good way to try it out, with dishes of zucchini fritters, chicken liver toast, and brussels sprout nachos.

**Bakery Bar,** 2935 NE Glisan St., Portland, OR 97232; (503) 477-7779; bakerybar.com; Comfort Food; $$. This delightful place, open and airy, serves some of the best breakfasts and baked goods in

Portland. There's lots of covered outdoor seating. It's a great place to go to order a special occasion cake or dozens of cupcakes that will taste as good as they look. And they look good. For my husband's birthday I ordered a mixed box of three dozen, six varieties I think, and they all met my lofty expectations. You won't lack for choices in baked goods, and the barista creates magic with the patterns of foam on the lattes and cappuccinos, using delicious Stumptown coffee. The scones are great, though I have a particular fondness for the coconut, which is mesmerizing. Breakfasts are equally delicious, including the egg dishes. Everything is baked at Bakery Bar, and you'll enjoy all of their offerings. I love Bakery Bar. There is something about it that draws me pretty often. They make terrific breakfast sandwiches on biscuits as light as a feather. The migas is good and there are hot sauce choices on the table. They have some of the best scones in town, and lots of people don't ever get to have their super-good cakes. And cupcakes. They get lost in the breakfast and lunch flurry.

**Beast, 5425 NE 30th Ave., Portland, OR 97211; (503) 841-6968; beastpdx.com; French; $$$$.** Naomi Pomeroy is a PDX food star. She is extremely talented, feisty, adorable, and a force, all in one. Her food is local, seasonal, and well thought out. Serious business and wonderfully delicious. As I have mentioned throughout, Beast's set menu is not something I would want every day. It is an interesting culinary journey with all kinds of flavors making music on your tongue. Beast has only 2 tables, so communal dining is the only way to go. It's fun chatting with the other people at the table and sharing the wonderful dining experience. There are quotations all over the walls, including a recipe for crème fraiche dough, which I have copied down and intend to make sometime soon. Other quotes are both interesting and funny. There are two seatings nightly for the six-course meal. Dinners often start with a soup and are followed by a house-made charcuterie plate consisting of tiny bites of wonderful foods like steak tartare, quail egg toast, *tete de cochon,* a savory *foie gras* bon-bon, and other morsels of creative and interesting offerings.

**Bollywood Theatre, 2039 NE Alberta St., Portland, OR 97211; (971) 200-4711; bollywoodtheaterpdx.com; Indian Street Food; $$.** As amazing as the food scene is in Portland, the Indian food has, in my opinion, been somewhat underwhelming. Not bad, but not great and fairly standard. There is an excellent lunch buffet in Hillsboro, but the majority, not so much. Bollywood Theatre has interesting Indian street food, and the room is fun and playful and many of the offerings are quite good. It's a casual place where you order, find a seat, and when the food is ready they bring it to your table. It's inexpensive and the portions are substantial. The potato samosa are 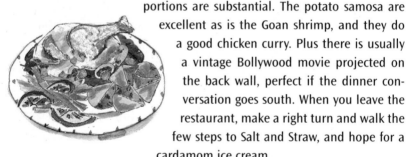 excellent as is the Goan shrimp, and they do a good chicken curry. Plus there is usually a vintage Bollywood movie projected on the back wall, perfect if the dinner conversation goes south. When you leave the restaurant, make a right turn and walk the few steps to Salt and Straw, and hope for a cardamom ice cream.

**Bye and Bye, 1011 NE Alberta St., Portland, OR 97211; (503) 281-0537; thebyeandbye.com; Vegan; $$.** I never expected to like this place. Although recommended highly by **Freehouse** (p. 82) Chef-Owner Eric Moore, I had my doubts. I had heard that it was a groovy hipster hangout, that's fine, but it is strictly vegan. Come on? Really? But I am happy to say that the food is really good. The food is prepared by people who know and clearly like food, and although some, in fact most, of my preferred foods are missing, the food is tasty, satisfying, and, yes, vegan. Drinks are quite good. There's lots of room inside and a patio with outdoor dining. My "meatball" sub was surprisingly quite good, the sauce thick and rich, and the soy cheese worked. It doesn't make me want to be vegan, but it makes me realize that if creatures from another planet come to earth and make us all be vegans, I can eat there several times a week and life won't be that bad.

**Ciao Vito, 2203 NE Alberta St., Portland, OR 97211; (503) 282-5522; ciaovito.net; Italian; $$.** Ciao Vito opened on Alberta Street well before it became one of the hippest spots in Portland. There really wasn't much going on at the time on Alberta Street except a very small and dedicated artistic community with a couple of yoga studios and creative spaces. Within a year Ciao Vito was busy and folks were starting to think of Alberta Street as a go-to destination. Ciao Vito serves superb Italian food in a town that sadly has quite a few mediocre Italian establishments. This is clearly a kitchen that totally gets what Italian food is all about, and from start to finish you will enjoy the classics as they were meant to be eaten. Fried meatballs are addictive—we had to get a second order—and the *sugo* with polenta is absolutely out of this world. On a recent visit I had a fantastic pork chop redolent with garlic, and awesome razor clams. The selection of wines is impressive, and if you are a grappa fan (to me it tastes like cough medicine), you will be thrilled. Oh yeah, the tiramisu is amazing.

**Cocotte, 2930 NE Killingsworth St., Portland, OR 97211; (503) 227-2669; cocottepdx.com; French; $$.** This lovely corner restaurant is in good company, sharing the street with PDX favorites **Beast** (p. 77), **Yakuza** (p. 93), **DOC** (p. 80), and **Autentica** (p. 75). The two women running the kitchen, Kat Liebman and Zoe Hackett, prepare French bistro meets the Northwest bounty using spectacular ingredients and a constantly changing seasonal menu. The food is delicate yet full of flavor and style. The *poulet en cocotte*, a milk-fed, confit-fried half chicken and the dish that the restaurant is named for, is as good a representation as I have had. The creamy chicken liver mousse was paired with a berry jam and some crisp and flavorful house-made pickles. I am a

# Regina Cocotte

Cocotte restaurant serves this lovely drink in their cozy and comfortable restaurant, and it is just a perfect complement to the fine French food.

(Serves 1)

>   2 ounces (4 tablespoons) aviation gin
>   ¾ ounce (4½ teaspoons) Lillet blanc
>   ¼ ounce (1½ teaspoons) Farigoule (French thyme liqueur)
>   1 dash Angostura orange bitters

Stir and garnish with a lemon twist.

snail fan, starting years ago with the classic escargot Bourguignons, with garlic and butter. The Cocotte version, on my most recent visit, featured the snails in a velvety Mornay sauce, with leeks and thinly sliced French bread. Desserts are well prepared and continue the French theme paired with the Northwest bounty.

**DOC, 5519 NE 30th Ave., Portland, OR 97211; (503) 946-8592; docpdx.com; Italian; $$$.** DOC is an absolutely charming restaurant, designed by Owner Dayna McErlean, whose eclectic, sophisticated, and sometimes playful style has created something unusual and quite special. To enter the dining room, patrons walk through the pretty small kitchen. It's different, but it works, making you feel like you are in someone's home rather than a restaurant. The kitchen takes up about a third of this restaurant's space. These two talented guys turn out remarkably good Italian-meets-Northwest cuisine, with careful attention to every detail, and there is the sense that these dishes are just as they should be, beautifully paired ingredients at the height of their potential. On a recent visit, both the squash carpaccio and the risotto, snap peas, nasturtium, and chives were masterful, and the Swiss chard and porcini lasagna, topped with a perfectly fried egg, was one of the most divine dishes I have ever had. The flavors and textures combined to form the perfect plate. DOC, bravo!

**Dove Vivi, 2727 NE Glisan St., Portland, OR 97232; (503) 239-4444; dovevivipizza.com; Pizza; $$.** Hold on to your hats, pizza lovers. Pizza here most closely resembles the deep-dish pizza of Chi-town, but with Oregon-sourced top ingredients and a chill PDX vibe. And with a cornmeal crust. When we were told about Dove Vivi by Gabe Rosen, the Chef-Owner of **Biwa** (p. 39), Gabe recommended not thinking about Dove Vivi as pizza, and he was right. Sort of. It's different for sure, and absolutely delish. It's a family affair, with husband and wife Delane and Gavin Blackstock and Delane's sister Memry. Pizzas are topped with amazing combinations of the freshest ingredients. There is a pizza with fresh corn that I hesitated to order but wished I had when someone at the next table gave me a bite. The crunchy crust is as good as the toppings, and the salads are always inspired. That pizza is great, and don't pass up the kale salad. Yes, I said kale. See Dove Vivi's recipe for **Heirloom Tomato Salad** on p. 210.

**Franks Noodle House, 822 NE Broadway, Portland, OR 97232; (503) 288-1007; franksnoodlehouse.com; Chinese; $$.** The house-made noodles are the reason this place is considered one of the best Asian food spots in Portland. The fresh noodles are perfect in taste and texture, and all of the entrees served with them are top rate. Vegetables are fresh and the meats and fish are of good quality. The noodles with black pea sauce is unusual and a must try, and the stir-fried noodles with pork are served with a yummy sauce and cabbage, peppers, and onions. The appetizers are good as well; we really enjoyed the dumplings and the fresh salad rolls. Kung Pao chicken is also excellent. The place is super busy and the staff pleasant and helpful, but you never seem rushed.

**Freehouse, 1325 NE Fremont St., Portland, OR 97212; (503) 946-8161; freehousepdx.com; Bar; $$.** Opened by former **Victory Bar** (p. 68) partner Eric Moore, this place showcases a good selection of beer and cocktails and all the best that Olympic Provisions has to offer, along with a superior mac and cheese. The brats and the hot dogs are

perfect, and the charcuterie plates are a great way to sample Olympic Provisions' recent offerings. The Italian sausage with peppers was making me think of Little Italy in New York, and the staff is warm and hospitable. There is seating out back, and the place is friendly and not expensive. If there is an old BMW motorcycle out front, then Eric is in and that's a plus. He knows everything about the Portland food scene, and he is such a pleasure to talk with.

**Grant's Philly Cheese, 15350 NE Sandy Blvd., Portland, OR 97230; (503) 252-8012; Philly Cheesesteak; $.** For those of you who have never had a Philly cheesesteak in Philly, Grant's sure comes pretty damn close. Certainly the best version I have had in Portland, the thinly sliced chopped sirloin with all the toppings, including Cheez Whiz, has made me a regular. Grant's offers chicken steaks as well, and hamburgers and hot dogs, but the way to go is the beef version with provolone or the whiz. That whole sandwich is the ultimate treat, washed down with a cold drink and maybe a side of cheese fries, just in case the cheese lover in you hasn't had enough.

**Kir, 22 NE 7th Ave., Portland, OR 97232; (503) 232-3063; kirwine bar.com; Wine Bar; $$.** This is a lovely little wine bar in a groovy neighborhood. It has a French feel and a great selection of mostly French wines and simple, tasty eats. Prices are fair and the atmosphere is quite relaxing, charming, and hip. The salt cod brandade is delicious, and there are good olives and warm almonds with honey, a delightful combination. On a recent visit I thoroughly enjoyed the mussels steamed in cream with Pernod. So good.

**Lemongrass, 1705 NE Couch St., Portland, OR 97232; (503) 231-5780; Thai; $$.** Thai food is popular in Portland, and there are many good choices. When I first came to town it was always Pok Pok, which is still great, but there are a number of other restaurants that rock Thai cuisine. Lemongrass is putting out some excellent Thai food; in fact the papaya salad is the best I have had in Portland. The pad Thai is my daughter's favorite, and the larb is spicy and just right. I recently enjoyed a special that was terrific: chewy rice noodles in a coconut sauce topped with vegetables and crispy fried noodles. Just delicious. They do Thai iced tea just right, and the whole dining experience is worth repeating frequently.

**Natural Selection, 3033 NE Alberta St., Portland, OR 97211; (503) 288-5883; naturalselectionpdx.com; Vegetarian; $$.** Dining at Natural Selection, a vegan and vegetarian restaurant on Northeast Alberta Street, I could imagine eating that way again. Maybe forever. There is nothing the least bit predicable or boring about the offerings. Every course was meticulously prepared and presented in masterful combinations of thrilling tastes and textures. Chef Aaron Woo, not a vegetarian himself, wanted to offer superb food for the non-carnivores, who are often limited to the same vegetables and rice I was eating daily many years ago. Chef Woo is warm and even-tempered, which is reflected in the serenity of his restaurant, and the style in the food and the decor is conducive to a special evening of relaxation. The menu deliberately limited; in fact, there are four courses, each with two choices. My husband and I had one of everything, and each dish was more beautiful and sensual than the next. Not for one moment did I yearn for a piece of beef or miss the ubiquitous chicken breast—under, over, or in the middle of anything. The food is delicate, yet satisfying. It seems that you can taste every meticulously chosen ingredient, and the flavors are never overpowering; rather, they work in harmony and the experience is astoundingly fabulous. They also have the coolest bar in town, an old industrial rolling cart where drinks are prepared for table service only. Before going to dinner, I had anticipated a possible after dinner stop for a venison burger at Victory Bar, but when the meal was over, getting a burger was the last thing on my mind. I left feeling impressed, sated, and happy. OMG, what a great restaurant!

**Navarre,** 10 NE 28th Ave., Portland, OR 97232; (503) 232-3555; **navarreportland.blogspot.com; Mediterranean; $$.** Navarre is a food lover's delight. It is completely unpredictable, except in the quality of its dishes. The small and large plate ordering system is an opportunity to try many things on the inspired menu. Dishes are tastes of Spain, Italy, France, and I think pretty much anywhere else that inspires the talent in the kitchen. The small plates are just that, but the large plates will make their way around a table of 4 or 5. Mushrooms are earthy and cooked right, the breadless crab cakes will stun, and the thinly sliced leg of lamb is astonishingly tasty and tender. The beauty at Navarre is that deliciousness doesn't stop after the entrees. Cakes are spectacular. The red velvet is the best I have had, and the almond cake moist and magnificent. This restaurant is a dream. See Navarre's recipe for **Red Velvet Cake** on p. 208.

**Ned Ludd,** 3925 NE Martin Luther King Jr. Blvd., Portland, OR 97212; (503) 288-6900; **nedluddpdx.com; American; $$$.** Ned Ludd, which opened its doors in 2008, is in a category of its own. All the cooking in the restaurant is done in the wood-burning oven, meaning that the staff has got their chops. So to speak. Jason French could very well be the spokesman for the American Craft kitchen movement, talking about community and keeping things fresh and local. A smoked cod with mussels and horseradish was phenomenal, as was the pork and beans, oven-roasted with just-picked greens. I love the duck breast with the mashed rutabaga redolent with earthy flavors. The stuffed ruby trout is perfumed with fennel and citrus, and it is a perfect dish to show off the magic of the oven.

**Ox, 2225 NE Martin Luther King Jr. Blvd., Portland, OR 97212; (503) 284-3366; oxpdx.com; Argentinean; $$$$.** I greatly anticipated, along with the rest of Portland, the opening of Ox. For some reason it took me 6 months to get there. This Argentinean, meat-centric restaurant is doing some seriously good food, though waiting in line for 1 to 2 hours at normal dining times on any given night is likely. I will only do that at Dominick's on Arthur Avenue in the Bronx. Because we were 7 for dinner, we were able to get a reservation. We tried just about every meat dish on the menu, and a bunch of salads and sides. The rib eye was a great steak, as was the skirt steak. I am not a blood sausage fan, but people liked it. And the asparagus risotto and the salad with beets and lemon was a nice light hit of green. Desserts were rich and the last thing we needed, but we managed to enjoy every bite.

**Pambiche, 2811 NE Glisan St., Portland, OR 97211; (503) 233-0511; pambiche.com; Cuban; $$.** Cuban cuisine is a meld of Spanish, African, and Caribbean influences, resulting in a richly flavored and well-spiced cuisine, often served with rice and beans, a staple of Cuban life. Pambiche is a fun place to get the best Cuban food in town. It is always busy with folks who appreciate the food and welcoming atmosphere. The restaurant is small and super colorful and when the weather allows there is plenty of outside seating. Chef-Owner John Connell Maribona is Cuban-American and ridiculously handsome. Am I allowed to say that? Maribona attributes his love of food to the women in his life. Pambiche is great from beginning to end, Cuban comfort food at its flavorful best. There is nothing as soul satisfying as the *ropa vieja* (shredded beef), which translates as "old clothes," or the *ajiaco*, a stew that is considered by many to be the national dish of Cuba. It is piled high with tropical fruits and vegetables, along with pork and beef. And the desserts rock.

**Petisco,** 1411 NE Broadway, Portland, OR 97232; (503) 360-1048; petiscopdx.com; American; $$. This is a casual neighborhood place to get a bite to eat and a glass of wine or beer. Petisco is a family-run restaurant with a simple menu and a big heart. They started out small and under the radar, and have grown to a nice place for the folks in the neighborhood and visitors. I have now been there twice, one lunch, one dinner, and I love having a place to go in that part of town. My rare roast beef sandwich with manchego cheese and a horseradish sauce was just fine, and when I was there for dinner, the cremini mushroom risotto was cooked perfectly and satisfying in that way risotto should be. Apparently the french toast at brunch is a winning dish, and their fruit crisps, which vary by season, are toothsome. Yes, toothsome.

**Podnah's Pit Barbecue,** 1625 NE Killingsworth St., Portland, OR 97211; (503) 281-3700; podnahspit.com; Texas Barbecue; $$.

OK, barbecue fans, here we go! Podnah's Pit is the best barbecue in Portland. And Chef-Owner Rodney Muirhead is the nicest pit guy. He is so friendly and warm, and it's a pleasure doing business with him. Rodney does Texas barbecue brisket simply: salt, pepper, and 10 hours of smoking. You add your own sauce and it is a dream. The meat tastes beefy and rich. The pulled pork cooks for 12 hours and is mixed with a killer vinegar sauce. You can't go wrong at Podnah's unless you feel too full and don't take the leftovers. Believe me, you will regret it later.

**Random Order, 1800 NE Alberta St., Portland, OR 97211; (971) 340-6995; randomordercoffee.com; Pie; $$.** I headed out with a few friends last week to Alberta Street, seeking something delicious. We stopped at Random Order, knowing we would be in safe hands. All the pies were perfection—the three cream pies, the triple berry, the salted caramel apple, and the mouthwatering blueberry rhubarb pie, made lovingly with the first rhubarb of the season. This is not unusual at Random Order, where nothing but the freshest seasonal ingredients are used in everything they make. The bakery has a homey feel, with mismatched tables and chairs of all heights and sizes. It is in the super funky Alberta neighborhood, and there are times when there are actually crowds hanging out on the street sipping latte and just chilling out. Owner Tracy Olsen has a sustainable business model and maintains close relationships with her vendors, all local farmers and grocers, in order to show her support for the neighborhood economy. Random Order serves savory pies and casseroles, including the hand pie filled with herbed cream cheese for those occasions when you don't have the time to sit down, relax, and drink the coffee. Hand pie to go—I do it all the time. With a recent addition of cocktails, tangy margaritas, and fruity sangria, this is a destination worth visiting any time of day and well into the evening.

**Salty's on the Columbia**, 3839 NE Marine Dr., Portland, OR 97211; (503) 288-4444; saltys.com; Seafood; $$$. On a sunny day you can't really beat the location of this family-owned PDX restaurant that serves lunch, dinner, an award-winning Sunday brunch, and happy hour, right on the Columbia. Every seat has a view of the water, and though the restaurant gets more coverage for the view than the food, I have had several excellent meals there. Salty's celebrates every seafood arrival, and the kitchen does a great job with crab, salmon, halibut, and oysters. On a recent visit I had a great crab cake starter, which I followed with a cioppino that was bursting with flavor and full of fresh, perfectly cooked fish and seafood. The Sunday brunch buffet is pretty amazing. It is one of those giant buffets that has everything, and it's all fresh and good. There are platters of seafood, waffles and eggs, ham, prime rib, and crazy desserts. This is not a typical Portland experience, and when I have folks in from out of town, we try to get there on Sunday to enjoy the food and the amazing location. See Salty's on the Columbia's recipe for **Grilled Steelhead Salmon with Citrus Salt & Bacon Rhubarb Chutney** on p. 189.

**Shandong**, 3724 NE Broadway, Portland, OR 97232; (503) 287-0331; shandongportland.com; Chinese; $$. Good Chinese food is not that easy to find in Portland. Very good Japanese, Vietnamese, and Thai food, but the regions of China, not so much. When we first ate at Shandong, we were so happy to find an excellent example of the cuisine of Northern China, one of my favorite areas for culinary delights. Dumplings and wontons are crisp and perfectly fried, not greasy, and the sweet and sour soup was the best I have had in PDX. The beef and pork dishes were also excellent, and we totally loved the house-made noodles, done just right. The service is attentive and the place is modern, clean, and comfortable.

**Simply Vietnamese**, 2218 NE 82nd Ave., Portland, OR 97213; (503) 208-3391; simplyvietnamese.com; Vietnamese; $$. I have enjoyed several meals at this restaurant, which serves the kind of Vietnamese food I think you would get in Vietnam. It is certainly not simple. On my last two visits I had goat, which I have only had in France, and these two dishes were interesting and enjoyable executions. The wings were quite wonderful as well, and the only dishes we didn't love were the standards available at so many places in Portland. The staff is friendly and this is a great opportunity to explore the more unusual offerings of this interesting cuisine.

**Smallwares, 4605 NE Fremont St., Portland, OR 97213; (971) 229-0995; smallwarespdx.com; Asian Fusion; $$.** I had an interesting meal with my friend Pauline at Smallwares. It was a mix of Asian and strange, but it worked and the food was quite delicious. We sat outside and enjoyed the bustling Alberta Street crowd as we feasted on such dishes as octopus, pumpkin miso and chili, carrot gnocchi with nori puree, and my favorite dish: fried kale, Canadian bacon, mint, and fish sauce. I would never have put those things together, but I am certainly glad they did. We loved the oxtail curry with coconut and scotch bonnet peppers, and for dessert the blood orange Jello with tahini fluff and saffron brittle was pure fun. And for the wee ones they have rice or noodles with a choice of additions, like chicken, for a couple of bucks.

**Spints, 401 NE 28th Ave., Portland, OR 97232; (503) 847-2534; spintspdx.com; German; $$.** Had it not been for a Dish Crawl I covered for OPB, I would never have found Spints. The crawl went there for dessert and I was so impressed that I went for dinner. The food was really good, Germanish, and I loved my pork schnitzel a lot. The fried chicken was also done very well, served with mashed spuds and grilled onion gravy. The baker, Laurie Donaldson, worked at Chez Panisse, so I had to finish everyone's dessert at the table. The chocolate espresso torte was super rich, the bread pudding light and luscious, and the totally homemade s'mores awesome. They have a great beer selection, and word is that brunch, a latke fest, is *wunderbar*!

# Ten Under Ten

There are lots of great dinner buys all around Portland. You can sit down, be served, be full, and leave without spending more than 10 bucks. You can certainly do that at lots of carts, but sometimes you want to go in, sit down, and take a load off. The list includes a decent variety of cuisines, and these places are all really good. You may want to spend more, you just don't have to.

**Bollywood Theatre,** *2039 NE Alberta St., Portland, OR 97211; (971) 200-4711; bollywoodtheaterpdx.com.* Eggs masala and a PBR under 10.

**Bunk Sandwiches,** *211 SW 6th Ave., Portland, OR 97204; (503) 972-8100; 621 SE Morrison, Portland, OR 97214; (503) 477-9515; bunksandwiches.com.* An unbelievably good grilled cheese sandwich and a creamy tomato soup. It's a steal cuz it may be the best in town.

**Burgerville,** *see burgerville.com for locations.* I would normally not suggest fast food, but this is a horse of a different color. Food is great, no crap, seasonal and local when possible. Burgers are sooooo good.

**Fat Albert's Breakfast Cafe,** *6668 SE Milwaukie Ave., Portland, OR 97202; (503) 872-9822.* This comfort breakfast is a bargain, loaded with all of the best in the category: 2 eggs, 3 strips bacon, cheddar on whole wheat or sourdough toast with home browns (diced potatoes) on the side. No charge for mayo, mustard, or hot sauce.

**Good Taste,** *18 NW 4th Ave., Portland, OR 97209; (503) 223-3838.* Any of the fresh and delicious chow meins or even the pepper and salt prawns in the shell will not set you back more than 10. No atmosphere, great food.

**Helsers,** *1538 NE Alberta St., Portland, OR 97211; (503) 281-1477; helsersonalberta.com.* The Scotch Egg and Potato Pancakes is filling enough to get you to dinner. It's a hard-boiled egg wrapped in bratwurst, lightly breaded, and fried golden brown. Served with three potato pancakes and horseradish cream, it is kind of a good monster breakfast or lunch. Yes, under 10.

**Kolbeh,** *11830 SW Kerr Pkwy., Lake Oswego, OR 97035; (503) 245-1662; kolbehpdx.com.* Absolutely fabulous lunch buffet for under 10. And it is so flippin' good.

**Por Que No?,** *4635 SE Hawthorne Blvd., Portland, OR 97215; (503) 954-3138; 3524 N. Mississippi Ave., Portland, OR 97227; (503) 467-4149; porquenotacos.com.* Bryan's Bowl offers a choice of meat or veggies in a bowl with beans, rice, salsas, guacamole, queso fresco, crema, cilantro, and either chips or three house-made tortillas. Yes, it's amazing.

**Sushiville,** *1514 NW 23rd Ave., Portland, OR 97210; (503) 226-4710.* Lots of rolls for under $3. It's a conveyer belt so look for what the sushi chef has just put out. If it's been going around the belt a long time, it is no longer desirable sushi. Sometimes someone will order something special or unusual and the chef will make extra and around it will come. Grab it. It's never great sushi, but this is good sushi at a great price. Soups and bento also a bargain.

**Ya Hala,** *8005 SE Stark St., Portland, OR 97215; (503) 256-4484; yahalarestaurant.com.* Lamb gyro, a ground lamb shoulder marinated in the chef's blend of spices, yogurt, garlic, and feta spread. Possibly the best food deal in the world.

**Swedeedees,** 5202 N. Albina Ave., Portland, OR 97217; (503) 946-8087; sweedeedeepdx.tumblr.com; Comfort; $$. This is a sweet breakfast and lunch spot that does a great job with baked goods, and their egg dishes are excellent. I had terrific corn cakes with bacon that was cooked perfectly and awesome. Cinnamon rolls are moist and wonderful and the pies are as well. Everyone who works there is super nice, and while I was deciding what to order, the woman at the table next to mine put a piece of her breakfast burrito on my plate. And that's what I ordered. Extracto coffee is served, which is fine by me, and the whole experience is delightful.

**Tabla Mediterranean Bistro,** 200 NE 28th Ave., Portland, OR 97232; (503) 238-3777; tmbistro.com; Mediterranean; $$. Tabla is a pretty terrific restaurant, with a great dinner special. For 30 bucks you get a three-course meal that will be delicious and interesting, and portions will be generous. Pastas are excellent, and I love the choices of seasonal crostini. The duck confit is in a wine reduction with a hint of orange, and the wild mushrooms on a polenta bed were deeply flavored and the polenta perfect. Although dessert is not included in the set-price meal, I would strongly urge you to have the panna cotta: hazelnut with a brown sugar streusel. Need I say more?

**Toro Bravo,** 120 NE Russell St., Portland, OR 97212; (503) 281-4464; torobravopdx.com; Tapas; $$$. Toro Bravo is perhaps the best tapas place in Portland. I'm not the only one who thinks so, hence the up-to-2-hour wait on occasion. When I first moved to Portland, it was the talk of the town. Everybody loved it. I generally don't mind long waits if the food is great, but I know some people don't like it. Toro has many types of tapas, powerful sangria, and is a bit of a scene. If you get there at 5 you will get a seat right away, and perhaps be halfway done when the throngs arrive. Not really.

**Tula Gluten Free Bakery and Cafe, 4943 NE MLK Boulevard, Portland, OR; (503) 764-9727; tulabaking.com; Bakery; $$.**
Certainly no one can deny that gluten free has become a far easier way to live than it was, say, 3 years ago. And since it seems that every other person I meet eats that way, it's a good thing. There are whole sections in supermarkets dedicated to this diet, and the products are getting better all the time. I think Tula has some of the best gluten-free products I have had. Gluten-free baked goods are difficult to make well; either the texture is bizarre or the flavor is just wrong. I have had both the sweet and savory offerings at Tula and honestly, I would never know that they were without gluten. I loved my lemon ricotta muffin so much that I bought four and dropped one off at each of my gluten-free friends' houses. I am a fool for an olive oil cake, and Tula's version, with orange and almond, was awesome. In the savory department the spinach, mushroom, and ricotta tart and the cheddar scone blew my skirt up, as my son Nick would say. He doesn't wear a skirt, he just says that. Also, I have nothing against men who wear skirts; they are fun and comfortable and often seen around Portland. Also in Glasgow I bet.

**Yakuza, 5411 NE 30th Ave., Portland, OR 97211; (503) 450-0893; yakuzalounge.com; Japanese Izakaya; $$.** Yakuza is an extraordinarily beautiful restaurant. Chef David Gaspar De Alba has a light hand, and everything tastes pure yet dramatic. The izakaya-style food is a great balance of tastes and textures, always fresh and always beautiful. The menu changes with the daily deliveries, and on a recent visit, the cheese-stuffed squash blossoms, battered and fried, were light and a brilliant rendition of that classic dish. Scallop tempura with shredded phyllo and creamy spicy sauce is delicate and unusual. Along with the upscale small bites, you can also order perhaps the best burger in Portland, so this place is perfect after all. Cocktails are awesome, a sugar snap pea martini—yes, it's true—was surprisingly tasty, and desserts are a great excuse to stick around. See Yakuza's recipe for **Ahi Tuna Poke** on p. 219.

**Zilla Sake House**, 1806 NE. Alberta St., Portland, OR 97232; (503) 336-4104; zillasakehouse.com; Sushi; $$. Zilla is a very fun and funky place to go for outstanding sake and sushi. This place has gone through a number of finding-itself changes and has now settled into a spot that all comes together beautifully, with beautiful food, people, and drink. The selection of sake is huge, and Zilla is a perfect place to try to find your favorite. The sushi is always absolutely fresh, and the people who work at Zilla are super fun and helpful. Sake is an acquired taste, but once you've got it, Zilla will take you on some pretty special sake journeys.

# Specialty Stores, Markets & Producers

**Dashen**, 3022 NE Glisan St., Portland, OR 97232; (503) 234-7785. This is a great little shop that has every product I have tried to find, particularly focusing on the south of the border items, from Mexico and Central and South America. I have used the frozen pastry shells for making empanadas, and enjoyed the *dulce de batata* from Argentina. It comes in cans with chocolate or vanilla, as well as the quince paste. It's kind of bizarre, but you take it out of the can as a whole and cut it in wedges to enjoy with cheese, fruit, and crackers. I love it and it's so different. The man who runs the shop is as sweet as can be, and although there is nothing fancy about the store, shopping there is fun, informative, and prices are right. Like **Barbur World Foods** (p. 33), you may find yourself looking at cans or jars of yummy-looking things and have no clue what they are or what's in it.

**Foster & Dobbs**, 2518 NE 15th Ave., Portland, OR 97212; (503) 284-1157; fosteranddobbs.com. Foster & Dobbs Authentic Foods is a small but extremely well-stocked shop that celebrates artisanal foods and products from small producers. The shop features European and American farmstead cheese, cured meats, craft beer, wine, and fine groceries. They are one of those places that doesn't stock a product unless they really love it. For me it's a mini food museum, but nothing is old, don't get me wrong. My husband lived in France for many years, and he found wines there that he has never seen outside of France. Many products are from family farms and small businesses dedicated to being local and using old recipes and techniques. I think this shop has a great vibe, and the shopkeepers are very knowledgeable about their products. And they do mail order.

**Gartner's Country Meat Market,** 7450 NE Killingworth St., **Portland, OR 97218; (503) 252-7801; gartnersmeats.com.** The meat, at this kind of out-of-the-way market, makes it always worth the trip. On holidays you need to take a number to be served, but tons of people work there and things move along pretty fast. While waiting you can buy an inexpensive hot dog or sausage and the time goes faster. I have gotten everything from the marinated short ribs to a huge, beautifully dry aged prime rib, reasonable and great quality. The selection of sausages is enormous, and I think I have had them all. These people know what they are doing. And they have the largest dog bones I have ever seen. My dog friends Boss and Bella love them.

**Mercado don Pancho,** 2000 NE Alberta St., **Portland, OR 97211; (503) 282-1892.** The little market attached to this tasty *taqueria* is the go-to place for picking up ingredients for Latin foods. They carry all kinds of beans and rice and terrific skirt steak at a great price for fajitas or just grilling and eating. Their fresh tortillas are great, the tomatillos are huge and fresh, and considering its size, the selection is pretty sweet. And try the habañero hot sauce, but do it with caution.

**Missionary Chocolates,** 2712 NE Glisan St., Portland, OR 97232; (503) 961-3262; missionarychocolates.com. Missionary Chocolates began in 2008 when Melissa Berry, a naturopathic physician, was in her last year of medical school. What started out as gifts for her vegan mother quickly became a company, as a few months later her dairy-free truffles won first place at the Northwest Chocolate Festival in Portland. This unexpected and deserved success changed what was a home-based kitchen experiment in chocolate into a thriving company. The truffles are exquisite, with interesting seasonal flavors that are pushing the envelope but never too far. The Meyer lemon is out of this world, and the spicy cinnamon chipotle is also very yummy. And this is the very interesting part: the mission of the company has always been to build an inpatient, integrative healing center in Portland, funded by chocolate. We hope you find the allergy-friendly truffles a deliciously good addiction—they are just what the doctor ordered!

# Northwest Portland

Northwest is a lovely part of the city. The Pearl is in Northwest Portland, and the shops and restaurants have lots to offer. There is a wide range of choices: some of the most expensive places in the city but also some spots to get a good meal at a very reasonable price. They are found among great little shops and lovely old apartment buildings and stately homes.

## Foodie Faves

**Andina,** 1314 NW Glisan St., Portland, OR 97209; (503) 228-9535; andinarestaurant.com; Peruvian; $$$$. Andina serves the best Peruvian food in Portland. It is located in the upscale Pearl neighborhood and seems to be a popular spot for celebrations, both for date night and groups of friends or business associates. The ceviches are all very good, but I personally love the green mango with passion fruit and prawns. The potato cakes (*causa*), particularly the green bean and cheese, taste so good we often get two if we are a good-size group. And that's the way to go there. Maybe you can get everything on the menu! Piquillo peppers are stuffed with cheese, quinoa, and serrano ham. Empanadas are as good as they get, flaky pastry stuffed with tender beef, raisins, and olives. They are as good as the empanadas my Argentinean friend Ines makes, and that is saying something. The lamb shank, slow-cooked in the traditional northern Peruvian style with cilantro and black beer, is one of their best entrees, although the wild mountain mushrooms wok-fried with onions, tomato sauce, garlic, and aji runs a very close second.

**Bar Mingo,** 807 NW 21st Ave., Portland, OR 97209; (503) 445-4646; Caffe Mingo; 811 NW 21st Ave., Portland, OR 97209; (503) 226-4646; barmingonw.com/caffemingo.html; Italian; $$. Bar Mingo was developed for two, actually three reasons. First, the space next door to the well-loved Caffe Mingo became available, and it was impossible to pass up for Owner Michael Cronin. Second, it would be a place for the Caffe Mingo diners to have cocktails and wines while waiting for their table next door. (Cronin takes no reservations, much to his loyal clientele's dismay.) And third, they wanted a place that would be a bar as much as a restaurant, a place to drink and dine with smaller portions and prices, perfect for tasting and sharing. Bar Mingo's chef, Jerry Huisinga, is an advocate of simple, seasonal food not covered with heavy sauces. Huisinga is a well-respected member of the Portland food community. The mussels, hard-to-find chicken livers, and the best *cacio e pepe* in town make Bar Mingo a monthly tradition for my family. And don't leave without having a house-made cannoli, perfect, and a true espresso. The restaurant Caffe Mingo has the feel of Italy, and the always-perfect tomatoes, fabulous bread, and small but well-selected wines add to the authenticity. The wait is rarely very long and is always worth it. Chef Brett West of Caffe Mingo has been with Michael for over 9 years. The menu is homage to homey Italian food, with everything made from scratch and only the freshest products. The pizzas are thin-crust wonders of the finest ingredients, the pastas handmade and extraordinary. All the items on the menu are winners, and from your first bite of their amazing bread and olive oil to the velvety panna cotta, you will leave a happy camper. See Caffe Mingo's recipe for **Pan-seared Salmon** on p. 217.

**Bent Brick,** **1639 NW Marshall St., Portland, OR 97209; (503) 688-1655; thebentbrick.com; Eccentric Northwest; $$$.** Bent Brick is intense Portland cuisine. No surprise as it is the second "child" of Scot Dolich, of **Park Kitchen** (p. 110). The crowd is smart hipster central, the entrance is pretty sexy, and the food is pretty strange. To me they push the envelope sometimes a tad too far; however, when it works it is pretty darn terrific. And there are lots of people who like that kind of food experience. The sausages are interesting, my favorite being the duck and sage (sounds like a kid's game), and I liked the seafood sausage very much. The oyster mushroom salad with crisp wild rice was well done, and the duck fat jojos with ranch dressing—boy, I would like to have them again. Soon.

**Besaws,** **2301 NW Savier St., Portland, OR 97210; (503) 228-2619; mbesaws.com; Comfort; $$.** You really can't go wrong at Besaws as long as you are hungry and love all things breakfast. The scrambles are outstanding, omelets excellent, and the Croque Madame is rich and ridiculously good. The service is excellent, everyone is friendly, and while you wait for your break-fast table, you can help yourself to coffee that makes the wait a little easier to take.

**Blue Hour,** **250 NW 13th Ave., Portland, OR 97210; (503) 226-3394; bluehouronline.com; Northwest; $$$.** Located in Portland's upscale Pearl district, Blue Hour is a large, lovely room with profes-sional service that is friendly and knowledgeable. There is outdoor seating that is covered so you can sit there even on chilly or gently raining evenings and be warmed by outdoor heaters. Chef Dolan Lane is at the helm, and his food is seasonal, thoughtful, and delicious. Last week I enjoyed a Dungeness crab sandwich, beautifully paired with avocado, bacon, and a lemon aioli. My dining companion enjoyed the Petrale sole in caper garlic butter. The dinner menu is full of wonderful-sounding entrees, and according to my friends Janet and Neil, the roasted pork chop and the black cod were both excellent. Speaking of excellent, the pineapple jasmine sorbet and the green tea panna cotta were just that.

**Brix Tavern, 1338 NW Hoyt St., Portland, OR 97209; (503) 943-5995; brixtavern.com; Comfort American; $$.** This is good American comfort food, with standout dishes including anything cooked on the rotisserie. The pizzas are good and the prime rib Cobb salad is hearty and different. I am a sucker for truffle anything, and their truffled mac and cheese is crusty and comforting. I think cheese has magic powers. The rib eye is cooked well and the shared trio of beef platter is a great idea, very well executed.

**Byways, 1212 NW Glisan St., Portland, OR 97209; (503) 221-0011; bywayscafe.com; Comfort; $$.** This is an old-fashioned diner-style restaurant in the fashionable Pearl neighborhood. They serve breakfast and lunch and do both artfully and generously. Breakfast offers most of the usual suspects along with some less common items. The blue corn pancakes are made even more magnificent served with the honey pecan butter, and the french toast is made with challah, which is always great. Burgers are good at lunchtime as are the sandwiches and salads. They do an excellent patty melt, something I can never pass up. The chicken Cobb sandwich on baguette is crazy good as well. And get a piece of whatever the coffee cake is: it will rock.

**Cafe Allora, 504 NW 9th Ave., Portland, OR 97209; (503) 445-4612; caffe-allora.com; Italian; $$.** The pastas at this small and comfortable restaurant in the Pearl neighborhood have all been prepared with a skilled hand, and everything is authentic and satisfying. Years back I spent a couple of summers in Italy, and the pasta at Cafe Allora comes very close to my pasta gold standard. The *amatriciana* is spicy and amazing, and the carbonara is creamy deliciousness. I always start with their excellent Caesar salad and end with a cup of espresso and a strong desire to return! If only they would make the *pici* I had in Chiusi, a small Tuscan town.

**Cafe Nell,** **1987 NW Kearney St., Portland, OR 97209; (503) 295-6487; cafenell.com; French; $$.** This small restaurant in Northwest Portland serves very good French/Northwest food, comfort food, in a 70-seat restaurant that feels homey and relaxed. The guys who own the place, Darren and Van Creely, are super warm and friendly, making you feel like you are dining in their home, which is just what they had in mind. Their dishes mainly reflect the French classics, but they also offer weeknight specials of varying ethnicity at super-fair prices; my favorite is Wednesday, when shrimp and grits is on the menu. With an emphasis on freshness, simplicity, and seasonality, Cafe Nell is a delightful spot to spend a long relaxed evening being treated like a guest in an old friend's home.

**Coppia,** **417 NW 10th Ave., Portland, OR 97209; (503) 295-9536; coppiaportland.com; Italian; $$$.** Based on the glorious food of the Piedmont section of Italy, Coppia does a good job of re-creating some of the specialties of the region. Although most people seem to have a love/hate relationship with anchovies, sadly more hate than love, everyone on earth should try *bagna caudo*, an absolutely mesmerizing dish of simple ingredients. Yes, one is the anchovy, and if it's not cooked I am not a fan, but when cooked, I tell you magic happens. Often just four ingredients—anchovy, garlic, butter, and oil—this dish is served warm and you are meant to dip bread or vegetables into the fragrant, magnificent sauce. If you doubt me, just make a simple pasta and in a pan melt the anchovies and garlic in a butter/ olive oil mixture and toss with the cooked pasta. Maybe add chicken or broccoli. It is sinfully good. Anyway, in addition to *bagna cauda*, Coppia serves risotto, salt cod, and an amazing Piedmontese skirt steak, all great, all the time.

**Davis Street Tavern, 500 NW Davis St., Portland, OR 97209; (503) 505-5050; davisstreettavern.com; Northwest; $$$.** I kind of love the way they organize their menu: Fingers, Forks and Spoons, Forks and Knives, and Hands. The burgers are under the Hands category. The cauliflower and green bean tempura is delish, as is the roasted beet and Asian pear salad. Sea scallops when seared right are wonderful, and these were cooked perfectly (Forks and Knives). There is a lively bar scene here, and the cocktails are strong and keep the crowd smiling. Happy hour is a good buy and the foods are interesting with lots of choices. The cocktails on the menu sounded great, but I used this opportunity to once again fall in love with the Lemon Drop.

**Fuller's Coffee Shop, 136 NW 9th Ave., Portland, OR 97209; (503) 222-5608; Diner Food; $.** This casual and old-fashioned horseshoe counter-style diner is pretty great. It reminds me of the Oyster Bar in Grand Central Station in NYC, only smaller. And no fish to speak of. I think they can't seat more than 25 or 30 people, but I have never had to wait, though I also haven't tried on the weekends. Maple syrup, whether it is for pancakes or french toast, is served warm, which is a lovely treat, and the coffee keeps flowing. They make their own loaves of bread, and their simple sandwiches are excellent. It's a great place to get a BLT, tuna, or egg salad sandwich. There are some tables outside. The bread, if they have enough, can be purchased whole, which I have done a couple of times. In fact, last time I made a very good bread pudding with three-quarters of it, and wow, awesome.

**Gilt Club, 306 NW Broadway, Portland, OR 97209; (503) 222-4458; giltclub.com; American; $$$.** Having passed by Gilt Club a bunch of times in its downtown/Old Town Portland location, I just assumed that its name told it all, and that it was a drinking or dancing spot. Over the last couple of months, I started hearing some positive buzz about the food at Gilt Club, and that it actually was not a club at all. Former Gilt Club Chef Chris Carriker had done a sold-out Plate and Pitchfork dinner with Chef Rick Gencarelli from Lardo, and the reviews were nothing but raves. My last dinner there was as good as my first. I had bacon-wrapped dates with some sort of blue cheese, and Bruce started with their excellent pork pâté. My entree was a cooked-just-right bavette steak, and Bruce loved his pasta with wild mushrooms. Desserts have always been rich and delish, and this was no exception. I had a great time with the strawberry petit pot with strawberry macaroons, and Bruce and I shared his fried doughnuts with smoked cheddar and bourbon syrup. Bruce also has not stopped talking about his BLT Cocktail, which was made with tomato-infused vodka, lemon juice, and basil leaves. It is served in a martini glass with a "bacon salted" rim and garnished with a drop or two of lemon olive oil and another basil leaf. Now in Portland you can easily find maple bacon doughnuts or pear blue cheese ice cream. Both of these Bruce readily ridicules, he's pretty "old school," but not this BLT Cocktail. Fortunately he was driving so one had to be enough!

**Good Taste, 18 NW 4th Ave., Portland, OR 97209; (503) 223-3838; Chinese; $.** What this place lacks in atmosphere, and it does, it makes up in home-style, authentic Chinese food. There are the required meats hanging in the window, a very decent congee, and yummy dishes like their chow fun, seafood chow mein on crispy noodles, and hearty and satisfying soups. They do a good job with fresh vegetables like bok choy and baby spinach. It gets crowded at lunch, and does a decent take-out business. They make the wontons in-house; in fact, if you eat there during off hours, you will see them being made. My favorite dish is the barbecue pork over eggs and rice. Although it is not ranked high with curb appeal, do not be dissuaded; the food is simple Chinese prepared well.

**Irving Street Kitchen,** 701 NW 13th Ave., Portland, OR 97209; (503) 343-9440; irvingstreetkitchen.com; Southern Soul; $$$. Described as Southern soul with a Northwest sensibility, Irving Street Kitchen has some unusual-sounding offerings, but honestly, they are not as strange as they sound. I had crispy chicken-fried oysters that I liked a lot, and Bruce had the asparagus and melted lardo salad with a seared egg, and it was also quite enjoyable. That said, I think brunch is this restaurant's strong suit. The sugar and spice doughnuts are killer good, as are the sticky buns and the . . . well, all the baked goods are amazing. The salmon gravlax benedict was yummy, loved the fried chicken and waffles, and the soft scrambled egg nachos were clever and very very good. Their drinks are also wonderful—possibly the best Bloody Mary I have had in months. Win, win.

**Isabel,** 330 NW 10th Ave., Portland, OR 97209; (503) 222-4333; isabelscantina.com; Eclectic; $$. I don't get there very often, but when I do, I am so happy. For me it's all about their breakfast and lunch, though they do serve a good dinner. Breakfast choices are inspired, with favorites being the blackberry pancakes and the artichoke scramble, served with crisp rosemary potatoes. The roast beef hash with horseradish cream is amazing. For lunch try the Buddha bowl, a dish of steamy lemongrass and coconut milk broth with shiitake mushrooms, noodles, veggies, chili flakes, cilantro, and green onions. Marinated tofu, chicken, or carnitas are an option. The chicken quesadilla is excellent as is the lettuce wrap, with marinated chicken, cukes, lime, and peanut sauce. On warm days, sitting outside is quite delightful. It's a busy but quiet spot, and the prices are reasonable and the staff pleasant.

**Jamison, 900 NW 11th Ave., Portland, OR 97209; (503) 972-3330; jamisonpdx.com; American; $$$$.** This restaurant is in a beautiful spot in the Pearl. Overlooking a city park, Jamison has one of the best outdoor seating opportunities in the city. The restaurant is elegant and rustic; much of the room is constructed from a series of barns that once graced the area. Though not inexpensive, the food at Jamison is a wonderful celebration of the Northwest bounty. Oysters, charcuterie, and cheeses are all well chosen, and the small plates are great appetite-whetting delights. The buckwheat crepes and the clams were so good, and the large plates did not disappoint. The duck breast was maple glazed and fork tender, and the short rib was stellar. Brunch gets very good reviews, and sitting outside on a nice day having an awesome breakfast sounds good to me.

**Le Happy, 1011 NW 16th Ave., Portland, OR 97209; (503) 226-1258; lehappy.com; Crepes; $$.** This place is so Portland. It is funky, small, slow, and the crepes are great. Crepes are made to order and made from buckwheat and white flour, eggs, milk, and a dash of salt. If you are in a rush, eat somewhere else, because the kitchen is tiny and doesn't hold enough people to get your food out in a hurry. However, when it does arrive, the crepes and their fillings are as good as it gets. The savory crepes are hard to pass up, but if you are intending to get a dessert crepe, have a spicy steak salad or the EU Chipotle, with greens, rice cakes, avocado, and some other stuff with chipotle vinaigrette. If, however, you are going for a savory crepe, my personal favorites are the caramelized onion and goat cheese or the smoked salmon gruyère sauce and scallion. The dessert crepes, particularly the simple butter, sugar, and lemon and the coconut cream, are out of this world. Maybe do the sharing thing; you get to try more.

# CHAINS AND MULTI-SITE SHOPS AROUND TOWN

**Elephant's,** *see elephantsdeli.com for locations.* Elephant's calls itself a delicatessen. In my mind that is an understatement. To me, the only thing that makes me think "deli" is that they have, and slice, meat. The huge store is European in feel, selling both food items and things for the home that are sophisticated and unusual. I go there to buy people cool gifts, both edible and not. It's the kind of stuff you don't see everywhere: beautiful glassware, interesting plates and candles, unusual oils and delicacies. I always want to buy something, and that's not generally the case for me. But certainly it is the food that draws the people. They have a ton of choices, a small display area with some trattoria-inspired foods, and then all the prepared foods that you can buy by the portion or the pound. They make good pizza, very good calamari, ditto for the fish and chips. But one must not miss the soups. I know a bunch of people who, if they find they may be getting a little sniffle, will get over to Elephant's to get a pint or quart of soup to go. All the soups are good, but from my first taste of Mama Leones, I felt it needed to be shared. I bought a pint for all my friends. It is delicious, chunky yet velvety, with a tomato flavor that is mellowed by the cream, and is, next to chicken soup, the world's best comfort food.

**New Seasons: Arbor Lodge,** *see newseasonsmarket.com for locations.* New Seasons is a strictly Portland chain. I have yet to be disappointed by anything I have purchased there, and if there is an issue with something, I have been told the employees will do everything in their power to make it right. The meat and fish are fresh and of the highest quality, and the folks behind the counter know their areas. They are super accommodating, will order what you need, and it will come in on time. They have an interesting seasoning selection and you can have anything you buy pre-rubbed. I love that. In addition to very good prepared food and all the groceries you could want, New Seasons has serious selections of health and wellness products, and the staff is knowledgeable and helpful. And helpful and friendly are the key words here. Everyone employed at New Seasons seems happy to be there. It is unbelievable.

I have a cooking conversation every time I check out, recently de the best way to make a pork roast with my food buddy Bosco, New Seasons in Lake Oswego. I have never been in a place with that many nice people at one time.

**Olympic Provisions,** *1632 NW Thurman St., Portland, OR 97209; (503) 894-8136; 107 SE Washington St., Portland, OR 97214; (503) 954-3663; olympicprovisions.com.* Olympic Provisions is home to Oregon's first USDA-approved salumeria, established in 2009. With two locations in Portland, both shops also have restaurants that serve their amazing charcuterie along with wonderful creative food. Salumist and Owner Elias Cairo carefully crafts "American Charcuterie" using the highest-quality local ingredients. Attached to the NW location is a large meat curing facility, which has allowed Olympic Provisions to make a wider number of products. Cairo has crafted 12 different types of salami based on the regional flavors you would find in France, Spain, Italy, and Greece. Each salami type and flavor profile is true to the region or country's style from which it originates (i.e., Saucisson d'Alsace has the flavor profile of what you would find in the Alsace region). I think that Olympic Provisions' hot dogs may be the best I have had. I love a Nathan's dog, but these have those beat. They are just too long for the bun! Not a huge problem, just saying.

**Zupan's: Burnside,** *2340 SW Burnside Ave., Portland, OR 97210; (503) 497-1088.* **Lake Grove,** *16380 Boones Ferry, Lake Oswego OR 97035; (503) 210-4190.* **Macadam,** *7221 SW Macadam, Portland, OR 97219; (503) 244-5666;* **Belmont,** *3301 SE Belmont St., Portland, OR 97214; (503) 239-3720; zupans.com.* Zupan's is a small chain of stores that carries top quality products. The prices are high, but you will not be let down. The counter staff in every department is helpful and knows their stuff. Shout out to Jeremy Alcatraz, yep, that's right, who manages the store on Macadam. Their soups and prepared foods are excellent, and occasionally they will have sales that are pretty decent. Produce is phenomenal, wine and beer selection excellent, and they have very lovely plants and flowers all year long.

**Lovejoy,** 939 NW 10th Ave., Portland, OR 97209; (503) 208-3113; lovejoybakers.com; Bakery/Sandwiches; $$. In what may be the heart of the Pearl District, the light-filled Lovejoy Bakery is making a name for itself in a tough town to make your mark. They serve spectacular sandwiches, my favorite being the roast beef with caramelized onions and cheddar with a nice slather of horseradish aioli. Beef and horseradish together always makes me happy. For lunch today I had the cream of tomato soup with a grilled cheddar and fontina sandwich that was crusty on the outside and heaven on the inside. Cookies are great; had a pumpkin with brown-butter frosting that was studded with currants and walnuts, and the triple chocolate was rich and chewy. Traffic flows in the bakery pretty much all day, and they have a very good selection of day-old breads and pastries that seem to fly off the shelf. Last week, I made a very good bread pudding with the day-old almond croissants I couldn't finish the day I bought them. Next time I'll only buy one at a time. Never!

**Noisette,** 1937 NW 23rd Pl., Portland, OR 97210; (503) 719-4599; noisetterestaurant.com; American; $$$$$. Black American Express cardholders, listen up! Your dining experience at Noisette will be an 8-course tasting menu. It's a pretty incredible dining experience, albeit a very expensive one. The food is elegant and interesting, and this is what we had for dinner the night we ate there: Maine day boat lobster, crushed gold and red beets with avocado terrine, basil emulsion, and Meyer lemon, Oregon coast albacore tuna tartare, black garlic puree and breakfast radish salad with toasted croutons and duck liver vinaigrette, butternut squash soup, salish alder smoked salt and crème fraîche, smoked Idaho white sturgeon, chive-scented fingerling puree with Oregon hedgehog mushrooms, Yukon Gold confit and bearnaise sauce, mushroom pasta tortellone, yellow foot chanterelles and chive beurre monté, moulard duck liver, toasted brioche with organic Granny

Smith apples and calvados sauce, wagyu culotte and Painted Hills short ribs, kale-fingerling puree with brussels sprout leaves, crushed celery root and compressed radish salad with short rib sauce, Valrhona chocolate soufflé, manjari chocolate, and red wine reduction. We left quite happy. And hopefully we will go again next year if we can save up. Maybe we'll mortgage one of our dogs to defray the cost!

**Oba! Restaurante,** 555 NW 12th Ave., Portland, OR 97209; (503) 228-6161; obarestaurant.com; New Latin; $$$. The foods of South America are deftly prepared at this colorful and festive Northwest restaurant. The menu is quite interesting, and the food tastes as good as it is described. The bacon-wrapped stuffed jalapeños were spicy but not too, and my entree, the *bife a micalense*, a steak topped with caramelized banana, bacon, and mustard cream sauce, was a terrific blend of unusual ingredients. The half chicken roasted over mesquite was delightful, served with a tomato cucumber relish and potatoes. For dessert we shared a warm caramel apple cake; it was a perfect end to a delightful meal. I'll be back! See Oba! Restaurante's recipe for **Bife a Micalense** on p. 183.

**Paley's Place,** 1204 NW 21st Ave., Portland, OR 97209; (503) 243-2403; paleysplace.net; Northwest; $$$. Paley's Place Iron Chef winner Vitaly Paley has been running his popular restaurant in an old Victorian house in Northwest Portland since 1995. The restaurant has about 50 seats and is sophisticated while still remaining friendly and warm. Paley creates his menu based solely on the products of the Pacific Northwest. The local organic foods use sustainable methods. The escargot bordelaise with marrow and garlic was outstanding, as were the crispy sweetbreads served with herb spaetzle and mushrooms in a morel cream sauce. The cocktails are done well—my first Lemon Drop experience was here, and I have been a fan ever since.

**Paragon, 1309 NW Hoyt at 13th; Portland, OR 97209; (503) 833-5060; paragonrestaurant.com; American; $$.** When I first moved to PDX, I ate at Paragon weekly. Honestly I have never had a bad meal; in fact, the food is reliably delicious, the menu has lots of tempting offerings, and the bar menu rocks as well. The corned beef sandwich off the bar menu is great, and the half chicken and the skirt steak are

wonderful. The drinks are good and creative, and the bar scene seems quite active. I don't know if they always have it, I am guessing it's there during apple season, but the brown butter apple cake was amazing and I had to bring a slice home for Olivia. Yes, it had bacon.

**The Parish, 231 NW 11th Ave., Portland, OR 97209; (503) 227-2421; theparishpdx.com; Creole/Seafood; $$.** I like The Parish. I like the guys who own it, Tobias Hogan and Ethan Powell. For the Pearl neighborhood the prices are super reasonable and the small menu certainly delivers the best of the offerings. Love the duck gumbo as much as the oyster po'boy, and all the sides rock. For several years I have been enjoying this crew's other restaurant, **Eat** (p. 118), and it's nice to have one on the west side of the river. Have the pecan pie for dessert if you have even a little room; it is yummy.

**Park Kitchen, 422 NW 8th Ave., Portland, OR 97209; (503) 223-7275; parkkitchen.com; New American; $$$.** The food and the service at Park Kitchen are sure bets. The staff is familiar with everything on the menu and will describe anything on the menu in explicit detail if you are interested. Knowing what each dish is like helps the servers guide you in the right ordering direction. Since the menu is composed of small plates and large plates, it is helpful to have guidance on how much to order and what foods complement each other. Sometimes I find that at Park Kitchen and sister restaurant **Bent Brick** (p. 99), the actual dish is not quite what you expect it to be. So ask. The food has always been excellent, occasionally a bit far out for me, but most people just love it. On my most recent visit I thoroughly enjoyed the gin-marinated clams and the shaved Virginia ham with the in-season, right-this-second rhubarb. Large plates were interesting, and we tried the lamb with pickled cardoons and the morel-stuffed cabbage, which was interesting. The sticky date pudding, my new favorite dessert, was excellent.

**Piazza Italia, 1129 NW Johnson St., Portland, OR 97209; (503) 478-0619; piazzaportland.com; Italian; $$.** This is a family spot in the Pearl neighborhood. Very casual and friendly. When there is a soccer game, the crowds are electric and the food is always reliable. I think that their lasagna is pretty amazing, they do a good job with their bolognese, and the shrimp scampi is light and full of garlic, as it should be. There are seats outside and they have a deli counter so you can buy some Italian taste treats. Everyone who works there is over-the-top nice and helpful, and the service is fast and the room fun. Soccer rules here.

**Red Onion, 1123 NW 23rd Ave., Portland, OR 97210; (503) 208-2634; redonionportland.com; Thai; $$.** Red Onion offers traditional Thai favorites and they are done with the skill of a kitchen that clearly knows its business. The spicy chicken and shrimp with crispy basil, roast duck with tangerine sauce, papaya salad, and drunken noodles are favorites, and everything else I have tried is just right. The food is not unusual Thai food, just the standards done really well. Chef extraordinaire Dang Boonyakamol has had three successful Portland area restaurants. Dang is from Chiang Mai in Northern Thailand, and the word is that he has been cooking since he was a child, when his mother forced him to cook in the kitchen instead of playing outside with his friends. He probably wasn't too happy back then, but he seems happy now, and so are his customers.

**Ringside West,** 2165 W. Burnside St., Portland, OR 97209; (503) 223-1513; ringsidesteakhouse.com; Steak House; $$$$. Let me start by saying that I love a good steak house. I love beef and pretty much every cut of steak. That said, if I go to a steak house and they serve prime rib, I am compelled to order an end cut with the bone. If they don't have an end cut I go with steak. And sometimes I call ahead and have one reserved. I have done that twice at Ringside and it is a perfect execution. Caramelized and tender, it has a great beefy flavor, and when you add a bit of horseradish sauce, I am over the moon. My dining companions always order steak there and everyone raves. They do a great job and the sides, the onion rings, are wonderful, and salads are excellent as well. Desserts look good but I honestly have been too full to order one. Maybe next time I won't finish my prime rib. Naw, that won't happen.

**Serrato,** 2112 NW Kearney St., Portland, OR 97210; (503) 221-1195; serrato.com; Mediterranean; $$$. On a busy evening 300 diners is not unusual at this spacious and comfortable restaurant. Serrato has a rustic Italian vibe. Whether you are a party of two out on a date, or a large bunch of work buddies who want to celebrate in a friendly and chill atmosphere, dining at this popular restaurant is a sure bet. The pizzas are good, with the toppings always reflecting farm-delivered freshness. Tuna tartare is refreshing, light, and full of flavor. There are many entrees I would love to have again, but in this seasonal culinary world you never know. The entrees I have enjoyed recently include a perfect lamb osso bucco and the grilled sea scallops. Generally I like my sea scallops seared, tongue twister, but grilling these beauties works just fine. The chocolate cobbler is one of my favorite desserts in Portland, and the crème brûlée gets very high marks for great taste and texture. There is a large lively bar that draws the after-work set to

# SERRATO SPICY MIKE

This is a drink that tastes like a smoothie and is just delicious. Kurt Fritzler is a master mixologist.

(Serves 1)

    Dash simple syrup
    Dash fresh lemon juice
    2 ounces (4 tablespoons) mango puree
    1 ounce (2 tablespoons) Mazama pepper vodka
    1 ounce (2 tablespoons) Sub Rosa saffron-cumin vodka

In a shaker glass filled with ice, combine all the ingredients. Shake well and strain into a chilled martini shell. Garnish with lime wedge.

this energetic and elegant neighborhood restaurant serving dishes from Italy, France, and the Mediterranean region, all with a Portland spin. Bartender Kurt Fritzler has been at Serrate for almost 30 years, and his cocktails are inventive and impressive, and his charming and upbeat personality has earned him a loyal following. He is the person to ask if you are looking for some special libation to accompany your meal. He totally has it down, and I have never been disappointed with his suggestions. He's a bartender's bartender.

**Stepping Stone Cafe, 2390 NW Quimby, Portland, OR 97210; (503) 222-1132; steppingstonecafe.com; Comfort; $$.** If you are able to eat the stack of Frisbee-size pancakes, you get a Polaroid of yourself on the wall of the restaurant. I actually think I could do it—they are very good pancakes—but there is something that stops me from trying. Not sure if it is a wall of shame, certainly decadence. All the portions at this place are big, and all the food is good. Super-casual and a fun place to linger over a great cinnamon roll made into french toast or a very decent burger. They open most days at 6 a.m. and stay open till 10 p.m., so you can get there and have breakfast any time of day, which is great because sometimes there is nothing like ending the day with a superb Canadian bacon and cheddar scramble. It's not just for breakfast anymore! Their motto is "you eat here because we let you," but don't be put off. It's nice they let you; you won't be disappointed!

**Trader Vic's, 1203 NW Glisan St., Portland, OR 97209; (503) 467-2277; tradervicspdx.com; Polynesian; $$.** This fun chain is making a comeback. We dined in the lounge and ordered "Cosmo Tidbits," which was the original pu pu platter, consisting of spareribs, crab rangoon, crispy prawns, and the sliced pork. I also couldn't resist the duck tacos and the egg rolls, crispy skin made in-house. Someone at the next table traded a shrimp for a few cheese bings, yummy panko-crusted treats. The huge wood-fired oven roasts meat, poultry, and seafood to  perfection and all the dishes come out smoky with hints of sweetness. When I agonized about which mai tai to order, the lovely waitress suggested I go for the flight of mai tais, consisting of pineapple, guava, and mango concoctions. That was dangerous but they were all delicious and refreshing. I have had flights of wine, beer, scotch, and bourbon and always found them informative and helpful. After my fifth sip, I barely remembered my name, let alone which drink I preferred. But I think it had a little umbrella in it!

**23 Hoyt, 529 NW 23rd Ave., Portland, OR 97210; (503) 445-7400; 23hoyt.com; Northwest; $$$.** This gentrified PDX neighborhood is host to a number of spots that serve good food and alcohol. 23 Hoyt is a large, two-story restaurant that reflects the feeling of this upscale part of town. Beer braised beef cheeks with preserved lemon polenta is magical, as is the pan-roasted salmon with flavors of sweet caramelized fennel and charred onions. 23 Hoyt has one of the best happy hours in town, and it's a great way to try some of the items on the regular menu at a fraction of the cost. Before you leave, have a couple of the salted chocolate chip cookies; they are out of this world.

**Wildwood, 1221 NW 21st Ave., Portland, OR 97209; (503) 248-9663; wildwoodrestaurant.com; Northwest; $$$.** At one time Wildwood was the "it" restaurant in Portland. The chef was famous, the food innovative, and everyone wanted to eat there. Although those days have passed, I have had nothing but good meals there. I prefer to sit in the bar and prefer that menu, and the food is excellent, the drinks are good, and the staff is super-nice. The burger, which they grind in-house, is pure and lovely decadence topped with pork belly and a fried egg. A cardiologist's dream! I love the skillet-roasted asparagus spears with miso-mustard, fried shallots, and once again the inevitable fried egg, the seasonal pizzas, and I can't keep my hands out of the truffled popcorn; it is amazing.

## Specialty Stores, Markets & Producers

**City Market, 735 NW 21st Ave., Portland, OR 97209; (503) 221-3007; facebook.com/pages/City-Market-NW/120795881303728.** This pricey market is a food lover's dream. Although I have never found it to be the friendliest market, I am there to shop and not find new companions. It's not a rude vibe, but it's a serious one. Sort of the opposite of New Seasons, where I want to hug everyone who helps me, and I know they would hug me back. Not everyone is looking for that kind of service. The store has different departments that operate independently. The butcher shop has a limited but superb selection of meats and some prepared foods, and they make a great beef jerky. The fish is fresh and completely seasonal, and the produce is beautiful. This is one of those shops that you can spend way too much time in. You'll find little jars of honeys and mustards and a ton of stuff you'll want to bring home to your kitchen. The cheeses are great and the cheesemonger knowledgeable. Parking in the back makes it a breeze.

**Phil's Uptown Meat Market,** 17 NW 23rd Pl., Portland, OR 97210; (503) 224-9541; philsuptownmeatmarket.com. This was one of the first places I bought meat when I first moved to Portland. Pricey, but I have never been anything but thrilled with my purchases. A couple of years back I ordered a prime rib for a dinner with the Jays and it was stellar. I remember that after dinner I took some of the leftovers and made an amazing roast beef hash, with onions and potatoes. And we put an egg on it, since we lived in Portland, where you can put an egg on almost anything. Also, every day they have a dude out front grilling up beef, chicken, and pork and making a great bento for a great price. And when you are done with that, head down the street for a scoop of Ben and Jerry's. I mean, you're right there.

# North Portland

North Portland is a diverse mixture of residential, commercial, and industrial areas. It includes the Portland International Raceway, the University of Portland, and massive cargo facilities of the Port of Portland. Slang names for it include "NoPo" (shortened from North Portland) and "the Fifth Quadrant" (for being the odd man out from the four-cornered logic of SE, NE, SW, and NW).

## Foodie Faves

**Baowry,** 8307 N. Ivanhoe St., Portland, OR 97203; (503) 285-4839; **baowry.com; Asian; $$.** The building that now houses the Baowry was once a crack house. The renovation turned this spot into the home of a very popular food cart, one more switch from wheels to brick-and-mortar. On my first of two visits I enjoyed the buns immensely, and the small and large plates were quite good too. The Peking duck for two was different, but the duck was prepared well and I enjoyed the dish. I tried an eel and avocado bowl that was like a hand roll without the seaweed. Just the other night we ate only buns, and they were cooked perfectly and we left happy each with a brand-new Baowry tee shirt.

**Cha! Cha! Cha!,** 3808 N. Williams Ave., Portland, OR 97212; (503) 281-1655; 3433 SE Hawthorne, Portland, OR 97214; (503)

236-1100; 2635 NE Broadway, Portland, OR 97232; (503) 288-1045; 4727 NE Fremont, Portland, OR 97213; (503) 595-9131; 1208 NW Glisan St., Portland, OR 97209; (503) 221-2111; chachachapdx.com; Mexican; $$. There are 9 locations of this Mexican food restaurant that has decent prices and good food. Specials are particularly tasty, and the margaritas pack a punch. Serving standard Mexican fare, the service is quick and the staff is friendly. For me, the best thing on the menu are the mole enchiladas; I get meat with all the toppings. Yummy. The tamales are inconsistent, but when they are good, they are very good. I have listed my favorite locations.

**Eat: An Oyster Bar,** 3808 N. Williams Ave., Portland, OR 97227; (503) 281-1222; eatoysterbar.com; Seafood/Cajun; $$. Portland has no shortage of chill, homey restaurants serving good food at an affordable price. Eat fits the bill but also has the distinction of being one of the few oyster bars in town. And many of the best oysters available come from just off the shores of coastal Oregon and Washington. The oysters are spectacular. There are often between 10 and 15 super-fresh varieties, with the majority of them coming from the west coast. When they are fried, they are crisp and creamy and terrific. The food at Eat is Cajun/Creole, which is a blending of many of our best-loved cuisines. They do a super flavorful jambalaya, with a variety of hot sauces on the table. Everything is homemade, the people who work there are super nice, and they really are good at dishing up Southern hospitality. The recipes are classics; the étouffées and the gumbos are rich and spicy. To wash them down, there's good beer, traditional Southern sweetened iced tea, and a fine selection of whiskeys, especially in the bourbon category. It's a delightful place, very reasonably priced, friendly, and fun.

**Equinox,** 830 N. Shaver St., Portland, OR 97227; (503) 460-3333; equinoxrestaurantpdx.com; American; $$. Equinox is a comfortable restaurant with a strong commitment to serving seasonal cuisine using the best of Northwest ingredients. They do an excellent Painted Hills beef burger with hand-cut fries, and the pan-seared chicken breast is excellent with the creamy garlicky mashed potatoes. On a recent visit I enjoyed a lamb stew, and the rib eye is well cooked and well priced. And rib eye prices have gone crazy. Pastas are also done well with a pork bolognese the most recent standout dish. There is always a fruit crisp dessert offering, and it is always a divine way to end an excellent meal.

**Fishwife, 5328 N. Lombard St., Portland, OR 97203; (503) 285-7150; thefishwife.com; Seafood; $$.** Seafood lovers, take note, this is some awesome fish at great prices. North Lombard may be a tiny bit of a schlep for some, but if you love fish and seafood, the quality and prices here are, I think, impossible to beat. Love the shrimp and clam chowder, and the Oregon bay shrimp cocktail is a big portion of super-fresh sweet shrimp. Salmon is done many ways, and all are great venues for this local fish. Fried oysters and scallops are perfectly prepared, and the pastas with seafood are hearty and heavenly. Save room for dessert because the cobblers and the bread pudding are warm and begging to be topped with a scoop of ice cream. You will go home happy.

**Laughing Planet, 3765 N. Mississippi Ave., Portland, OR; (503) 467-4146; Healthy; $$.** I happened in here just last week in search of a smoothie. My local Jamba Juice went out of business and I had a craving. Smoothies are for me liquid comfort food. Some crave bourbon; for me it's a smoothie with banana and pineapple. This spot is kind of a throwback, featuring healthy food that is affordable and nutritious.

minds me of a place I loved in Brattleboro, Vermont, called The
mon Ground. Oh well, I digress. They offer tasty burritos and bowls,
ps, salads, fresh juices, and homemade cookies. My smoothie was
delish! And the vegan cookie assortment was not bad at all. Considering
all the good stuff that's missing.

**Lincoln,** 3808 N. Williams Ave., Portland, OR 97227; (503) 288-
6200; lincolnpdx.com; Mediterranean/Northwest; $$$. The food at
Lincoln is modern, influenced with flavors of the Mediterranean and a
powerful Northwest sensibility. The menu changes to reflect seasonality.
Jenn Louis and husband David Welch have created an elegant
restaurant with fine food and impeccable service. This is
one great restaurant! Yeasted polenta fritters and fried
squash with aioli and pecorino-Romano are amazing.
I loved the bull's blood beets, and the cured scallops with
preserved lemon, fennel, and bottarga will be in my food
memory forever. The cassoulet is the best of French comfort
food, and the polenta with veal ragu is super. Jenn is a master of
pasta, so don't leave Lincoln without trying at least one. I must con-
fess that fish is not my favorite, but the fillet of sole with fregola sarda,
pine nuts, wild oregano, and Meyer lemon kind of had me rethinking
the fish thing. I'll say it again: This is one great restaurant!

**Lovely's Fifty Fifty,** 4039 N. Mississippi Ave., Portland, OR
97217; (503) 281-4060; lovelysfiftyfifty.com; Pizza; $$. Appropriately
named, this cozy pizza spot on Mississippi serves good food at reason-
able prices. Salads are creative and fresh and they do a fine job with
roasted vegetables and soups. On a recent visit I started with the oven-
roasted cauliflower with dried fruit and pine nuts. My husband had
the potato soup with sorrel and green garlic. Yum, green garlic! Pizzas
are done just right, and toppings are seasonal and well designed. I am
crazy for the mushrooms with fontina and tartufo pecorino. Fontina
has become my favorite cheese for pizza. When it melts it is a dream.

They serve the food on a collection of mismatched plates, which is a style that always adds a bit of coziness to a restaurant, and this one doesn't need much more: It's already super chill and comfortable. The house-made ice cream, gelato actually, is fantastic. It is as good as some of the places where people wait online for a long time. They should go here: no wait and very delicious. Every flavor I have tried is soul satisfying, with my current favorites being dark chocolate amarena cherry and the flowering almond. A very nice place to have dinner in a very cool part of town.

**Mextiza, 2103 N. Killingsworth St., Portland, OR 97217; (503) 289-3709; mextiza.com; Mexican; $$.** This second "child" of Oswaldo Bibiano's is a sampling of dishes from all over Mexico. Where **Autentica** (p. 75) focuses on foods from Oswaldo's native state of Guerrera, Mextiza ("pieces of Mexico") allows you to try a varied sampling of the best of his country. The slow-roasted goat is a perfect way to be introduced, and the *doraditas*, shredded pork in a chili sauce, is magnificent. I love the *jarocho con jocoque*, a fried corn tortilla topped with black beans and a choice of toppings. I am always debating between the mushrooms and the *carne asada*. My young friend Mikey tried the tongue sandwich; frankly I was appalled, but he loved it and declared it the best he had ever had. When there is a tamale on the menu, order it, as this is an opportunity to get this hard-to-perfect dish at its best. Brunch is served on Sunday and it is also amazing. On my last visit I had the best enchiladas of my life, and I have eaten hundreds of them in my day. And the scrambled eggs with mint, sautéed spinach, and a grilled tomatillo habañero sauce is something I have been trying to re-create at home. Close, but no cigar.

**Mississippi Pizza, 3552 N. Mississippi Ave., Portland, OR 97227; (503) 288-3231; mississippipizza.com; Pizza; $$.** For a while Mississippi was the best, and probably only, gluten-free pizza in Portland. Having several gluten-free friends, we were there often, and the pizzas, both gluten free and regular, were quite good. Pizza toppings were plentiful and there are excellent beers on tap. Although there are many more GF pizzas in town, Mississippi still stands out as one of the best. The place is full of hipsters, hippies, and families out for a very reasonable yummy pizza lunch or dinner. On occasion you can wait for the pizza, but the place is fine for hanging out and a bit of people watching. And sometimes there is live music. I try not to go during those times, but that's just me.

**Muddy's,** 3560 N. Mississippi Ave., Portland, OR 97227; (503) 445-6690; muddyspdx.com; Comfort Food; $$. Portland has no shortage of places serving awesome comfort food. Maybe it's all the rainy days, but hot coffee drinks and their hearty breakfast and lunch have quite a following. Muddy's does this fare quite well, with great quiche, soups, stratas, and amazing french toast. I think quiche, when done properly, is a great lunch with a salad, in spite of the book from the '80's, *Real Men Don't Eat Quiche*. Ha! Sandwiches are generous and the coffee drinks are done well. And today's men do eat quiche!

**The Old Gold,** 2105 N. Killingsworth St., Portland, OR 97217; (503) 894-8937; oldgoldpdx.com; Bar; $$. This place is rad. They have good bar food and a terrific selection of beers, wine, and lots of bourbons and whiskeys. Not fancy, not trendy, just well-prepared bar food, great egg sandwich, super fries, and yummy curry popcorn served in a big bowl. Salads are fine and recently I enjoyed a roasted pork sandwich with a perfect Moscow Mule. They often have the sought-after bourbon Pappy Van Winkle, not cheap but liquid gold going

down. They drink it a lot on the TV show *Justified*; I am guessing that it is now even harder to get a bottle. Plus Old Gold is the first place I've seen that adds a "pickleback" for their whiskey lovers. One dollar for a shot of pickle juice after your shot of neat whiskey—how can you go wrong?

# BURGERVILLE

I confess I am not a fan of fast food. That said, I am in love with this chain of fast-food restaurants in Oregon and Washington. To me it is as good as, if not better than, the fast-food places people rave about, "In and Out" for one. No secret menus or California glitz. Their burgers are really honest and good, and you never get strange bits in the meat that make you wish you hadn't stopped in. It's good quality, and it tastes like it. Of course there are all kinds of ways to order the burgers, with all kinds of toppings and sauces, one to three patties, the whole show. I like the double cheeseburger and the Tillamook bacon burger, though take my word for it, don't eat it in the car. It's a mess! But a delicious mess that is fine in the restaurant or your house. They have at least two veggie burgers and a fish sandwich, too. An ad agency guy revealed to my husband that when they had a special ice cream promotion, they had to bring in freezers. There were NONE in Burgerville. Everything is fresh daily! Now that's something in the fast-food world.

I love that they are seasonal, local when possible, and that they try to use products that are purchased and grown with integrity and quality in mind. During strawberry season they have yummy shakes and strawberry lemonade as well as berries in salads. During Walla Walla onion season their fried onions are sooooo good. So are the rosemary fries. The deep-fried asparagus with a garlic aioli is pretty impressive for fast food. It is fast, and it is delicious. They make a great Arnold Palmer if you are at the drive-in window; somehow they always get the proportions perfectly. A few weeks back, my daughter Olivia came home with a bag that was a burger but clearly not Burgerville. It was another brand. I was in shock. I asked Olivia what made her make that awful choice. She said that the line at Burgerville was way too long. Well, that wouldn't have stopped me, I said in a huff. But with teenagers, you have to pick your battles!
**Burgerville,** *check website for locations; burgerville.com.*

**Pause Kitchen and Bar,** 5101 N. Interstate Ave., Portland, OR 97217; (971) 230-0705; Bar Food; $$. Pause is cool. Located out on Interstate in North Portland, they serve up excellent pub food, including a very good cheeseburger and, when it is on target, amazing mac and cheese. They have excellent sliders; sometimes they hit the spot better than a burger, not sure why. Their meat loaf is quite good as well, and the portions are generous. The place is big and there is a patio or back area for being one with nature. Prices are low and they have a good beer selection. My favorite thing of all is that kids can get noodles with butter and cheese, and it's free. I LOVE THAT.

**Por Que No?,** 3524 N. Mississippi Ave., Portland, OR 97227; (503) 467-4149; 4635 SE Hawthorne Blvd., Portland, OR 97215; (503) 954-3138; porquenotacos.com; Mexican; $$. This place is super popular with PDX hipsters and families and hipster families. They do a great job with tacos and bowls, and the prices are incredible. I have to say that the spot on Mississippi is quite small, but there is outside seating and it's worth the squeeze sitting inside on a rainy day. I was there once during a huge rainstorm and we ended up sitting with people we didn't know. They were awesome and we all shared our food and beer and it was super fun. The food is excellent, not fancy, just tasty and filling.

**Posie's Bakery and Cafe,** 8202 N. Denver Ave., Portland, OR 97217; (503) 289-1319; Comfort Food; $$. This homey cafe offers excellent coffee and properly done scones and muffins. Their Morning Glory muffin is possibly the best I have had in Portland. I have always loved a rare roast beef sandwich with Havarti cheese, and Posie's does it well. The staff is friendly and you never feel rushed to leave. Last week I was there with a couple of friends and we shared 3 of their cupcakes: a chocolate, a carrot, and a red velvet. There were all pretty terrific, and I have just ordered a cake from them for the friend who completely flipped over the carrot cupcake. 'Cuz that's what friends are for.

**Proper Eats Market and Cafe, 8638 N. Lombard Ave., Portland, OR 97203; (503) 445-2007; propereats.org; Healthy; $$.** Local and seasonal is the name and tone of the game here. The other game is learning about all these healthy and strange-sounding foods, and when you try them, you will be pleasantly surprised at their lack of similarity to cardboard or rabbit food. This type of food can be done deliciously if placed in the right hands. They cater to the vegan, gluten-free folks, but meat eaters can do well with satisfying yet meatless dining options. The ingredients are of good quality, and the employees are really nice and helpful. Proper does soups and bowls and interesting wraps, like the slaw and sunseed spread in a collard leaf. The hummus and guacamole are good and they serve beer and wine. Sometimes that kind of food feels just right. And other times it makes me want to head right to Burgerville. On a run.

**Tasty n Sons, 3808 N. Williams Ave., Portland, OR 97212; (503) 621-1400; tastyntasty.com; Eclectic; $$.** Tasty n Sons is one of my favorite eateries in Portland. I love it for breakfast, lunch, happy hour, and dinner. The room is a nice size, and there is a communal table so if you are eating alone you can probably get a social thing going on there. Getting a table at a traditional hour will probably not be easy, and if you are able to go early or late, or even in between, you can get in right away and will be delighted. It is a super-hip crowd, both working and eating, and the food is all over the place: Moroccan, Spanish, Mexican, and cowboy, and it all works together beautifully. I find that with the variety there is something for everyone, at every meal. And the wonderful Tasty Burger is available, at happy hour, for a tiny bit of money and a very big and good burger. The *shakshuka*, red pepper and tomato stew, is brilliant and the pork cutlet is crisp and cooked just right. Bloody Marys are outstanding, and they have iced tea with a side carafe of more iced tea. I totally love that. It doesn't happen everywhere!

**The Tin Shed, 1438 N. Alberta St., Portland, OR 97211; (503) 288-6966; tinshedgardencafe.com; Comfort; $$.** This casual spot offers breakfast, lunch, and dinner 7 days a week. The place is cool with terrific outside seating and was actually one of the first hipster spots on Alberta Street. Most of the food is kind of bar foodish, with good sandwiches, mac and cheese, and excellent sliders. Egg dishes are hearty and good, and I love their oatmeal, full of bananas, raisins, different seeds, and pure maple syrup. Best of all, there is a dog menu, with tasty treats for Fido of bits of chicken, beef, or pork with rice. One of these days they will probably offer a vegan option; it would be so Portland.

**Trebol, 4835 N. Albina Ave., Portland, OR 97217; (503) 517-9347; trebolpdx.com; Mexican; $$.** This is a fun Mexican restaurant. Colorful and casual, impressive tequila selection, and the food is consistently on target. Trebol does a good job with salads and starters; I particularly love the guacamole with serrano chilies and caramelized garlic. Blue cheese stuffed prawns were different and excellent, and the crunchy shelled taco sampler was like a "flight" of tacos, and a great way to try a bunch. For entrees the slow braised chicken with greens was tender and full of flavor, and they do a seafood stew that has a combination of fresh fish and a rich stock. My favorite is a ravioli stuffed with cactus, chilies, and cheese. Wow, it is awesome. One normally does not see ravioli on a Mexican menu, and I was reluctant, but now when it is available I have to order it, for me or for the table! My excuse for getting a dish that is up for grabs. Trebol does fun specials throughout the week, serving *flautas* one night and tacos another, and the food is paired with an alcoholic beverage and costs around $10. Also, they do cooking classes that are informative and fun.

**Cherry Sprout Produce Market,** 722 N. Sumner St., Portland, OR 97217; (503) 445-4959; cherrysprout.com. Nice little neighborhood market that has very good prices on produce and the employees are super friendly and helpful. Got a great rhubarb recipe from someone there just last week. Their wine department has over 120 different kinds of wines. As much as Cherry Sprout likes to go local, their wines are mostly from distant shores. As wonderful as local wines can be, due to some legit reasons they are often a bit pricey. The shop specializes in the "under $10" bottle of wine: 75 percent of their entire stock is priced under $10. I have purchased many of their selections and have been pleased by how well you can do for such a low price. Delightful place to shop; the wine guy is a sweetheart.

**The Meadow,** 3731 N. Mississippi Ave., Portland, OR 97227; (888) 388-4633; atthemeadow.com. If someone had told me 10 years ago that there would be a salt and chocolate store that was actually successful, I think I would have been skeptical. But it's there and it's a trip. It's a lovely little shop that has some flowers and some cookbooks, but mostly people come for the salt and the chocolate. I don't actually know if the shop has more kinds of salt or chocolate, but it seems to me that there is a pretty serious amount of choices. Salts are kind of amazing, with their texture, color, and place of origin. You can spend hours. Then you can go out, grab lunch, and come back in for chocolate and maybe some flowers for your favorite person.

**Mr. Green Beans,** 3932 N. Mississippi Ave., Portland, OR 97227; (503) 288-8698; mrgreenbeanspdx.com. This store is cool. Many years

# COFFEE

Portland and coffee. It's a natural, sorta like peanut butter and jelly. Or Stewie and Brian.

Portland is way up there on the list of coffee shops per capita. I mean, it is so much easier to find a coffee shop than a bank. Or a hardware store. A hat shop closes and becomes a coffee shop. And then they sell hats as well! They are everywhere. And I'm not just talking Starbucks. Maybe it's because of the rain; people either need that pick-me-up on a long, gray day or a great mocha latte to take the damp chill out of their tattoos. Also, people in PDX, at least  compared to New York City where I came from, have lots more leisure time. That's part of what Portland is about. Not wasted time by any means, just time to do what you want. There are so many great places to stop, get out your iPad, have a chewy cookie and a serious cup of joe*. Or have a business meeting. I've seen as many as seven people meeting for a "coffee shop" conference. Coffee is serious business here in the Pacific Northwest. And big business. Portland has spoiled me. In most places it is hard to get a good cup of coffee. Here, it is hard not to. Baristas are highly respected, like the chef or bartender, and if so inclined can talk about coffee for hours. Many, many coffee shops roast their own coffee beans. News of a good, new roaster can cause a tsunami of spilled lattes from people dropping their cups, running to taste the newest and greatest!

I was not a coffee drinker before moving to Portland. Maybe a couple of cups a week. Now, it's not so much that I need it to get me started, I just love the way it tastes. I love iced coffee. There's a place in Lake Oswego, a coffee shop named **Chuck's Place,** and they make their iced coffee ice cubes from black coffee. That's perfect. Instead of the ice melting and watering the coffee down, you have coffee till the last drop. Hot or cold, light or dark, topped with foam or a sprinkling of cocoa, I am now one of the many in PDX proud of the quality of our beans.

A few weeks ago, I was shopping on Mississippi, a super cool neighborhood, and went into a coffee shop named Mr. Green Beans. Small shop packed with all kinds of roasters, coffeemakers, filters, all the "stuff." Around the ceiling, on shelves, were quite a few hot-air popcorn poppers. I had no idea why they were there. Until today. It seems there are lots of people around town, roasting their own green coffee beans in the place where the popcorn kernels usually go. It makes sense, though I haven't tried it.

This is how I hear it's done:

One thing, before you start, use a popcorn popper that has side vents inside the machine, at the base of the interior funnel. You are going to put the beans in the place where you would put the kernels. Roast for somewhere between 3 to 5 minutes. Use two colanders to cool down the beans as quickly as possible, transferring the hot beans from one colander to another. Set up a large bowl to catch the pieces of skin or hull from the roasting beans. You can only roast around 4 ounces at a time. The coffee takes about 3 to 5 minutes, depending on the darkness of the roast. Keep the machine in a ventilated place, and hang around; this is a fun project but needs babysitting. Allow to cool thoroughly before storing or using. It won't be the best you ever had, but it will be awesome. And it will be uniquely yours.

*A cup of coffee. The term originates from former US Navy Secretary Josephus Daniels; when Daniels banned alcohol from Navy vessels, soldiers instead drank coffee and grudgingly came up with the term.

ago, like 25, I had a coffee bean roaster and loved it. I forgot all about it till I happened upon Mr. Green Beans. Lots of awesome stuff, great folks to talk to. Every coffeemaking contraption is there, everything from the Jetsons to the science lab. There's a lot to learn about coffee, and if you want to, the folks there will be thrilled to engage. And that whole street is so awesome.

# Cities & Towns around Portland

There are lots of little towns and cities around Portland that serve up some fine food. They are for the most part rather inexpensive, and good to know when you hit the road. Many of them are ethnic spots, and a few are worth a trip out of town. And remember you are probably always kind of near a Burgerville, and maybe you will be lucky and it will be Walla Walla onion season.

## Beaverton

**Chinatown Restaurant,** 14125 SW Walker Rd., Beaverton, OR 97006; (503) 641-4153; chinatownrestaurant.com; Chinese; $$. Right near the Nike campus, the dim sum at this simple place in a strip mall is excellent. In fact, all the food is terrific. They have a lot of dim sum choices and they have never been off the mark in either execution or quality of ingredients. The staff is very helpful, and we have discovered some wonderful new treats due to their suggestions. Out on 82nd Street, the area of town with many Asian restaurants, you can wait for hours for a table, but here I have never had to wait.

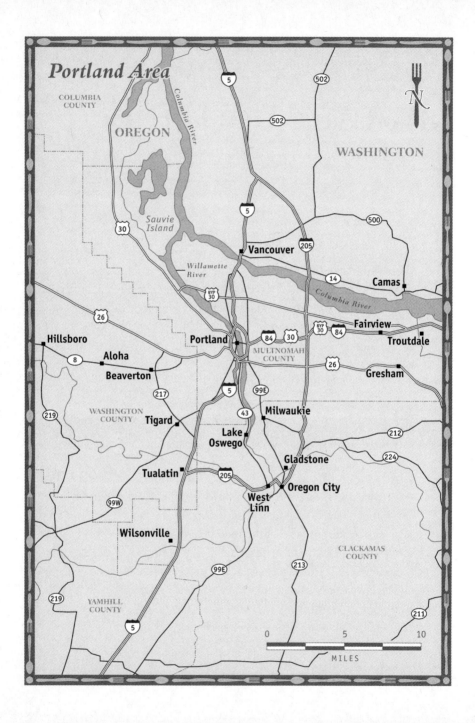

**Decarli,** 4545 SW Watson Ave., Beaverton, OR 97005; decarli restaurant.com; Italian; $$. I have never been disappointed with a meal at this large but friendly and rustic Italian restaurant. You can taste the freshness of the ingredients, and the seasonal menus reflect the best of what is local and the creativity in the open kitchen. I always get steak tartare and usually no one wants to taste and that is fine with me. Bruschetta varies and never ceases to wow us, and the pastas are inspired. The pan-roasted brick chicken is perfect, and when they have short ribs, I am amazed at how tender and tasty they are. Desserts are homey, and they offer just what you crave: crisps, gelato, and an outstanding salted caramel cheesecake.

**Monkey Subs,** 6087 SW 185th Ave., Beaverton, OR 97007; (503) 649-7827; Sandwiches; $. This sub shop has a wide variety of sandwiches and I have yet to be disappointed. People rave about the French Dip but I stick with the fresh bread piled high with top-quality cold cuts. I get the Monkey Wrench with everything, a whole not a half, and I am stuffed and happy. The people who work there are super nice, and Victor the owner is a great guy.

**Nakwon,** 4600 SW. Watson Ave., Beaverton, OR 97005; (503) 646-9382; Korean; $$. Former Blazer Ha Seung Jin, the first native Korean on an NBA roster, calls this the best Korean restaurant in Portland. They have tabletop grills, and the meat and other ingredients are of high quality. They bring out plates of accompaniments to eat with your barbecue, and they keep bringing more when you finish them. They offer a phenomenal seafood pancake and their soups are outstanding. And cooking your own food at the table is fun. I remember, many years ago, taking my dad to one of these places. He got in a really bad mood because he didn't think it was right that he had to cook his own food.

# Beaches. Not the Movie.

The Oregon coast is breathtakingly beautiful. Huge rocks jut out of the water and are majestic and dramatically rugged. There are sleepy beach towns, and towns that get more tourists and have the usual beach side stuff. Beaches, however, are rarely crowded; it's windy and the water is freezing, but the beaches are so close to Portland and so magnificent and peaceful that they are an ultimate in relaxation. And there's some good food too.

**Bowpicker Fish & Chips,** *1634 Duane St., Astoria, OR 97103; (503) 791-2942; bowpicker.com; Fish and Chips; $$.* I try to hit this spot every time I am in Astoria. Once a fishing boat, it is now the place to go for the best fish and chips in town. There are two choices here, small or large, and both come with thick-cut steak fries and ketchup and tartar sauce. They have lots of hot sauces and malt vinegar and outdoor picnic tables. The last three times I was there we ate in the car, and it was a bit of a mess but so worth it.

**Bread and Ocean,** *154 Laneda Ave., Manzanita, OR 97130; (503) 368-5823; breadandocean.com; Bakery/Sandwiches; $$.* I have spent several nights in Manzanita, a charming untouristy spot on the coast. The town is laid back and tiny, and there is nothing to do except hang out on the beach and relax. Which is wonderful. I often will go to Bread and Ocean to get lunch to go, but in the mornings their baked goods draw relaxed crowds purchasing the perfect cinnamon rolls or the special daily breads. Friday's polenta bread is my favorite, although sometimes I make sure we get to the beach by early Thursday. I hate the thought of missing the stout cheddar bread by just one day. Stellar.

**Bridgewater Bistro,** *20 Basin St., Astoria, OR 97103; (503)-325-6777; bridgewaterbistro.com; Seafood; $$$.* Astoria is a cool town that feels a bit like you have stepped back in time. It has been getting increasingly more popular and more restaurants and shops are opening up. Bridgewater has a great location at the mouth of the river, and the restaurant is open and full of light. The seafood is fresh and the offerings are varied and everything has always been wonderful. The seafood is prepared by a chef who knows how to showcase this kind of food. There is a delicious Asian-inspired stew of whatever is in season, and the Dungeness crab, when available, is amazing. This place is fairly expensive; however, you can't beat the view or the quality of what is offered.

**Fulio's Pastaria**, *1149 Commercial St., Astoria, OR 97103; (503) 325-9001; fulios.com; Italian; $$.* There is a wonderful Italian dish that I used to see on the menus of restaurants in Manhattan's Little Italy, home of some mob shootings and some amazing meals. The dish that I loved and have missed is called spedini, and it is the house specialty at Fulio's. Rounds of homemade mozzarella are skewered with slices of baguette, then baked until the bread crisps. It's then bathed in a buttery garlic sauce that's studded with capers and diced tomatoes. (Sometimes it has melted anchovies in the butter sauce, which is great.) The restaurant serves the dish with additional bread, because they know you will ask. It would be criminal to leave any of that sauce on your plate.

**Kelly's Brighton Marina**, *29200 Hwy. 101 N, Rockaway Beach, OR 97136; (503) 368-5745; kellyscrabs.com; $$.* Fresh is the key here. At this busy marina you can actually rent a boat and go out and do your own fishing or crabbing. And people love that. Personally, I prefer to have the people who work there do that for me, and I thank them and happily eat the catch right there, knowing that it couldn't be fresher. The crab is so fresh and sweet there was no need to add anything.

**Pacific Oyster**, *5150 Oyster Dr., Bay City, OR 97107; (503) 377-232; Seafood; $$.* All kinds of seasonal oysters, hand shucked and as fresh as is possible. There is a full menu, and the ciopinno and the deep-fried razor clams were great, yet if you are an oyster lover, that is definitely the way to go. The oyster stew was wonderful, and I found that if the oysters are fresh there is no such thing as too many.

**Pop's Sweet Shop**, *567 Pacific Way, Gearhart, OR 97138; (503) 738-8484; popsgearhart.com; Candy; $.* My friend Madeline had been telling me about the scones at Pop's for quite some time. Last week on a trip to the coast I stopped in, and boy was she right. The scones were absolutely perfect: moist and buttery and wonderful. Pop's is also known for its fudge and local Tillamook ice cream. The town is quaint, and sitting in the garden enjoying your espresso is a treat in itself.

**Roseanne's Cafe,** *1490 Pacific Ave., Oceanside, OR 97134; (503) 842-7351; roseannescafe.com; American; $$.* The location on a hill-top overlooking the ocean is a perfect setting for the wonderful food prepared in the kitchen. The staff is friendly and professional, and the menu, which changes daily, offers superb, creative food that showcases the local bounty. I have never had a less than great meal, and have never had a cobbler as good as their homey scrumptious Marion berry version. It is a killer.

**Silver Salmon Grille,** *1105 Commercial St., Astoria, OR 97103; (503) 338-6640; silversalmongrille.com; Seafood; $$$.* I think that the name implies that the salmon is the best way to go here, although other entrees have been quite good. Their salmon dishes, however, are truly excellent, and there is a wide variety of preparations that showcase this local and loved fish. The salmon filled with a Dunge-ness crab, bay shrimp, and smoked Gouda stuffing is rich and awe-some. I also love the salmon fillet coated with spices and blackened in a hot cast-iron pan, as it should be. The lime chive aioli served with it was a perfect pairing. And oh the chocolate pudding cake is amazing and I want it right now.

**Waves of Grain Bakery,** *3116 S. Hemlock St., Cannon Beach, OR 97110; (503) 436-9600; wavesofgrainbakery.com; Bakery; $.* This town, during the summer months, can be teeming with tourists, and be kind of a drag. However, the giant rocks jutting out of the ocean, and the vast and beautiful beach make that all go away. And while you walk along the beach looking at brightly colored starfish and sea anemone, try to be eating either the cheese biscuits, the simple version with a spot of jam, or the crunchy-topped streusel muffins that are offered in various seasonal fruit flavors. The bran muffins are pretty terrific as well, and not to be missed. And the seagulls like them too.

**Uwajimaya,** 10500 SW Beaverton Hillsdale Hwy., Beaverton, OR 97005; (503) 643-4512; uwajimaya.com; Asian Supermarket; $$. This chain of Asian products started in Washington, and Beaverton is lucky to have their only Oregon location. It's an adventure; the produce is unusual and terrific, and frozen foods like dumplings and all kinds

of noodles make the experience seem like you are in a food museum. Prepared foods are mixed, but it's fun to try some of their unfamiliar items. In the market is a bookstore that is the largest chain in Japan, named Kinokuniya. And the restaurant, Hakatamon, serves absolutely wonderful Japanese food. The restaurant has a pork and kimchee dish over rice that is out of this world. Highly recommend.

**Yuzu,** 4130 SW 117th Ave. Suite H, Beaverton, OR 97005; (503) 350-1801; Sushi; $$. The sushi at Yuzu is fresh and the cooked food is wonderful. Stellar ramen, and the pork belly and black cod were among the best I have had in the area. There is a large Asian community in Beaverton, and we often head out that way for authentic and reasonably priced Asian food of all kinds.

# Canby

**Thai Dish Cuisine,** 108 N. Ivy St., Canby, OR 97013; (503) 263-9898; thaidishcuisine.com; Thai; $$. Honestly, I never expected to find delicious Thai food in Canby, Oregon. This little farm town doesn't have much to draw people there and I just never expected to find a restaurant that is so good. And Thai food, what a lovely surprise. The appetizers we have tried have been excellent, particularly the salad rolls and the fried tofu with plum sauce. Soups are very good as well and the coconut soup, *tom ka gai*, is absolutely wonderful. Noodle dishes are way above average, and the spicy basil noodle is amazing. The prices are very reasonable, and the family that owns the restaurant is a delightful bunch.

## Eugene

**Brails,** 1689 Willamette St., Eugene, OR 97401; (541) 343-1542; **brailseugene.com; Breakfast; $.** Not being much of a drinker, I have never quite grasped the "best hangover food" so popular, not surprisingly, in this and other college towns. On the rare occasions that I have been in that miserable state, the last thing I want to do is eat, although that may be just what the doctor or roommate ordered. That said, I can appreciate a good breakfast and have been very happy with Brails, even perfectly sober! The Joy's Special is a heaping plate of hash browns with ham, tomatoes, onions, green peppers, swiss, and cheddar cheese. And because that isn't decadent enough, it is covered with their home-made country gravy, made daily. I would highly suggest ordering their biscuits, with or without more of that rich and dangerous gravy. Maybe a little jam and some good hot coffee and give your arteries a break.

**Glenwood,** 1340 Alder St., Eugene, OR 97405; (541) 687-0355; **glenwoodrestaurants.com; Breakfast; $.** Another hangover joint, this spot does a great job with all kinds of scrambles. Honestly, eggs are the last thing I would eat if I were hung over, but I must be in the minority based on the crowds here. The 13th Street scramble, my favorite, features eggs scrambled with mushrooms, bacon, bell peppers, olives, onions, jack, and cheddar cheese. They also make some light and flaky

 biscuits, served with a house-made raspberry jam that is exactly what you hope it will be. And at lunchtime, don't miss the creamy tomato cheese

# Eugene, home of the Ducks

Eugene is a city of roughly 160,000 people. It has some awesome farmers' markets in its downtown area, as well as some great activities to do, rain or shine. Try the kitschy Voodoo doughnut shop, see a concert at WOW concert hall, go for a beautiful hike up Spencer Butte, visit the Jordan Schnitzer Museum of Art (on campus), go for a run on any of the famous running trails, go see a football game, if you can get tickets, at Autzen Stadium, go see a track meet at Hayward Field, a brewery tour at Ninkasi, and best of all go try some of Eugene's unique restaurants. Eugene is a very active city, with more bikes than cars, more recycling bins than garbage cans, more beer than liquor, more die-hard college football fans than any other city in the country. Eugene was ranked one of the top 10 best college towns in the nation a couple years back. The best way I guess to describe this quirky town's vibe is by stressing the fact that driving around Eugene, even though it is a town that is growing and has some trendy urban areas, you can often find yourself feeling as if you were transported to a '70s co-op where a friendly smile is worth more than money and spending a large portion of your day outside is not a scheduled daily activity but a lifestyle. Even though it's cloudy or rainy 60 percent of the days year-round, there is something special and honest about this town.

soup with earthy pumpernickel rolls. The cheesy, soupy goodness is perfect on a rainy Eugene day. And believe me, there are lots of them.

**La Perla, 1313 Pearl St., Eugene, OR 97401; (541) 686-1313; laperlapizzeria.com; Italian/Pizza; $$.** They have wonderful thin-crusted true Italian pizzas with anything on them from fresh house-made mozzarella to eggplant and capers. They also offer very good seasonal salads, my favorite currently being the *insalata d'arugula*, which is baby arugula tossed in a wild huckleberry vinaigrette with marinated figs, walnuts, oven-crisped prosciutto, and shaved Parmesan. The restaurant has an open kitchen so you get to pass the time watching for your pizza to go in and out of the oven.

**Marché, 296 E. 5th Ave., Ste. 310, Eugene, OR 97401; (541) 342-3612; marcherestaurant.com; French; $$$.** I have only been to Marche for brunch, but they do an impressive business at lunch and dinner. It is a pricey restaurant for Eugene, and a place that is popular for celebrations, like graduations and all A's. The Croque Madame, which is raclette cheese, ham, béchamel, and a fried egg on their *pain de mie*, is one of the best I have ever had. I am a sucker for that sandwich, and they do an excellent rendition. Marché is a French restaurant that prides itself on using fresh ingredients that you would find in the local Eugene farmers' markets. They have a wood-fired oven, large bar area, private dining room, and large outdoor patio with awnings, umbrellas, and a lush garden.

**Off the Waffle, 2540 Willamette St., Eugene, OR 97405; (541) 515-6926; offthewaffle.com; Breakfast/Lunch; $.** Liège waffles (made from yeast-based dough and containing imported Belgium pearled sugar that caramelizes throughout the waffle) are served here and they are super popular. They offer both sweet and savory waffles, and although it is wrong, I have had a meal with one of each. Really I should have more willpower, but I don't get to Eugene that often! My favorite sweet waffle is called the Overachiever. It is their signature waffle topped with Belgian chocolate chips, sliced bananas, and then drizzled with their house-made dark chocolate sauce. My savory waffle choice is called Goat in the Headlights, topped with chèvre, avocado, fresh basil, two sunny-side-up eggs, smoked paprika, and fresh coriander then drizzled with extra-virgin olive oil. This place is a unique spin on fun breakfast food—who doesn't love a waffle or two?

**Papa's Soul Food Kitchen, 400 Blair Blvd., Eugene, OR 97402; (541) 342-7500; Southern Soul; $$.** I love this place for its fun atmosphere, creative menu, and awesome soul food. They do a good job with their crispy fried catfish, and their yams and fried okra are perfect. Their bread pudding is comfort food on steroids and they have live music to tie it all together. This place has a great Southern feel and I will head back the next time I am in Eugene.

**Prince Puckler's, 1605 E. 19th, Eugene, OR 97403; (541) 344-4418; princepucklers.com; Ice Creamery; $.** Prince Puckler's is an ice cream shop a couple blocks from the U of O campus. The flavors are interesting and still appealing, and they do some magic with sundaes and malts. President Obama has enjoyed ice cream there, his favorite being the mint chip. I like to get the Euphoria Sundae with their bittersweet nugget ice cream. This sundae has slices of bananas on the bottom layer and then ice cream and then drizzled, or should I say doused, with their euphoria chocolate fudge sauce over the top. Whipped cream on top, of course, and a few sprinkles of roasted almonds. Their Euphoria Chocolate Fudge is super thick and has a bittersweet taste to it, wildly rich and amazing!

**Sweet Life Patisserie, 755 Monroe St., Eugene, OR 97402; (541) 683-5676; Bakery; $.** Dessert shop that has cupcakes, chocolates, gelato, cakes, wedding cakes, tortes, pies, tarts, pastries, espresso, and tea. This place is a Eugene "must" if you are visiting. They have an incredible selection of beautiful desserts. My favorite things to get are the decadent German chocolate cake or the fresh coconut macaroons that are kind of gooey in the middle. There's a coconut theme going on here.

**Ubon Thai Kitchen, 690 Oregon 99, Eugene, OR 97402; (541) 689-0033; Thai; $$.** This super delicious, and very reasonable, Thai restaurant is a true family labor of love. There's seating in the owner's home by a cozy fireplace as well as plenty of covered outside seating attached to the trailer where the food is cooked. The Pad Thai is as good or better than any I had eaten recently, with a peanut sauce that was light and full of flavor. The *pad sa moon pai* is a wide rice noodle dish full of fresh vegetables, ginger, tofu, and lemongrass, and it is also excellent. Owners Bill and Pla grow much of the produce in their back garden, which is always a great discovery. I must mention that I washed my food down with a terrific Thai ice tea.

**Uly's Taco Cart, W. 13th Ave. and Olive St., Eugene, OR 97401; Tacos; $.** Uly's menu is super basic, serving just tacos for cheap, served on double layered corn tortillas (choice of meat: carnitas, steak, or

chicken) with your choice of cheese, sour cream, onions, cilantro, and their special tasty sauce. Open Friday and Saturday from 11:00 p.m. to 2:30 a.m.; there is always a long line of tipsy and hungry students waiting outside of the cart every night excited for these one-of-a-kind tacos!

**Vero Espresso, 205 E. 14th Ave., Eugene, OR 97401; (541) 654-0504; Cafe; $.** Beautifully artistic coffee drinks and tempting pastries and sandwiches draw crowds to this homey spot that attracts students, laptops in tow, who drink and eat and do homework. They have very good waffles, and I think they do a terrific latte. In Portland, expectations are always high, and they live up to people's expectations.

**Voodoo Doughnuts, 22 SW 3rd Ave., Portland, OR 97204; (503) 241-4704; 1501 NE Davis St., Portland, OR 97232; (505) 235-2666; 20 E. Broadway at Willamette Ave., Eugene OR 97401; (541) 868-8666; voodoodoughnut.com; Doughnuts; $.** Talk about "Keep Portland Weird." This popular bumper sticker might have been created after a trip to this famous, and pretty bizarre, Portland doughnut shop. Lines form out the door at odd hours of the day or night, and the newly upgraded shop on the west side has all sorts of odds and ends, I mean stuff that you can buy so you never forget this doughnut experience. Another way to remember it is to get married there. A real wedding, with doughnuts and coffee for six people, will cost you about $300. I am guessing that you can get an assortment, which would include some unusual toppings and flavors. And shapes. The cream-filled doughnut shaped like a phallus is very popular, as are the round doughnuts topped with Captain Crunch or Fruit Loops, and my personal favorite, the maple bacon. I am ashamed to admit I can never eat just one. My son Nick, who will eat bacon on anything, said it was "a damn good doughnut." And don't panic, there are vegan doughnuts too.

## The Gorge

The Columbia River Gorge is a canyon of the Columbia River. Up to 4,000 feet deep, the canyon stretches for over 80 miles winding through the stunning Cascade Mountains. The river forms the boundary between Washington and Oregon, and the gorge furnishes the only navigable route through the Cascades and the only water connection between the Columbia River Plateau and the Pacific Ocean. That said, the most important fact about The Gorge, as it is simply called here in Portland, is it is absolutely spectacular.

The Gorge has protected status, which is officially referred to as the Columbia Gorge National Scenic Area, and it is a hugely popular recreational destination. Hiking trails abound, with trailheads about every 3 feet! I've hiked up to Angel's Rest with its view of the Columbia River. My friend Graeme brought his bulldog, Boss, along. Everyone knows how bulldogs love to hike very steep trails! When we reached Angel's Rest, Boss, who had been a grouch during the entire walk, came alive because the summit is populated by hungry, begging, fearless, and very speedy chipmunks. Boss immediately chased one over the side, disappearing from sight. The summit is about 2,000 precipitous feet above the Columbia, or should I say the highway running alongside the Columbia. Boss ran off the rock ledge and wound up on a 3-by-4-foot outcropping about 2 feet below. After regaining our composure, and putting a leash on Boss, we did have to chuckle at the sight from below if in fact Boss had flown off the top! But Boss usually makes us chuckle no matter what he does.

The Gorge transitions between temperate rain forest to dry grasslands in only 80 miles, hosting a dramatic change of scenery while driving down I-84. In the western, temperate rain forest areas, forests are marked by maple trees and Douglas fir. In the transition zone (between Hood River and The Dalles), vegetation turns to Oregon white oak, ponderosa pine, and cottonwood. As I write this on the banks of the neighboring Willamette River, the cottonwood "cotton" is flowing by, making it feel like the river has a layer of snow! Then on the eastern end the forests make way for expansive grasslands, with occasional pockets of ponderosa pine. Driving east from Boise, Idaho, you see some of the most beautiful high desert scenery around. Just breathtaking.

The area of the Gorge is one of the most beautiful places I have ever seen. From Oregon to the hills of Washington, the vegetation looks like miles and miles of lush green velvet. The colors are browns and greens and it is magical. The main town, Hood River, is a gem in the middle of all this unforgettable beauty.

The area around Hood River is fertile farmland used mainly for the growing of fruit. It is an easy day outing from Portland, and picking apples with the majestic, snow-covered Mt. Hood off in the distance is just mesmerizing. Plus the apples are delicious!

**10 Speed Coffee Bar,** 1412 13th St., Hood River, OR 97031; (541) 386-3165; 10-speedcoffee.com; Coffee; $. There are a bunch of spots outside Portland to get delicious coffee. In the Gorge, 10 Speed's many locations are a sure thing. The places are welcoming and the bike theme is so Oregon. They serve very well-made pastries, including scones and freshly baked doughnuts. I had a ham and cheese croissant on a recent visit that was excellent. And their coffee art is pretty special too. This spot is my favorite, but check out their website for other locations.

**Bette's Place,** 416 Oak St., Hood River, OR 97031; (541) 386-1880; bettesplace.com; Comfort; $$. Open till 3 p.m. 7 days a week, this place rocks breakfast and lunch in a big way. The cinnamon roll was as big as my head and tasted great. A town institution since 1975, with baked goodies still made by the original owner. The omelets and more complicated egg dishes were just perfect. Muffins are wonderful and you will be happy and pretty full when you head out the door. Get a pie to go; they are terrific.

**Celilo,** 16 Oak St., Hood River, OR 97031; (541) 386-5710; celilo restaurant.com; Northwest Cuisine; $$. I have been there twice in the last couple of months. My first meal was excellent and we ordered lots of the "small plate" offerings. Mussels were cooked perfectly and the pasta with cremini mushrooms was satisfying in their earthy way. A beet salad was a refreshing addition to the meal as was the perfectly mixed Berry Drop, with a house-made vodka berry infusion. On the next visit we ordered entrees, and I was very pleased with my chicken confit. My friend Cathy had a lamb dish that she loved. Give yourself an extra 15 minutes and get the chocolate volcano cake; it was amazing. Since I don't live far from a real volcano, Mt. St. Helens, I should know.

**Columbia View Orchards,** 8467 Hwy. 30, Mosier, OR 97040; (541) 478-3750; columbiavieworchards.com; Fruit; $. Located in Mosier, just east of Hood River, this orchard has 45 acres that have been producing grapes for over 15 years. The grapes are mostly Pinot Noir, Merlot, Syrah, Chardonnay, Sauvignon Blanc, Grenache, and Primitivo, among others. The tasting room has a view that is unforgettable. The Pinot Noir is distinctive from the valley Pinot, as their grapes are battered by the strong winds prevalent in the area. This thickens the skins of the fruit and gives depth to the wine. The orchard produces cherries and pears as well. I once spent a couple of hours picking cherries and honestly I have never had better. They were plump and juicy and spectacular. They also produce a cherry port-style wine made from their cherries, and it is quite wonderful. The artfully decorated cherry stand sits on the east end of the property, on Highway 30, and is open during peak cherry season. For decades people have come from great distances to load up on their huge and flavorful varieties of cherries: Bings, Vans, Chelans, Sweethearts, Rainier, Royal Annes. The setting of this winery and orchard is as beautiful as I have seen anywhere. Absolutely mesmerizing. And the folks who run it are pretty sweet.

**Double Mountain Brewery,** 8 4th St., Hood River, OR 97031; (541) 387-0042; doublemountainbrewery.com; Brewpub; $$. Although beer is not my drink of choice, I have several buddies who love the beers brewed at this super-fun brewpub with really good pizza and sandwiches. The staff is so nice they seem to remember you even if you haven't been there in months. They sometimes have live music and have beer celebrations when they feel it's time. And they have a single hop IPA called Clusterf*ck. It almost makes me want to drink one.

**Draper Girls Country Farm, 6200 Hwy. 35, Mt. Hood, Parkdale, OR 97041; (541) 352-6625; drapergirlscountryfarm.com.** This year-round self-service fruit stand attracts hordes of people for the fun of gathering your own cherries, apples, pears, plums, and more. It all depends on what is in season. The cider mill produces Hood River's only 100 percent pure, licensed non-pasteurized apple cider. And it is incredibly delicious. Last year I roasted a pork butt and made a sauce with a cider reduction that was terrific. The orchards are beautiful and you are welcome to hang out and picnic, feed the farm animals, and buy some of their amazing jams. Buy a bunch of their cinnamon sugar dried apples. They are a treat!

**East Wind Drive-In, 395 Wa-Na-Pa St., Cascade Locks, OR 97014; (541) 374-8380; Burgers; $.** This roadside burger joint has been in business since 1939, and not much has changed. The burgers seem to get mixed reviews but the ice cream always gets raves. Whether it is a cone, a malt, or a scoop, people just love this place. This Cascade Locks burger shack serves huge cones and cups of ice cream, and the tropical soft serve is wonderfully refreshing.

**Everybody's Brewing, 151 E. Jewett Blvd., White Salmon, WA 98672; (509) 637-2774; everybodysbrewing.com; Brewpub; $$.** Just across the river from Hood River is the lovely town of White Salmon, Washington. This cozy brewpub features a terrific sun-drenched back deck with spectacular views. They brew a lot of interesting beers and serve fresh salads and a very good burger.

**Full Sail Pub,** 506 Columbia St., Hood River, OR 97031; (541) 386-2247; fullsailbrewing.com; Brewpub; $$. In addition to brewing beer that people love, the company is pretty special. The business started with a bunch of folks who wanted to work in a non-corporate, nontraditional environment doing something they were passionate about. It was in that spirit that Full Sail became an independent, employee-owned company in 1999, divvying up the company between the 47 employees. It is a happy place to drink. And eat. They do shared plates of the food that beer drinkers want to eat and they do it well: wings, fries, cheesy bread, and a killer artichoke dip. They have good burgers and very good salmon fish and chips. For dessert try a Beer Float, three scoops of Tillamook vanilla ice cream served in a pint glass with your choice of beer. I was sad at first until I discovered that they do that with root beer for the younger folks or the old ones who aren't beer lovers. Win, win.

**Kaze,** 212 4th St., Hood River, OR 97031; (541) 387-0434; facebook .com/pages/Kaze-Japanese-Restaurant/121477461196045; Japanese; $$. The food is fresh and the servers are cordial at this traditional Japanese restaurant in this lovely town. The fish

was fresh and there were some very interesting and well-done rolls. I particularly loved the roll with battered and fried soft-shell crab. The service can be a bit slow but sushi is often that way; after all, you wouldn't want your sushi to be undercooked. LOL!

**Nora's Table,** 110 5th St., Hood River, OR 97031; (541) 387-4000; norastable.com; American; $$. My husband and I recently had a terrific meal at this restaurant just off Hood River's main street. I had a curry that was surprisingly good for a nonspecific ethnic restaurant, and Bruce thoroughly enjoyed his lamb ragu on a bed of pasta. The staff is super friendly and the service was excellent. Some seats give you a view of the kitchen if you like to watch. People are also raving about their breakfast, and I must say the offerings sound great. I want to have the cardamom pancakes. Who wouldn't?

**Sixth Street Bistro,** 509 Cascade Ave., Hood River, OR; (541) 386-5737; sixthstreetbistro.com; Eclectic; $$. I have been to the bistro several times and have found the locally sourced food and drink to be top-notch. I enjoyed the fish and chips and had a chicken satay for my meal that was an appetizer but a very generous portion. The hand-cut fries are terrific, as are the burgers they accompany.

**Solstice Wood Fire Cafe,** 415 W. Steuben St., Bingen, WA 98605; (509) 493-4006; solsticewoodfirecafe.com; Comfort; $$. This is my favorite place to get pizza in the Gorge. There is a huge wood-fired oven and the pizzas are crisp and topped with fresh ingredients. They do a good mac and cheese with chorizo, and pastas are delicious. There is outdoor seating on sunny days but just as lovely is sitting inside by the warmth of the fireplace on chilly, winter days.

**Trillium Cafe,** 207 Oak St., Hood River, OR 97031; (541) 308-0800; American; $$. Soups, sandwiches, and salads are pretty reliable at this spot that serves traditional American food. The meat loaf was first rate and the burgers and fries were quite delectable. The staff is very friendly and the service is good. At times people say it can be a bit too loud, but honestly I have never found that to be an issue.

# Timberline Lodge/Mt. Hood

Built in the late 1930s, this historic landmark sits at an elevation of 5,960 feet, within the Mount Hood National Forest. It is a popular tourist attraction, drawing more than a million visitors annually. It is noted in film for serving as the exterior of the Overlook Hotel in the scary and fantastic movie with Jack Nicholson and Shelley Duvall called *The Shining*. The building is immense and fabulously situated with views that are astonishingly beautiful. There is snow on the mountain year-round, which makes it possible for people to ski year-round. The mountain is visible from Portland and looks different and haunting at times, surreal at other times.

One of the things that people love about Portland is that within 90 minutes you can get to the beach or to the mountain. And Portlanders love to do both. The lodge was constructed between 1936 and 1938 as a WPA project during the Great Depression. Workers used large timbers and local stone, and placed intricately carved decorative elements throughout the building. President Franklin D. Roosevelt dedicated the Lodge on September 28, 1937. In his remarks, he commented on the reasons for the project: "This Timberline Lodge marks a venture that was made possible by WPA, emergency relief work, in order that we may test the workability of recreational facilities installed by the Government itself and operated under its complete control.

"Here, to Mount Hood, will come thousands and thousands of visitors in the coming years. Looking east toward eastern Oregon with its great livestock raising areas, these visitors are going to visualize the relationship between the cattle ranches and the summer ranges in the forests. Looking westward and northward toward Portland and the Columbia River, with their great lumber and other wood-using industries, they will understand the part which National Forest timber will play in the support of this important element of northwestern prosperity. Those who will follow us to Timberline Lodge on their holidays and vacations will represent the enjoyment of new opportunities for play in every season of the year. I mention specially every season of the year because we, as a nation, I think, are coming to realize that the summer is not the only time for play. I look forward to the day when many, many people from this region of the nation are going to come here for skiing and tobogganing and various other forms of winter sports." Thank you, FDR, for making it happen!

**Blue Ox Bar, Timberline Lodge.** Tucked away just behind the main lobby, the Blue Ox is a favorite watering hole steeped in history and tradition. It features pub-style pizza and handcrafted microbrews from the Mt. Hood Brewing Company. Don't miss the glass murals of legendary Paul Bunyan and Babe the Blue Ox.

**Cascade Dining Room, Timberline Lodge.** Casual by day, romantic by night, this fine restaurant serves seasonal food with creativity and top-quality ingredients. There is a lunch buffet that is quite bountiful, and dinners are excellent. After a day of skiing, hiking, or boating, there is something wonderful about stepping into the Cascade Dining Room and choosing from an impressive wine and cocktail list and varied and interesting menu. My most recent dinner included 8 of us, so happily I was able to taste lots of entrees. Writing a book about food paves the road for lots of tastes and sharing.

The salt-roasted beets with goat cheese was an excellent combination; in fact, it has inspired me to pair the two at a recent dinner party. The duck egg in a cast-iron skillet was amazing, served with potato chips made in-house along with mushrooms and bacon truffle butter. The arugula salad was fresh and wonderful combined with the applewood bacon crunch. The most popular entrees were the marinated Cornish hen and the elk sirloin medallions with a red wine demi-glace. Additionally, the rib eye steak for two was melt-in-your-mouth tender and tasted wonderful with the cheddar mashed potatoes.

Hopefully you will save room for dessert, as both the vanilla orange cream cake and the fried dulce de leche cheesecake were extraordinary.

# Government Camp

**Glacier House Bistro and Pizza, 88817 E. Government Camp Loop, Government Camp, OR; (503) 272-3471; glacierhaus .com; Eastern European; $$$.** We started the meal with the Alpine plate, an interesting array of sausage, ham, pâté, and pickled vegetables. In addition we enjoyed the potato croquettes, panko crunch on the outside and creamy in the middle with scallion and Parmesan. Lovely. Both the goulash and the pork schnitzel entrees were generous portions and well executed. I love a crispy pork product. Government Camp was built as a camp for the government workers building the Timberline Lodge in the late 1930s. It was a WPA project and is now a National Historic Monument.

**Huckleberry Inn, Government Camp Loop, Government Camp, OR; (503) 272-3325; huckleberry-inn.com; American; $$.** During ski season this restaurant is a pretty good steak house, and just being "on the mountain" is an awesome place to be. The prices are not too bad for a steak place, and the chicken piccata was quite good on my last visit. The huckleberry pie is what steals the show. Have a scoop of ice cream on the top, and you will feel like you are on top of the world.

# Hillsboro

**Swagat, 1340 NE Orenco Station Pkwy., Hillsboro, OR 97124; (503) 531-9500; swagat.com/hillsboro; Indian; $$.** Personally I love a good Indian buffet. I don't get Indian food that often and I want to try everything. At a good buffet you do just that. I love taking my time and eating the lunch in courses. The food here is always fresh; you never feel like you are eating last night's leftovers. They do a busy lunch and trays of hot food are replenished constantly. The chicken saag was creamy and dreamy and the tikka masala excellent as well. We have gone with our good friends Kathy and Richard and we always have fun and we always have plenty.

**Syun, 209 NE Lincoln St., Hillsboro, OR 97124; (503) 640-3131; syun-izakaya.com; Japanese; $$.** In the basement of what was once the Hillsboro Library, Syun's food is authentic, beautiful, and superb. Our daughter Olivia lived in Japan for 6 months and she found the food to be as authentic as any she has had in this country. They have some dinner specials that are quite reasonable, the staff is nice and helpful, and the food is served on lovely plates, which adds to the delightful experience. There are so many sakes, you can never expect to taste them all, although you will want to!

## Lake Oswego

**Blast Burger, 315 1st St. #101, Lake Oswego, OR 97034; (503) 305-8088; blastburgers.com; Burgers; $$.** This is a very good burger located in Lake Oswego. It is thick and juicy and I love all the toppings. The burger with fried jalapeños, roasted Anaheims, pickled Serranos, chipotle aioli, and pepper jack cheese is my favorite, but I have never had a burger there I didn't like. Also, they carry Random Order pies, so I would eat there even if the burgers were awful. But they're not, they're great.

**Casa Del Pollo, 15910 Boones Ferry Rd., Lake Oswego, OR 97035; (503) 344-4354; casadelpollo.com; Costa Rican; $$.** I have become a regular at this family-run Costa Rican restaurant that smells so good I have no idea how anyone drives by without stopping. The chicken is super tender and has a perfect amount of smoke in the flavor. The beans and rice are better than average, and their green sauce is fresh and fabulous. The taco platter, again I go for the chicken, is enormous and terrific. They have vegetarian options and some good breakfast food, all day long.

**Chuckie Pies, 430 5th St., Ste. A, Lake Oswego, OR 97034; chuckiepies.com; Pizza; $$.** Lisa and Chuck Ryan own the terrific coffee shop named **Chuck's Place** (below) in Lake Oswego. They are great people, generous and fun. Now they have a pizza place in town. It's called Chuckie Pies—there's a theme here—and it's a perfect addition to the thin-crust pizza-lacking town of Lake Oswego.

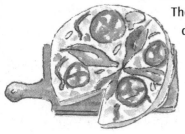

The pizza is Neapolitan style, with house-made dough, fresh mozzarella, and ricotta. Classic salads with great ingredients, simple but tasty desserts. A selection of hand-crafted cocktails, wines, whiskey, and Italian beer will be on tap to accompany you on your fantastic pizza voyage.

**Chuck's Place, 148 B Ave., Lake Oswego, OR 97034; (503) 675-7861; chucksplaceonb.com; Coffee; $.** Chuck's is the go-to coffee shop in L.O. Chuck and Lisa Ryan run this large yet cozy coffee shop and home office (people set up for hours with their computers or business meetings), and they do so as if it was their home. Chuck is hilarious and makes my day. No one can insult you like Chuck! He always has a funny comment that is served up with warmth and a twinkle in his eye. Lisa knows her stuff, and is a pleasure to talk to about food, politics, and her two cute boys. The coffee is Illy and the ice cubes are frozen coffee if you want them to be. And the baked scones and cookies are the bomb.

**Crave Bake Shop,** Kyra's Bake Shop 460 5th St., Lake Oswego, OR 97034; (503) 212-2979; cravebakeshop.com; Bakery; $. When this bakery opened, I figured it would last at the most 6 months. Never thought the gluten-free thing would last, goodbye, Crave. Not true at all. The cupcakes are so good I have friends who buy them and they have no gluten issues. And I get it. There is nothing lacking in these beauties; taste and texture are absolutely perfect. Business is great and the folks are nice. My faves are the chocolate with vanilla bean Italian meringue and the carrot cake with creamy cream cheese frosting. In the 100th episode of Food Network's *Cupcake Wars*, Crave Bake Shop went head-to-head in the finale and came out on top! Woot.

**The Firehouse Pub,** 23 A Ave., Lake Oswego, OR 97034; (503) 697-3903; firehousepub.net; Pub; $$. For the last 4 years, on Wednesday nights, my husband and his buddies D'Mark, Graeme, Lyle, and sometimes John go to this bar for wings and conversation. Sometimes the wings are better, sometimes the conversation, but they always enjoy the vibe at this friendly neighborhood bar. The burgers are decent, chili with everything rocks, fries are fine, and they love the tots. But it's more about the atmosphere and wonderful staff. Occasionally they have music on Wednesday, and if they do, the guys switch their night to Thursday! How can you solve the world's problems with live music in the background?

**Kolbeh,** 11830 Kerr Pkwy., Lake Oswego, OR 97035; (503) 245-1662; kolbehpdx.com; Persian; $$. I have never been to this restaurant for dinner, not sure why, but the lunch buffet is really special. I have taken lots of friends there, and everyone marvels at the quality of the food, the price, and the unlimited iced tea. The buffet choices all seemed prepared for the occasion, not last night's leftovers, and it is really a terrific food deal. I love the little meatballs and the ground beef kebobs. The salads are fresh, the pita is warm, and there are always mediocre to good cookies for the final sweet bite. Go anyway, the cookies aren't so bad, just pale beside the delicious buffet.

**Pine Shed BBQ,** 17730 Pilkington Rd., Lake Oswego, OR 97035; (503) 635-7427; pineshedribs.com; Barbecue; $$. This place has a strange setup but excellent barbecue and totally amazing mac and cheese with bacon. It's a shed with outside tables and they have a storefront in the same strip mall where you can go and eat inside. You order and they bring you the food. It's odd because usually it's just diners, no staff, and I feel like I'm in a classroom and the teacher left but that's just me. The ribs are excellent, both beef and pork. I would stay away from the pastrami if you have ever had good pastrami, like from

Katz's in New York. I have found that in Portland and surrounding areas most of the pastrami tastes like they took a brisket and kept it in a box of potpourri for a month. If Katz's would open a cart in Portland, it would be amazing.

**Scratch,** 149 A Ave., Lake Oswego, OR 97034; (503) 697-1330; scratchfoodsllc.com; American; $$$. Scratch is a small, mildly upscale spot that has good food and friendly staff. Their menu caters to those who want to eat locally and healthfully. They do wonderful work with greens and vegetables, serving creative dishes that are sure to please. On a recent visit I loved the roasted beet, red onion, and goat cheese salad, which I followed with a perfectly roasted game hen with an outstanding potato gratin. Bruce had the steak that was cooked perfectly, seared on the outside and medium rare on the inside. We decided to share the chocolate lava cake, which, after one bite, I wanted to tell Bruce to get his own.

**Senor Taco**, 333 S. State St., Lake Oswego, OR 97034; (503) 635-8226; **Mexican; $.** My daughter Olivia had been trying to talk me into dining at this place forever. Finally she prevailed and I was pleasantly surprised. The food is made to order, standard Mexican fare, and it's good and fresh. We have since eaten there quite a bit, and if you are looking for well-done, fast Mexican food that's cheap and portions huge, this may be your place. I know it's one of mine.

## Milwaukie

**Busters BBQ**, 11419 SW Pacific Hwy., Tigard, OR 97223; (503) 452-8384; 1355 NE Burnside St., Gresham, OR 97030; (503) 667-4811; 17883 SE McLoughlin, Milwaukie, OR 97267; (503) 652-1076; bustersbarbecue.com; **Barbecue; $$.** This family-run operation serves Texas-style barbecue, dry rubbed and smoked for hours. I've never been to Texas, and would have only gone there for the barbecue, so this has saved me a trip. Folks who know say that it is authentic, and I just know it's good. I usually go for a combo of three smoked items, and have never been disappointed in anything. I have also gotten food by the pound when I don't have the time and crave ribs, either beef or pork. Only once did I have room for the pecan pie. It was excellent.

**Enchante**, 10883 SE Main St., Milwaukie, OR 97222; (503) 654-4846; enchantechocolatier.com; **Chocolate; $$.** Wow. This stunning storefront looks as good as the chocolates taste. Not inexpensive; however, I think it may rival or even surpass some of Portland's best-loved chocolate shops. The pecan clusters are studded with toffee bits, and the praline almonds are so good I ship them to my brother in Maine monthly. They do a fine chocolate-covered Oreo, and for your France-loving friends pick up a foil-wrapped chocolate Eiffel tower. *Ces't magnifique!*

**Highland Still House, 201 S. 2nd St., Oregon City, OR 97045; (503) 723-6789; highlandstillhouse.com; Scottish; $$.** I completely adore this pub. It has an authentic Scottish feel, the staff is super  friendly, and the atmosphere relaxing and fun. The selection of whiskey (bourbon, scotch, rye, Irish whiskey) is unbeliev-able. If you are a single malt lover, this is an opportunity to try a glass of the labels you have only read about. Beer selection from revolving taps is impressive as well. And the food is fabulously done Scottish pub food, with a great Scotch egg, flaky pasties, and a giant plate of fish and chips that rocks. Desserts are terrific too; the sticky toffee pudding has been on my mind since last week. It is kind of mind-blowingly delicious. The ample parking lot is always full, a testament to the popularity of this gem of a pub.

**Loncheria Mitzil Mexican Eatery, 212 Molalla Ave., Oregon City, OR 97045; (503) 655-7197; Mexican; $$.** I love this quirky place in my new town. Mitzil is a terrific woman who cooks and entertains at her mostly family-run restaurant in Oregon City. You feel like you are eating in her kitchen at home. Salsa only in the summer when the tomatoes are ripe, and the chile rellenos are excellent and the prices are low. They serve a killer breakfast on Saturday. Search for them on Facebook for more info.

**Mi Famiglia, 701 Main St., Oregon City, OR 97045; (503) 594-0601; mi-famiglia.com; Pizza; $$.** The thin crust pizza is excellent here, with fresh toppings and friendly, fast service. I had an excel-lent Caesar salad and met some nice folks sitting at the bar a couple of weeks back. There is a nice neighborhood feel to this family and date-night spot, and having just moved to this town, I thought it was

# Oregon City, the end of the Oregon Trail

Oregon City is the first incorporated city west of the Rockies. Established in 1829 by Dr. John McLoughlin as a lumber mill near Willamette Falls, it was later designated as Oregon's territorial capital. It was the end of the Oregon Trail, sort of the last stop. Visiting its many museums and historical buildings allows you a glimpse of pioneer life in Oregon territory.

a delightful find. One warning: The delish calzones are big enough for 20! Not really, but expect to fill a doggie bag before leaving. Thanks, Jody and Mark.

**Singer Hill Cafe, 723 7th St., Oregon City, OR 97045; (503) 656-5252; singerhill.com; Coffee; $.** This family-owned restaurant has an absolutely charming vibe, and the food is good and the coffee is excellent. It's Stumptown Coffee of course. Not a place to go if you are in a hurry, but if you are able to sit and relax, this is the perfect spot. There are two vertical herb and flower gardens inside and one outside. The garage door windows open for plenty of fresh air and sun, if the weather permits. I have enjoyed a delicious cinnamon roll and good scones, and they make a nice sandwich. These folks care, and it shows.

**The Verdict Bar and Grill, 110 8th St., Oregon City, OR 97045; (503) 305-8429; verdictbarandgrill.com; American; $$.** Located across from the Oregon City courthouse, this restaurant and bar does a surprisingly good sirloin steak with a peppery whiskey sauce. The steak was cooked perfectly and the sauce had just the right amount of spice and booze. We enjoyed the salmon, and on a recent visit during happy hour, all day Thursday, we had a very decent cheeseburger and a good size Caesar salad. My neighbor Dave enjoys the fish tacos and the gnocchi. Word has it that they make a good Spanish coffee, but I have yet to try it. Let me know if you do.

## Sandy

**Joe's Donuts,** **39230 Pioneer Blvd., Sandy, OR 97055; (503) 668-7215; joes-donuts.com; Doughnuts; $.** This is a well-loved pit stop for folks heading up to Mt. Hood. It's also a destination in itself; people travel to get these doughnuts made the old-fashioned way. You can't miss it since it is painted in wide red and white stripes. Open 7 days a week. The doughnut variety is excellent and the coffee they serve is very good. I hate when you have a great doughnut and a lousy cup of coffee. I also hate when you have great coffee and a lousy doughnut. But at Joe's both are excellent. In Portland right now there is a new-ish doughnut shop and the doughnuts cost about $2.50. At Joe's the doughnuts cost either 95 cents or $1.50, and they are just as good, just not crazy flavors. These are doughnuts like mother used to make, if you were lucky, and I think they are all at the top of their category. My three favorites are the old-fashioned, the maple bars, and the raised glazed. I can never leave there without bringing a box home for friends. There is nothing like coming home to a box of doughnuts on your doorstep.

**Banning's Restaurant and Pie House,** 11477 SW Pacific Hwy., Tigard, OR 97223; (503) 244-2558; banningsrestaurant.com; **American; $$.** Banning's Restaurant and Pie House has been around for over 30 years. So they know how to make pie. I have had tastes of most of them, and the crust is flaky and the fillings are clearly made from scratch with high-quality ingredients. The restaurant is open 'round the clock, and I have to say I have had nothing there but pie and coffee. But that's okay; sometimes pie is all you need. Like love.

**Hmart,** 13600 SW Pacific Hwy., Tigard, OR 97223; hmart.com. This place is not the least beat upscale, modern, or pretty to look at. But the selection of Asian spices, produce, meats, fish, and poultry are impressive. There are cuts of meat for Korean barbecue and unusual products that you might not find in many places in Portland. And I am talking super unusual. Things written in languages nobody understands with no pictures, translations, or any help whatsoever. Prices are super inexpensive and I have always been happy with the quality.

# West Linn

**Mean Street Pizza,** 21700 Salamo Rd., West Linn, OR 97068; (503) 657-5799; meanstreetpizza.com; **Pizza; $$.** It took my friends Ed and Carole visiting from Chicago to steer us in the direction of this very good pizza place. It's like an old-fashioned pizza parlor; the people are so nice and the pizza is so good. Not fancy or artisan, just whole pizzas or by the slice that have good sauce and cheese, fold the way a slice should, and make us happy when we eat it.

# Woodburn

**Luis's Taqueria, 523 N. Front St., Woodburn, OR 97071; (503) 981-8437; luistaqueria.com; Mexican; $$.** Everything I have ordered at Luis's has been great, beyond what you think of as standard Mexican fare. The place is super casual, and the people behind the counter are friendly and have let me know if there is something special that day that they think I would like. The menu has standard Mexican offerings but with the freshest of ingredients, found locally in this farm town.

# Farmers' Markets

To say that these markets are outstanding is actually an understatement. Just beyond city limits you will find many, many small, independent farms. There are at least two serious farms right in Portland proper, The Zenger Farm and the 47th Avenue Farm. Many Portland neighborhoods have a farmers' market, and most run from spring through fall, with a couple remaining open year-round. The markets tend to reflect the vibe of the neighborhood, by the crowd they draw, the cooked foods they sell, and the type of produce and products available. The fruits and vegetables are fantastic in both quality and breadth of variety.

I never knew Oregon had a thriving local truffle scene to go with the thriving local IPA beer scene and the ubiquitous coffee scene. Most stalls will give samples of their wares, and I generally hit every stall a couple of times. Farmers' markets are wonderful to just wander around. The people are interesting, very interesting, there is generally a very positive vibe, and it's fun. If you hang around, you are bound to get some food tips; after all, many of PDX's top chefs shop there, too. The markets are a feast for the palate and the eyes, with colorful produce right from the garden. Also, there are usually plenty of prepared foods at the markets, from bagels to bratwurst, and terrific baked goods. And yes, coffee.

For a complete vendor list go to portlandfarmersmarket.org/index .php/vendors/complete-vendor-list.

# PORTLAND'S FOOD-RELATED
# NOT-FOR-PROFITS

Portland is a city with several nonprofit organizations bent on, if not eliminating, at least alleviating the problem of hunger in its under-privileged communities. Historically Portland has had a strong public consciousness for the homeless and the poor, dating from the 1970s when it was a mecca for the street people coming to protest the war in Vietnam and living in Portland's parks. There remains inequality in Portland as there is in every US city, but with the abundant farms and the long growing season, Portlanders are out to help.

## Community Supported Agriculture

The temperate Willamette Valley produces a bounty of vegetables and fruits, and is home to ranches and small meat and poultry farms. Many of these farms supply to restaurants and the farmers' markets, and some deal directly with families, offering contracts that allow for home use of what's best and in season. There are pickup points as well as delivery options, and peeps are learning about foods that they might otherwise never get to know, and eat, and you know just where your food is coming from.

In some cases you pay a fee at the start of the season, and occasionally part of the deal is working at the farm in some visitor-friendly capacity. The farm and ranch community is an interesting group of folks, and there are often stellar tips on what to do with that 3rd week of zucchini and chard!

We have found at our house that buying directly off the farms is deeply satisfying. We have ongoing relationships with several of the growers and have gained a connection to the place and people who grow what we are eating. It has definitely strengthened our con-nection to the source, and I think we all like that. Also, who better to get cooking tips from than the people who raise and grow the food. Another benefit for me is that I think I have become a better cook, experimenting with the many vegetables that I have come to love. Five years back I would have given kale away. Now I have developed 6 or 7 different recipes that show how awesome kale is.

One is a recipe for kale chips I wrote for *Parent's Magazine*. Try it, it's really good. Start with 1 bunch kale, rinsed and patted dry, and preheat oven to 300°F. Tear the kale into pieces and remove the thick spine of the leaves. Gently toss with olive oil and sprinkle with salt. Lay the kale on a greased baking sheet or parchment. Bake until the edges are brown but not burnt, 15 to 20 minutes. Watch carefully. Allow to cool and enjoy.

## Growing Gardens

This not-for-profit gets at the root (food pun) of hunger in Portland, Oregon. Growing Gardens organizes hundreds of volunteers to build organic, raised-bed vegetable gardens in backyards, front yards, side yards, and even on balconies. They support low-income households for 3 years with seeds, plants, classes, mentors, and more. Their "Youth Grow" after-school garden clubs grow the next generation of veggie eaters and growers! Through Learn & Grow workshops and work parties, this organization teaches gardeners all about growing, preparing, and preserving healthful food while respecting the health of the environment.

G.G. makes sure low-income people have the resources they need to grow organic vegetables at home. Through this work, community members meet over the backyard garden, through volunteering, by attending classes, and through sharing extra produce.

## Portland Fruit Tree Project

This grassroots nonprofit organization tries to provide solutions to a critical and growing need in Portland and beyond: access to healthy food. The Tree Project empowers people to share in the harvest and care of urban fruit trees, preventing waste, building community knowledge and resources, and creating sustainable, cost-free ways to obtain healthy, locally grown food. Because money doesn't grow on trees . . . but fruit does!

"We organize people to gather fruit before it falls, and make it available to those who need it most. We register fruit and nut trees throughout the city, bring people together to harvest and distribute thousands of pounds of fresh fruit each year, and teach tree care and food preservation in hands-on workshops."

**Oregon Food Bank**
OFB helps needy households fight hunger by distributing food from a variety of sources through a statewide network that includes its four branches located in Beaverton, Ontario, Portland, and Tillamook, 16 independent regional food banks, and 945 partner agencies. These local programs provide food directly to people who are hungry in the form of boxes of food for people to take home and cook or already-prepared meals. The OFB Network serves an average of 270,000 people each month. I have worked there on several occasions, and the people involved are committed and determined to eliminate hunger in Portland.

**Slow Food Portland**
Slow Food Portland seeks to connect people with the food they eat and the cultures, community, and production behind it. At the heart of their commitment is the belief that every individual has a right to healthy, good food in their daily life. Through lectures, tours, cooking demonstrations, volunteer days, and other local events, Slow Food Portland works to engage our community with the broader food movement. They partner with local and national activists, chefs, farmers, and organizations already working to make improvements in the food culture of Portland and beyond.

**Wild Food Adventures**
This not-for-profit focuses on the edible plants and forageable food in the Northwest and other parts of the country.

The organization strongly believes that this knowledge will allow folks to live more sustainable lifestyles and be better caretakers of the environment. As I mentioned earlier in the book, Oregonians are very serious about the environment. I think not recycling might be grounds for excommunication, or at least having to eat in heels and a suit.

There are lectures, expeditions, and workshops that address the past, present, and future of making the most of what just grows naturally.

**Beaverton Farmers' Market, 12455 SW 5th St., Beaverton, OR 97075; (503) 643-5345.** One of the largest markets in the Portland area with an estimated 20,000 shoppers each week. There are nursery growers, artisan food producers, noodle makers, and plenty of breads, pastries, pickles, and chocolate. There's live music and lots of places to sit and enjoy the festivities. I can easily spend hours there.

**Buckman Farmers' Market, SE Salmon St. and SE 20th Ave., Portland, OR 97214.** A family-friendly feel and great energy, this market is a great place to shop. Throughout the season they are going to do free cooking classes for kids. What a great way for kids to learn and enjoy fresh food in a cool environment. And on a less healthy note, they do a great Franks a Lot event with plenty of goodies to pile on your hot dog.

**Hillsdale Farmers' Market, SW Sunset Blvd. and SW Capitol Hwy., Portland, OR 97239; (503) 475-6555.** I love this one. It is open year-round and had many vendors. I find the market has a great energy, lots of variety, and there's parking at Wilson High School. It is also located behind Baker and Spice so you can get the world's best crumb cake.

**Hollywood Farmers' Market, 4420 NE Hancock St., Portland, OR 97213; (503) 709-7403.** A totally family-friendly market with lots of kids, dogs, and excited PDX shoppers. Important to many of the shoppers is the availability of good food to eat while shopping. Hollywood does pretty well on that score, with excellent tamales, fried rice from the **Ate-Oh-Ate** (p. 37) cart and a totally sweet mango lime popsicle.

**King Farmers' Market, NE Wygant St. & NE 7th Ave., Portland, OR 97211.** Small and laid-back, this market near the groovy Alberta

Arts 'hood has an interesting mix of hipsters and families. They have the usual fare, with some excellent prepared food and lots of tastes of seller's products. I had amazing salmon from a purveyor, and rumor has it that you can get great fresh oysters on alternate weeks. My friend Laura said that she had an amazing burrito a few weeks back.

**Lents International Farmers' Market, 11741 SE Foster Rd., Portland, OR 97266; (503) 282-4245.** This market has terrific produce and products from a wide variety of ethnic growers and producers. I have gotten fresh garbanzo beans and heirloom Russian tomatoes. There is a wide variety of hard-to-find Asian vegetables and herbs and plenty of international taste treats. It's a fun, festive atmosphere.

**Portland State University Farmers' Market, 724 SW Harrison St., Portland, OR 97201.** The most impressive in size and selection is the market at Portland State University, right in downtown Portland. People spend hours there, looking, eating, listening to music, and feeling fortunate. The market goes for blocks and has everything you need to put together some fine meals. And while you walk around, try to be eating something absolutely delicious, which will be super easy to do.

**Shemanski Park Farmers' Market, SW Park Avenue and SW Main Street, Portland, OR 97205.** A favorite with chefs in town. I have seen Jenn Louis from **Lincoln** (p. 120), David Kreifel from Laurelhurst, and have actually gone with Jobie Bailey and Brian Scibetta from **DOC** (p. 80) to watch them create their menu. It's not big but the selection is good and there are totally terrific tamales for sale.

# Trucks & Carts

The Portland food cart scene is pretty extraordinary and seems to be getting more so by the day. The carts are in parking lots, on sidewalks, and in "pods." I love that they are called "pods." So futuristic. Or the future is now. There are pods all around the city; some have names, some don't.

Food lovers know that some of the best food you can get is street food. Food that is cooked by regular people, many of whom learned at their mother's stove. Street food is generally not overly complicated, and ingredients tend to be simple and not extravagant.

The food carts in Portland reflect well over 50 cultures. For many people this is their first introduction to the foods of a specific country, and for some it is a welcome taste of home. The food is always reasonably priced and usually quick to prepare.

When you dine at a food cart, you are also supporting a small local business, one that might not have the funds to open a brick-and-mortar location. Hours for carts are generally limited, occasionally there is seating though often there isn't, and when a truck or cart is successful, they often find a location and become a "real restaurant" or use the money they have made to fund a different project. The carts bring some pretty sweet eats to the street for people who want a quick or inexpensive bite, as well as allowing folks to try foods of the hopefully growing ethnic communities in Portland.

**Bento Box,** 530 SW 10th Ave., Portland, OR 97205; (503) 250-3604; facebook.com/bentoboxpdx. Perfectly grilled chicken, never dry, very, very special sauce, rice and vegetables, super reasonable, big portions, and owned by the nicest family on earth. Tell them Laurie sent you.

**Big Ass Sandwiches,** 304 SE 2nd Ave., Portland, OR 97214; bigasssandwiches.com. Sandwiches (and big ones, at that) with my current favorite being the ham, bacon, and sausage. I know, it's almost a disgrace. But so good.

**The Big Egg,** 4233 N. Mississippi Ave. (at Skidmore), "Mississippi Marketplace" Portland, OR 97217; thebigeggfoodcart.blogspot.com/2009/09/big-egg-has-landed.html. The breakfast not to be missed is the grilled flour tortilla with scrambled egg, grilled potatoes, portobello mushrooms, and vintage white cheddar, with their house-made fire-roasted poblano salsa and yogurt-lime sauce. Spring for the bacon. Because you can. If you are a Portland resident, you have a certain bacon quota you need to meet each week, unless you can prove that you are a vegetarian or vegan.

**Brunchbox,** Southwest 5th Avenue and Stark Street, Portland, OR 97204; (503) 477-3286; brunchboxpdx.com. Breakfast and burgers, some monstrous in size, all delicious.

**Flavour Spot,** North Lombard between Denver and Greeley; (503) 289-YUMM; Corner of Mississippi and Northeast Fremont; (503) 282-YUMM; flavourspot.com. Waffle sandwiches (Dutch tacos) that are sweet or savory. I can't resist the Black Forest ham and smoked gouda. Sometimes I forget about how wonderful smoked gouda is. When I remember I have it in my house for several months.

**The Frying Scotsman, Southwest 9th and Alder Street, Portland, OR 97205; (503) 706-3841; thefryingscotsmanpdx.com.** British fish-and-chips, done just right.

**La Jarochita, 310 SW 5th Ave., Portland, OR 97204; (503) 421-9838; foodcartsportland.com/2008/02/25/jarochita.** Veracruz-style tamales in banana leaves and made-to-order Mexican flatbreads (*sopes* and *huaraches*) with various toppings. If you have ever tried to make tamales, you know that when you find someone who can, it's a solid gain.

**KOi Fusion, 4th and Ankeny, 6th and College, PGE Park, Portland, OR; Various Locations; koifusionpdx.com.** I cannot resist the dog, served with kimchee sauerkraut, Japanese mayo, and some barbecued Korean meat. Totally awesome taste combo.

**Nongs, 609 SE Ankeny St., Ste. B, Portland, OR 97214; (503) 740-2907; 411 SW College St., Portland, OR 97201; (503) 432-3286; SW 10th & Alder St., Portland, OR 97205; (971) 255-3480; khaomangai .com.** Chicken and rice, pork and rice. Sauce of fermented soybeans, ginger, garlic, Thai chilies, vinegar, house-made syrup, and soy sauce.

**The People's Pig, Southwest Washington and 10th, Portland, OR 97205; facebook.com/peoplespig.** Pork belly, porchetta sandwiches, ciabatta bread . . . heaven.

**Popped ART, Southwest Washington and 9th, Portland, OR 97205; facebook.com/poppedart.** Cracked black pepper and balsamic vinegar, sweet jalapeño lime, and yes, BACON WITH MAPLE SYRUP.

**Potato Champion Food Cart, Southeast Hawthorne Boulevard and Southeast 12th Avenue, Portland, OR 97214; (503)**

**505-7086; potatochampion.com.** Potatoes, fried and yummy, with many choices of sauces for dipping. Open crazy hours, often till very very late. Located in a pod with several other carts. Fun place for a late-night snack or dinner.

**Spella Caffe, West 9th Avenue at Alder Street, Portland, OR 97205; (503) 421-9723; spellacaffe.com.** This great cart roasts coffee beans off-site, then hand-pulls sublime espresso drinks. Dreamy, chocolate-flaked stracciatella gelato in the warmer weather, though I would eat it outside in a snowstorm.

**Tábor, Stark Street near Southwest 5th Avenue, Portland, OR 97205; (503) 997-5467; schnitzelwich.com.** From a truck that looks like a gypsy cart, Czech specialties like fried eggplant on ciabatta, slathered with paprika spread and horseradish. I love eggplant. This is a marvelous use of the underappreciated vegetable.

**Viking Soul Food, 4262 SE Belmont St., Portland, OR 97214; (503) 704-5481; vikingsoulfood.com.** Heavenly griddled potato flatbread with sweet or savory fillings. I guarantee you will be back.

**Whiffies Fried Pies, Southeast 12th and Hawthorne, Portland, OR 97214; (503) 946-6544; whiffies.com/index.html.** Savory and sweet pies deep fried but not greasy for your dining pleasure. It may seem decadent but I have had a savory one with a sweet one for dessert. It's so wrong and so right at the same time.

**The Whole Bowl, Southwest 9th and Alder, Portland, OR 97205; 1100 NW Glisan St., Portland, OR 97209; 4411 SE Hawthorne, Portland, OR 97214; (503) 757-BOWL; thewholebowl.com.** A comforting and healthy medley of brown rice, red and black beans, fresh avocado, salsa, black olives, sour cream, Tillamook cheddar, cilantro, Tali Sauce, and a lot of love.

**Wolf and Bear's, 113 SE 28th Ave., Portland, OR 97214; myspace.com/wolfandbearskitchen.** Vegan food, amazing falafel, and the Olea, which is homemade kalamata tapenade, labneh, grilled eggplant, roasted red peppers, grilled red onions, gorgonzola crumbles, caramelized walnuts, freshly cracked pepper, salad greens drizzled with tahini sauce, and olive oil on a warm pita.

**Wy'East Pizza, 3131 SE 50th Ave., Portland, OR; 97206; (503) 701-5149; wyeastpizza.com.** Thin crust pizza, fresh toppings; go for the Cloud Cap: mushroom, ricotta, roasted garlic, rosemary, and black pepper.

# Wineries &
# Wine Country

The Willamette Valley. Oregon's wine country is beautiful and easily manageable. There are bus and limo tours or you can just drive to the wineries themselves or to the tasting rooms in the towns. It's a lovely part of the state, and the trip from Portland is under an hour.

Pinot Noir is one of the oldest grape varieties to be cultivated for wine production. The grape variety is grown around the world but has, historically, been mainly associated with the Burgundy region of France. The name is derived from the French word *"pinot,"* which means pine, and the word *"noir,"* which means black. The vine produces tight clusters that resemble black pine cones.

The quality of a Pinot is based on a number of factors. Vineyards do best when they slope gently down toward the east, providing the vines with long sun exposure yet avoiding scorching afternoon heat. The soil should contain calcium carbonate, which offers good drainage. Volcanic and sedimentary soils are perfect for the best results. Well-drained soils have a higher average temperature, which assists ripening. Pinot Noir wines reflect the flavor of the soil, making the locations of the vineyards critical, even more critical when grown in cooler climates such as Oregon.

One of the most appealing qualities of Pinot Noir is its soft, velvety texture. When right, it is like liquid silk, lovingly caressing the palate.

Pinot does not have the same tannin profile as the bigger red varietals such as Cabernet Sauvignon, Zinfandel, and Syrah. Pinot Noir tends to be enjoyed earlier, typically 5 to 10 years past the vintage. Foods that are simple and rich work well with the complicated and subtle flavors of this elegant wine.

The Oregon wine industry took off in the '70s and '80s. Due to the similarity of the Oregon wine country and the Burgundy region of France, the Pinot Noir has become the signature wine of Oregon. In international competitions, Oregon Pinot has surpassed some of the finest French Burgundys. In 1987 the Drouhin family of Burgundy, one of France's highly regarded winemaking families, purchased 100 acres of land in the North Willamette Valley, founding the Domaine Drouhin Oregon winery.

I am happy to know Lynn and Ron Penner-Ash, owners of the very successful vineyard that bears their name. I have been to their winery for several tastings, and have called on Lynn, the winemaker of the vineyard, to work with me to feature a number of different style Pinots that reflect some of the best that the Portland area has to offer.

**Beaux Freres, 15155 NE North Valley Rd., Newberg, OR 97132; (503) 537-1137; beauxfreres.com.** Beaux Freres is dedicated to the production of estate-bottled Pinot Noirs that express the personality of the Pinot Noir grape, preserve the integrity of their vineyard, and reflect the character of the vintage. In pursuit of these goals, the Beaux Freres Vineyard has been planted with tightly spaced vines, crop yields are kept to about 2 tons per acre, and the grapes are harvested when physiologically (rather than analytically) ripe. In the vineyard, Beaux Freres follows the path of biodynamic farming, and in the cellar, winemaking philosophy is one of minimal intervention.

# Where to Eat in Wine Country

**Community Plate,** *315 NE 3rd St., McMinnville, OR 97128; (503) 687-1902; communityplate.com; Comfort; $$.* Both breakfast and lunch are pretty terrific at Community Plate. I had the most wonderful pork hash with caramelized onions, and I paid a dollar extra for a fried duck egg on top. Breakfast sandwich was sitting on a perfect biscuit and the granola was full of good stuff. Mac and cheese for lunch was yummy, and the pork loin and ham Reuben, sort of a Cubano, was so rich and deeply satisfying, as only something that decadent can be. On a lighter note, the chop salad was a great choice. If you wish they served dinner, go to their sister restaurant, **Walnut City Kitchen.** Yay!

**Jory,** *2525 Allison Ln., Newberg, OR 97132; (503) 554-2525; the allison.com; Northwest; $$$.* Located in the Allison Inn and Spa, Jory is a foodie's dream come true. Executive Chef Sunny Jin brings skill and creativity to his menu, and the food reflects the seasons and his great sense of food and wine pairing. I had an exceptional duck and sweet potato dish, and the halibut with chorizo was stunning. The dining room is large and lovely and you can sit at the counter in front of the open kitchen if you like. For dessert I had a strawberry rhubarb pie with an almond streusel that was sooooo good. On sunny days there is outdoor seating.

**Painted Lady,** *201 S. College St., Newberg, OR 97132; (503) 538-3850; thepaintedladyrestaurant.com; Northwest; $$$.* Steak is one of

**Bethel Heights,** 6060 Bethel Heights Rd. NW, Salem, OR 97304; (503) 581-2262; bethelheights.com. Twin brothers Terry and Ted Casteel, and their partners Marilyn Web and Pat Dudley, launched Bethel Heights Vineyards in 1984. The Bethel Heights team has recently expanded to include second-generation leadership and ownership, bringing youthful energy, talent, and passion into the blend. Located in the Eola Hills just my favorite foods, but I rarely eat it out these days. Too expensive, and I do a pretty good job at home. However, my friend Sam said it was one of the best he had ever had. And it was outstanding. Dry aged, great flavor, and tender as is possible, this was a great dinner. The 5-course tasting menu offers lots of choices and everything we ordered was wonderful. I had a trio of chocolates for dessert that was beyond-belief delicious.

**Red Hills Market,** *155 SW 7th St., Dundee, OR 97115; (971) 832-8414; redhillsmarket.com; American; $$.* If you are looking for a sandwich or totally great Cobb salad, you can't do better than this homey, friendly market. Local products are used when possible, and they serve Stumptown coffee so you know you will get a good cup. They have local beer and wine on tap, and the shelves are stocked with all the things you might want for a picnic lunch in wine country.

**Walnut City Kitchen,** *2580 SE Stratus Ave., McMinnville, OR 97128; (503) 857-0034; walnutcitykitchen.com; American; $$.* Everything is first rate at this lunch and dinner spot in McMinnville. Modern inside but still manages to feel inviting. The sandwiches are way above average and dinner excellent. The chickpea fritters were perfect paired with the romesco sauce, and the crab cake was outstanding. As for entrees, the roast chicken and the pork chop were perfectly executed. I had heard raves about the fries so we ordered a plate for the table, who was very hungry after a busy morning. Fries . . . yum.

west of Salem, the vineyard's wines are distinctively bright with focused red fruits and are extremely well balanced. Bethel Heights wines are consistently some of the best from the Willamette Valley.

**Brick House Vineyards,** 18200 NE Lewis Rogers Ln., Newberg, OR 97132; (503) 538-5136; brickhousevineyards.com. After a career as a network war correspondent, Doug Tunnel, owner/winemaker of Brick House Vineyards, came home to the Willamette Valley to produce estate-grown wines from the three great varietals of Burgundy: Pinot Noir, Chardonnay, and Gamay Noir. Brick House Vineyards has been certified organic since 1990 and Demeter Biodynamic since 2005. In what was once the farm's horse barn, Doug produces about 3,800 cases in accordance with both standards—native yeast fermentations and minimal handling to produce wines that are both elegant and profound in their simplicity.

**Domaine Drouhin,** 6750 Breyman Orchards Rd., Dayton, OR 97114; (503) 864-2700; domainedrouhin.com. Founded in 1988, Domaine Drouhin Oregon produces stunning Pinot Noirs and Chardonnays that are noted internationally for their pure expression of fruit, superior balance, silky texture, and classical elegance. The 225-acre estate is home to 90 acres of high-density vineyards, planted atop Oregon's Dundee Hills. Fourth-generation winemaker Véronique Drouhin handcrafts the wines, using traditional Burgundian techniques in their four-level gravity flow winery. It is Véronique's mission to handle the fruit gently, to let the wines reveal the true character of the vineyard and the vintage. The result is wines of lovely balance.

**Kookoolan Farms,** 15713 Hwy. 47, Yamhill, OR 97148; (503) 730-7535; kookoolanfarms.com. I met Chrissie at wonderful Barbur Foods where she was selling her pasture-raised chickens. We talked for a while about her being a farmer, and her chicken and her green walnut wine, and we said goodbye. I bought a chicken and the wine, and became a fan of both. The chickens are unbelievable, so moist, and they cook beautifully. Expensive, but a much better product than your average bird. The farm has different classes and events. The vegetables and herbs from there are always bursting with flavor, amazing quality. I am actually going to enter a recipe contest with their komboucha, which is so much more delicious than any komboucha I have ever had before. And there is just something magical about this place. There may be a little piece of everyone who would like to be a farmer. The getting up so early just ruins it for me! When farming starts at noon, I'm in!

**Penner-Ash Wine Cellars, 15771 NE Ribbon Ridge Rd., Newberg, OR 97132; (503) 554-5545; pennerash.com.** Penner-Ash embodies the spirit and passion of small producers focusing on Pinot Noir in the northern Willamette Valley, Oregon. Penner-Ash Pinot Noirs and Syrahs are often described as "elegant and earthy, structured and thoughtful." These qualities come from a fundamental notion of transparency. The wines are produced with a desire to break down barriers and to expose the winemaking mystery—to do away with pretense and bring us closer to the source. Winemaker Lynn Penner-Ash and her husband, Ron, started Penner-Ash Wine Cellars in 1998. In the winery, the focus is on small-lot indigenous yeast fermentation with extended cold soaks to extract a rich, fruit-focused, textured mouthfeel. Each lot is treated individually and, depending on the outcome, either blended into a reserve quality Willamette Valley Pinot Noir or bottled separately as a vineyard designate. A sustainable three-level gravity winery building is sited within the estate vineyard.

# Recipes

The generosity of the PDX food community is expressed through support of the neighborhoods where restaurants are located and an amazing willingness to help the less fortunate with fundraising efforts. Chefs have been extremely generous sharing recipes I never expected to get my hands on. Awesome.

# Bife a Micalense
## Portuguese Sirloin Medallions

*Oba! Restaurante is a fun and festive restaurant that serves terrific food full of flavor. This recipe has a lot of ingredients but is well worth the effort. It's not hard, and you probably have most of the staples in the house. Portuguese food has lots of spice and interesting flavor combinations. Perhaps make yourself a cocktail to go with it.*

*(Serves 2)*

1 tablespoon butter

1 ripe banana, peeled and cut in half lengthwise

2 tablespoons butter

2 tablespoons olive oil

Salt and pepper

4 medallions top sirloin (approximately ½ inch thick)

¼ cup white onion, cut in ⅛ inch strips

2 teaspoons minced garlic

4 teaspoons Dijon mustard

½ cup beef stock

½ cup heavy whipping cream

1 tablespoon chopped flat parsley

2 tablespoons crisp bacon, diced

Cilantro sprigs for garnish

*Heat a sauté pan over medium heat and add the tablespoon of butter and the banana. Cook the banana slowly to bring out the natural sugars, about 3–4 minutes on each side. Reserve and keep warm while cooking the sirloin.*

*Heat another pan over medium-high heat. Add the butter and the oil and warm until the butter melts and the foam subsides.*

*Season each side of the top sirloin medallions. Add to the pan and cook for 2 minutes.*

*Turn the top sirloin over and add the onions to the pan. Cook until the sirloin is at the desired temperature, approximately 2 minutes for medium rare. Turn the heat down so that the onions do not burn.*

Remove the sirloin from the pan and hold warm; meanwhile add the garlic and sauté for 1 minute to bring out the flavor.

Add the Dijon mustard, beef stock, and whipping cream. Cook until the sauce reduces and the cream thickens. You can put the cooked top sirloin back in the pan if it needs to warm a bit. Add in the parsley at the end to keep them green and fresh.

Put the sirloin on a plate and top with the caramelized banana. Top with the mustard cream sauce.

Sprinkle the sirloin with the chopped cooked bacon. Top with the cilantro. Serve with fingerling potatoes and vegetables.

Courtesy of Oba! Restaurante (p. 109)

# Albacore Tataki & Cucumber Sunomono

The next two recipes are from a dinner prepared by Gabe Rosen for a Growing Gardens' fund-raiser. Guests loved preparing their own nabe, a dish that is simple to make at home. Ingredients can be varied according to what's fresh, or just what you have in the fridge.

*(Serves 6)*

2 pounds very fresh tuna loin

16 ounces rice vinegar

8 ounces mirin

2 teaspoons salt

1 teaspoon sugar

1 cup dried wakame, rehydrated in cold water for 5 minutes, drained

2 tablespoons lemon juice

1 English cucumber

¼ cup sesame seeds

*In a very hot skillet sear the tuna loin on all sides, very quickly. Chill.*

*In a medium saucepan bring the vinegar and mirin to a boil, add the salt and sugar, stir and remove from heat. Add the wakame and half the lemon juice to the dressing. Allow to cool. Taste the dressing and add additional salt and lemon if desired.*

*Thinly slice the cucumbers and add to the dressing. Thinly slice the tuna and serve with the cucumber salad. Sprinkle with the sesame seeds and drizzle with lemon juice.*

Courtesy of Biwa (p. 39)

# Nabe

*A quick and easy one-pot meal.*

*(Serves 6)*

6 cups dashi soup
⅓ cup sake
4 tablespoons soy sauce
2 tablespoons mirin
2 cups grilled tofu
1 cup daikon radish
1 cup shredded Napa cabbage

2 cups shiitake mushrooms
2 dozen clams
2 dozen shrimp
12 thin slices pork belly
½ cup ponzu sauce
1 package udon noodles,
    precooked

*Put soup and sake in a large pot or an electric skillet. Bring to a boil on high heat. Turn down the heat to low. Season with soy sauce and mirin. Skim off any foam or impurities that rise to the surface. Add all ingredients except noodles and cook until done. Times will vary depending on what you are cooking.*

*When you have cooked everything you want, add the noodles, stir, and eat. The noodles will have the flavor of the ingredients cooked in the pot. Yummy. Yes, just add what you like*

Courtesy of Biwa (p. 39)

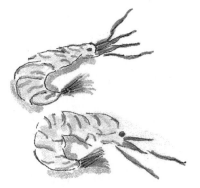

# Crema Cream Cake

*This is one of the most delicious cakes I have ever eaten. I have really never had anything like it and couldn't figure out how it was made. It's pure and rich, and I am so grateful that Crema Owner Collin Jones would share. He is a doll.*

*(Makes 1 cake)*

## Crust

2⅞ cups powdered sugar

2½ cups cake flour

1½ teaspoons baking powder

pinch salt

1 egg

¾ stick unsalted butter

3 tablespoons milk

1 teaspoon vanilla

## Filling

8 ounces cream cheese, softened

3¾ cups powdered sugar

3 eggs

1 stick unsalted butter

1 teaspoon vanilla

*To make the crust: Spray a 9 x 13-inch baking pan with baking spray. Line the pan with parchment, making sure the parchment covers the sides of the pan as well as the bottom. Spray the parchment.*
*Sift the dry ingredients into mixer, add egg, butter, and milk, and mix on low till the crust begins to pull together. Spread the dough in pan and be sure to pack into corners.*

*To make the filling: In a mixing bowl beat cream cheese till smooth. Add sugar on low and mix on high till smooth. Add eggs one at a time. On low, stream in butter and vanilla. Mix on high.*

*Heat oven to 350°F.*

*Pour filling batter onto crust and bake for 35–45 minutes. Cake should be golden brown and still jiggly in the middle. Cool completely and remove using parchment. Chill before serving and slicing.*

Courtesy of Crema (p. 45)

# Liptaeur Cheese

*The Liptauer Cheese from Gruner is such a fine blend of tasty ingredients and the delightful and super talented Chef Chris Israel was willing to part with his simple and wonderful recipe. It's just great.*

*(Makes 2½ cups)*

1 cup sieved cottage cheese

1 cup cream cheese

2 tablespoons minced chives

2 tablespoons finely chopped parsley

2 teaspoons paprika, or more to your liking

2 teaspoons caraway seeds

1 tablespoon finely minced shallots

Salt and pepper to taste

*Combine all ingredients and mix well.*

Courtesy of Gruner (p. 23)

# Grilled Steelhead Salmon with Citrus Salt & Bacon Rhubarb Chutney

*This restaurant has a spectacular setting on the Columbia River. Seafood is their specialty, and this recipe is great for company. When steelhead are running, this should most certainly be in your repertoire.*

(Serves 4)

### Citrus Salt:

Zest 1 lemon
Zest 1 lime

2 tablespoons kosher salt

### Salmon:

4 (6-ounce) steelhead fillets
¼ cup canola oil

Citrus salt

### Spring Medley:

24 asparagus spears
8 king trumpet mushrooms
4 heirloom carrots
2 ounces ramps

2 ounces olive oil
½ bunch oregano
1 teaspoon sea salt

### Bacon Rhubarb Chutney:

8 ounces applewood smoked
   bacon, diced
16 ounces rhubarb, medium
   dice
1 tablespoon minced garlic
2 cups apple cider vinegar
2 cups brown sugar
1 teaspoon chili flakes

1 teaspoon ground coriander
1 tablespoon chopped fresh
   thyme
1 tablespoon sea salt
1 teaspoon ground black
   pepper
½ cup sliced green onions

*Zest lemon and lime, place salt and zested citrus on plate and let air dry for 1 hour. Reserve lemon and lime.*

Take your fillets of wild steelhead and rub with canola oil, then season with citrus salt.

Make sure your gas grill is hot; otherwise, your steelhead will stick.

Place salmon on grill and cook to desired temperature.

To make spring medley: Toss all vegetables with oil, chopped oregano, and salt and place on grill, flipping over every 3 minutes till done.

To make chutney: In a large skillet, sauté diced bacon (till rendered) then add rhubarb, garlic, vinegar, and sugar and let reduce on a simmer for 20 minutes, then add chili flakes, coriander, and thyme, finish with salt and pepper and let chill in fridge for 1 hour. When ready to use, fold in green onions and let come to room temp.

When salmon and medley is finished, place on plate, top with bacon rhubarb chutney, and ENJOY!!

Courtesy of Salty's on the Columbia (p. 88)

# Pork Belly Cubano

*I think that the Cubano is my favorite sandwich. And getting Bunk to share their recipe was a generous and glorious coup. I have made this sandwich 6 times in the last 3 weeks. Thanks, Nick and Tommy.*

*(Serves 4)*

### Spice Mixture:

1 cup kosher salt

1 cup sugar

1 teaspoon ground fennel seeds

1 teaspoon nutmeg

1 teaspoon chili flakes

1 tablespoon chopped garlic

### Pork:

2 pounds naturally raised pork belly (pork shoulder can be substituted)

1 tablespoon molasses

4 (8-inch) French rolls

6 ounces prepared mayonnaise

10 ounces yellow mustard

A few splashes Mexican hot sauce

8 (¼-inch-thick) slices swiss cheese

8 ounces thinly sliced smoked ham

16 (⅛-inch-thick lengthwise) slices kosher dill pickle

2 tablespoons unsalted butter, softened

*To make the spice mixture: In a medium bowl combine the salt, sugar, fennel, nutmeg, chili flakes, and garlic. Rub the spice mixture over the pork belly or shoulder and cover with plastic wrap. Allow to cure in refrigerator for 2–3 days.*

*To prepare the pork: Heat a convection oven to 275°F. Brush the pork belly with the molasses, place in a roasting pan, and roast for 3–4 hours, until tender. If the belly starts to get too dark, cover it in foil. Take it out and let it rest.*

*To make the sandwich: Open the French rolls, and lightly spread the mayonnaise on one side. Squeeze the yellow mustard liberally over both sides. Throw down a few splashes of the hot sauce. Then, split the*

slices of swiss on the bread. Add a couple of slices of roast pork belly to each sandwich. Then, add the ham and pickle. Lightly butter the outside of the sandwich.

Heat a panini press or griddle. Add the sandwiches to the press and cook over moderate heat until the cheese is melted, about 6 minutes. Cut the sandwiches in half and serve.

Courtesy of Bunk Bar (p. 41)

# Pear Hazelnut Galette

This recipe from Lisa Schroeder of Mother's Bistro is exceptional. Yes, it's long, but so worth it. You can cheat a bit by buying a good quality piecrust dough. Some time, when you have time, make this pastry; you will be delighted with the results. All Lisa's tips are worth remembering; she is a star.

This free-form tart is great for those times when you want to make pie but are pressed for time or are a little intimidated by getting dough into a pie pan and making it look pretty. Here the pie dough is rolled out into a round circle (not necessarily a perfect one), fruit is placed in the center, and then the sides are folded on top, leaving the center open to expose the filling. In this case, the filling is frangipane—a rich, sweet blend of nuts, eggs, and sugar. The frangipane (see Note 1) cooks up into a dense, rich, nutty filling surrounding soft, juicy pears.

Many components of the galette can be made ahead. Toast the nuts and make the dough one day and the frangipane filling the next. The pears can be peeled, sliced, and covered with water and a squeeze of lemon juice (to keep them from turning brown) earlier in the day, even the day before. The whole galette can be made a day ahead and baked the next, so you can serve it warm soon after it comes out of the oven. I like to use hazelnuts and pears because they are both Northwest specialties—and they also happen to be a heavenly duo. Just be sure you use the freshest hazelnuts you can find—it really makes a difference.

(Serves 10–12)

## Galette Dough:

2½ cups all-purpose flour

1 teaspoon salt

2 teaspoons granulated sugar

½ pound cold unsalted butter, diced into ¼-inch pieces

1 large egg

½ teaspoon distilled white vinegar

5–6 tablespoons ice water

### Frangipane Filling:

¾ cup toasted hazelnuts, skins removed (see Notes 2 and 3)

½ cup granulated sugar

3 tablespoons unsalted butter

2 large eggs

¼ cup all-purpose flour

### Assembly:

2–3 Bartlett or d'Anjou pears, peeled and sliced ¼ inch thick (about 3 cups)

¼ cup granulated sugar

1 large egg

1 teaspoon water

*To make galette dough: In the bowl of a food processor fitted with the metal blade, add flour, salt, and sugar and pulse to combine. Alternatively, you can combine them in the bowl of a standing mixer fitted with the paddle attachment, or mix by hand in a medium-mixing bowl.*

*Add the butter pieces and pulse, mix, or cut in by hand with a pastry cutter, wire whisk, or two knives until butter is the size of peas.*

*Mix in egg, vinegar, and a few tablespoons of the water. Add more water, a little at a time, until dough begins to hold together. (If using a food processor, scrape the bottom and sides of the bowl periodically to make sure the water gets distributed evenly; otherwise, you may end up adding too much. You know you have added enough when you can squeeze a handful of the dough and it stays together in a malleable, but not sticky, ball.)*

*Turn the dough out onto a work surface and press into a ball. Flatten to a disk and wrap in plastic wrap; refrigerate at least 1 hour or up to 2 days (or freeze).*

*To make the frangipane filling: Place hazelnuts in the bowl of a food processor fitted with the metal blade and pulse until the nuts are finely ground. Transfer nuts to a bowl and set aside.*

*Place the sugar in the food processor bowl. Cut butter into ½-inch pieces and add to food processor bowl. Process until mixture is smooth. Add eggs, one at a time, mixing until smooth between additions and stopping at least once to scrape down the sides of the bowl.*

Add the flour and ground nuts. Pulse a few times until just incorporated. Using a rubber spatula, scrape the filling into a small bowl and refrigerate until ready to use.

To assemble: Remove dough from refrigerator and let sit at room temperature for 10 minutes (to make it pliable and easier to roll out). Line a rimmed baking sheet with parchment paper.

Meanwhile, place pears and sugar in a medium mixing bowl and toss to coat.

Unwrap dough on a lightly floured surface. Sprinkle a little flour on top and rub some flour on a rolling pin. Roll out the dough, from the center outward, giving it a one-eighth turn as you go, until it's about 14 inches in diameter and ¼ inch thick (it doesn't have to be perfect—it's not called a "rustic" tart for nothin', but try to get as close to a circle as you can). While rolling, use a bench scraper to lift the dough and flour the surface underneath it whenever it seems like it's starting to stick. Reflour the rolling pin whenever it starts to stick to the dough (see Note 4).

Transfer the dough to the baking sheet by rolling it loosely over the rolling pin and unrolling it carefully over the baking sheet.

Spread the frangipane mixture evenly in the center of the pie dough, leaving a 3-inch border bare around the perimeter. Pour the sugared pears over frangipane, or arrange them in concentric circles, if desired. Fold up the sides of the dough where the hazelnut filling ends, letting the folds overlap a bit. You should have a 2½-inch border of pastry around the top of the tart, and a wide opening in the center.

Place galette in the refrigerator for at least 30 minutes, or up to overnight. (This will help firm up the dough and keep it from spreading too much when baked.)

When ready to bake: preheat oven to 350°F. In a small bowl, whisk together the egg and water (this is called egg wash; it helps crusts look more golden brown and shiny when baked). Brush the dough (not the pears) with egg wash and bake for 1 hour to 1 hour and 10 minutes, or until the crust is light brown, the pears are tender, and the frangipane filling peeking up from between the pear slices looks glossy.

Serve warm with vanilla ice cream.

Note 1: Frangipane (fran-juh-pan) is a French term for a custardy mixture that includes finely ground nuts. It's usually spread in pastries and tart shells and often made with almonds, although you can use any of your favorite nuts. Because it's so deliciously nutty, it goes with almost any fruit.

Note 2: To roast hazelnuts, preheat oven to 275°F. Spread shelled hazelnuts in a single layer on a baking sheet. Toast for 20 to 30 minutes, or until the skins crack and the nuts turn light golden brown and smell fragrant. You can also roast them at 350°F for 10 to 15 minutes, but stay close by and check them periodically to be sure they don't burn. Remove nuts from oven and set aside to cool.

Note 3: The skins are especially tight on hazelnuts, but toasting loosens them a considerable amount. To remove the skins from toasted hazelnuts, place them in a colander with large holes. Put the colander in the sink and use a clean dishtowel to rub the nuts so the skins peel off. Shake the colander occasionally to encourage the skins to fall into the sink. Another way to remove the skin is to put the nuts onto a clean dishtowel and gather it closed. Let the nuts steam for 4 to 5 minutes then rub vigorously for 1 to 3 minutes. Rub longer to remove even more skin. Don't knock yourself out trying to remove every trace of skin for this recipe. It's really not that important for this recipe. But if you do attempt a recipe, particularly a cake, where all the skins must be removed because of the slight bitterness of the skins or because of their dark color, the quickest way to do it is to blanch them for 1 minute in boiling water spiked with baking soda (1 tablespoon per cup water). Then plunge the nuts in cold water and the skins will slip right off. In this case, you would roast them after they were peeled, at the lower temperature.

Note 4: The big trick to rolling out dough is keeping it from sticking to the work surface and the rolling pin. Although you don't want to add tons of flour, which would make the dough heavy, don't be afraid to reflour the work surface and the rolling pin occasionally. Otherwise, you'll get your dough all rolled out and you won't be able to get it off the work surface in one piece! A bench scraper makes it easy to dislodge the dough as it starts to stick and lift it a bit so you can dust some flour underneath or turn the dough if needed.

Courtesy of Mother's Bistro (p. 29)

# Roasted Cauliflower with Couscous

When you roast cauliflower you get that caramelization that takes the already wonderful vegetable to a heightened level of deliciounesss. This is healthy comfort food, with Mediterranean spice and love.

(Serves 4–6)

- 2 medium heads cauliflower, broken into florets
- 1 medium onion, peeled and sliced in wedges
- 4 tablespoons olive oil
- 2 cups drained canned white beans
- 3 cloves garlic, minced
- 1 teaspoon ground cumin
- ½ teaspoon cumin seeds
- ½ teaspoon black pepper
- Dash salt
- 1 cup golden raisins
- 1 cup spinach
- 2 cups cooked couscous, Israeli preferred
- ¾ cup plain Greek yogurt
- ½ teaspoon ground cumin
- 2 teaspoons lemon juice
- Salt and pepper to taste

Heat oven to 400°F.

Place the cauliflower and the onion wedges on a baking sheet and toss with 2 tablespoons of olive oil. Roast until tender, 35-40 minutes. Stir occasionally.

In a large skillet heat the remaining oil and sauté the beans, garlic, and spices.

Add the raisins and cook an additional 3-5 minutes. Add the spinach and allow to wilt, 2-3 minutes.

In a large bowl combine everything, including the couscous, and toss gently. Serve hot or at room temperature.

In a small bowl combine the yogurt with the cumin, lemon juice, and salt and pepper to taste. Serve alongside the cauliflower.

Courtesy of the author

# HAZELNUTS

Oregon is known for growing the highest quality hazelnuts in the world. Apparently the climate and the soil are the perfect environment for this popular nut. Almost 99 percent of our country's hazelnuts are grown here, and they appear often in everything from appetizers and soups through to dessert. I wasn't much of a fan before, although I always loved Nutella, but have come to like them, particularly after having them used in delicious and interesting ways by the PDX chefs. Jenn Louis does a great hazelnut crunch on her soft serve, and beets with salsa verde and hazelnuts was a terrific way to enjoy, in fact savor, the flavor of these often underappreciated nuts at the lovely **Firehouse** restaurant. In the recipe section you will find a delectable recipe, a pear hazelnut galette, from Lisa Schroeder, chef-owner of **Mother's Bistro.**

I have developed a couple of recipes that will allow you, too, to enjoy and appreciate these tasty nuts.

**Rhubarb Crisp**
**(Serves 8–10)**
*Topping:*

> 6 tablespoons unsalted butter, softened
> ¼ cup packed brown sugar
> 1 cup all-purpose flour
> Nutmeg
> Pinch salt

*Filling:*

> 1½ pounds rhubarb stems, cut into ¼-inch-thick slices
> 2 cups sliced strawberries
> 1 cup light brown sugar
> Pinch salt
> ½ teaspoon finely grated orange zest, plus 2 tablespoons
> 1 tablespoon cornstarch
> ½ cup orange juice
> ½ cup roasted hazelnuts, skins removed

Heat oven to 375°F.

For the top: In a bowl combine the butter, sugar, flour, nutmeg, and salt. Work with your fingers until the mixture begins to resemble coarse oatmeal. Set aside.

For the filling: In another bowl combine the rhubarb with the strawberries, sugar, salt, and the zest. In a small bowl, stir the cornstarch into the orange juice and mix well. Add the mixture to the fruit filling. Place the mixture into a small (approximately 6-cup) buttered baking dish. Transfer baking dish to a rimmed baking sheet.

Sprinkle with the crisp topping and the hazelnuts.

Bake until the topping turns golden brown and juices are bubbling (40–45 minutes). Cool for 20 minutes and serve, perhaps with a scoop of your favorite ice cream. You think vanilla, so do I, but strawberry is pretty good too.

**Hazelnut Chocolate Spread**
Your very own recipe!
**(Makes about 4 cups)**
    2 heaping cups hazelnuts, skin removed
    ¼ cup sugar
    1 pound coarsely chopped good quality bittersweet chocolate
    1 stick unsalted butter, cut in chunks
    1 cup heavy cream
    1 teaspoon vanilla
    ½ teaspoon salt
Heat oven to 350°F.

Spread the nuts on a rimmed baking sheet. Bake for about 15 minutes, shaking occasionally to brown evenly. The nuts should be dark brown when done. Allow to cool completely.

In a food processor combine the hazelnuts with the sugar until smooth.

Place the chocolate in a double boiler and melt, stirring occasionally. When fully melted, remove from the heat and stir in the butter. When the butter is incorporated, stir in the cream, vanilla, salt, and the hazelnut puree.

# Dungeness Crab, Fennel & Cantaloupe Salad

*I would have never thought to pair cantaloupe with crab.
So glad Chef Jobie Bailey did. It rocks.*

*(Serves 4)*

*(Serves 4)*

12 ounces Dungeness crabmeat

2 fennel bulbs, medium heads

½ cantaloupe, peeled and seeded

¼ cup roasted lemon vinaigrette (see recipe below)

2 tablespoons chopped chives

¼ teaspoon Controne chile flakes (or similar hot pepper flakes)

½ teaspoon lemon juice

Coarse sea salt to taste

Extra-virgin olive oil

Herbs for garnish (mint, basil, salad burnet)

### For the roasted lemon vinaigrette:

1 lemon

1 tablespoon plus ¼ cup extra-virgin olive oil

½ teaspoon plus ½ teaspoon kosher salt

¼ teaspoon ground black pepper

½ cup lovage leaves

1 egg yolk

2 tablespoons lemon juice

¼ teaspoon Controne chile flakes

½ cup grapeseed or other neutral oil

Ice cubes or cold water as needed

*Drain and squeeze the moisture from the crabmeat. Pick through the crabmeat to remove any pieces of shell or debris that may have been left from processing and place the crab in a medium-size mixing bowl.*

Using a mandoline slicer or sharp knife, slice the fennel paper-thin. If using a large head of fennel, remove the core first. Adjust the mandoline to about $\frac{1}{16}$-inch thick and slice the cantaloupe lengthwise. Reserve the cantaloupe for plating.

Combine the fennel with the crab, vinaigrette, chives, chile flakes, lemon juice, and salt. Taste and adjust seasoning if needed.

Divide the cantaloupe between four plates, spreading out into thin folds, and sprinkle with a little sea salt. Spread the crab over the melon, sprinkle with sea salt, and drizzle with olive oil. The salad can be garnished with mint, basil, salad burnet, or other complementary herb.

## To make the vinaigrette:

Preheat the oven to 375°F and place a sheet pan or cookie sheet in to heat. Split the lemon in half lengthwise; remove the center pith and all seeds. Slice the lemon into $\frac{1}{8}$-inch-thick half wheels. In a small bowl toss the lemon with 1 tablespoon olive oil, $\frac{1}{2}$ teaspoon salt, and black pepper. Pour contents of bowl onto the hot sheet pan. Roast for 8 to 10 minutes, stirring occasionally, until the lemon is soft and slightly charred. Remove from the oven and allow to cool to room temperature, approximately 10 minutes.

In a blender combine the roasted lemon, lovage, egg yolk, lemon juice, chile flakes, $\frac{1}{2}$ teaspoon salt, and one small ice cube. Puree on low until a paste is formed.

Once a paste has formed, with the blender still running, begin drizzling in $\frac{1}{4}$ cup olive oil. Once all the olive oil has been absorbed and emulsified, begin adding the grapeseed oil. After the first $\frac{1}{2}$ cup, turn off the blender and taste the dressing. Adjust the seasoning as necessary, and if the dressing is still too acidic, turn the blender on and add more oil, 1 to 2 tablespoons at a time, until the dressing becomes creamy. It should have the consistency of a thin mayonnaise. If the blender is having a hard time turning the dressing, turn the speed up and adjust the thickness of the dressing with cold water, or add more ice cubes.

Courtesy of DOC (p. 80)

# Seared Panzanella Chicken

*I am convinced that searing and baking is the way to go with chicken. Crisp on the outside, tender and moist inside. It's perfect.*

*(Serves 4)*

### For the salad:

1 cup olive oil
12 garlic cloves, peeled
4 boneless chicken breasts
4 boneless chicken thighs
16 good-size chunks day-old bread, drizzled with olive oil and coarse salt

⅓ cup pitted oil-cured black olives
4 cups chicken stock
Salt and black pepper to taste
¼ cup chopped parsley

1 bunch arugula, cleaned and dried on a clean dish towel
¼ cup sherry vinegar

¾ cup olive oil
1 tablespoon sugar

*Preheat the oven to 450°F. In a small pan, add one cup of olive oil and 12 cloves of garlic. Slowly caramelize the garlic until tender. In a skillet, pan sear the chicken pieces and place on a baking sheet until all pieces are seared. Place in the preheated oven to roast. Cut up chunks of day-old bread and drizzle with olive oil and salt (about four cubes of bread per person). Place in oven to toast.*

*Once chicken is cooked through, remove from the pan and keep warm. Discard oil from the pan and add pitted olives, the garlic, and chicken stock. Scrape the bottom of the pan to get all the crust. Taste, then add salt and pepper and chopped parsley. Remove toasted bread and place on plates. Spoon the sauce over the warm croutons. Top with the arugula salad dressed with sherry vinegar, olive oil, and sugar and warm roasted chicken.*

Courtesy of Roost (p. 61)

# Morel Mushrooms
## with Douglas Fir Tips & Snow Peas

*Morel mushrooms and Douglas fir tips, two sure signs that spring has arrived. Morels are deeply flavored, rich, earthy mushrooms. Douglas fir tips, sweet with the stored sugar of the trees, are sprightly, with a fresh citrus and lightly fragrant forest scent. Paired together, this dish sings of spring.*

*(Serves 4–6)*

1 tablespoon olive oil

½ pound morel mushrooms, cleaned and left whole if small, halved lengthwise or cut crosswise into rings if large

Salt and freshly ground pepper to taste

1 very small leek, white and pale green part only, finely chopped

1 garlic clove, minced

12–15 snow pea pods, zipped of their strings and cut in half

Several Douglas fir tips

*In a skillet large enough to accommodate all of the mushrooms in a single layer, heat the olive oil over a medium-high flame. When the oil is very hot, shimmering but not smoking, carefully add the mushrooms all at once and cook them over high heat, stirring occasionally, until any water that the mushrooms give off evaporates and the mushrooms again begin to sizzle. Reduce the heat to medium and cook the mushrooms for another 5 minutes, stirring now and then, until they are fully cooked and beginning to caramelize (they will not overcook, but may burn if the flame is too high—adjust accordingly if the mushrooms brown too quickly).*

*Season the mushrooms with salt and freshly ground black pepper. Add the chopped leek, minced garlic, and sliced snow peas to the pan, and continue to sauté, tossing frequently, until all of the aromatics and snow peas are*

tender (about 2–3 minutes). Adjust seasonings and remove the pan from the flame.

Pluck the needles from the stem of the fir tips and add them to the sauté. Toss the needles into the warm mushrooms and snow peas, and serve immediately, while the fragrance is fresh and the color is bright. (Note that if the needles are added to a pan that is very hot, they will crisp and darken, rendering them unpalatable and destroying their tender, citrus-like quality.)

Courtesy of Kathryn Yoemen

# MUSHROOMS

Kathryn Yoemen is a PDX food and recipe writer, cooking teacher, farmers' market chef, and one of Portland's mushroom experts. We have followed Kathryn around the markets to catch demos of her wonderful recipes with all kinds of mushrooms. She has given us two mushroom recipes, all worthy of your finest china. I have to mention the best thing I have eaten recently, and it is due to Kathryn: lion's mane mushrooms. They have the most wonderful texture and a flavor like a perfectly cooked scallop, but better. Slice the mushrooms and sauté them in butter for just a few minutes, till golden brown on both sides. Sprinkle with a bit of coarse salt and eat. When you live somewhere you can go foraging for mushrooms and see the variety and taste mushrooms you didn't know existed, you get stoked. Love them or not, mushrooms are kind of amazing. Bruce and I were at the restaurant Skin and Bones, in the afternoon before service, and their mushroom farmer came by with a 10-pound cauliflower mushroom. I immediately thought *Invasion of the Body Snatchers*, but then realized that we were all standing around Caleb as he held this unusual mushroom in his arms, and it was like we were looking at a beautiful baby.

# Curried Lobster Mushrooms with Late Summer Vegetables

These mushrooms, given their proximity to the Pacific Ocean, absorb the sea air, which lends them a flavor reminiscent of shellfish, particularly noticeable in their scent as they sauté.

Dense and woodsy, these mushrooms have a sturdy constitution and integrity of flavor that is able to stand up to curry spice. Both the flavor and texture of lobster mushrooms are enhanced by a cooking time longer than that of other wild mushrooms, making them an ideal choice for this preparation.

*(Serves 6)*

1 pound lobster mushrooms
4 tablespoons butter
Sea salt
Freshly ground black pepper
½ cup chopped onion
3 garlic cloves, minced
1 tablespoon curry powder, or to taste
Optional: 1 can (13.5-ounce) coconut milk and ½ cup broth (either mushroom, shellfish, or vegetable) or water

2 tablespoons extra-virgin olive oil
1 medium eggplant, peeled and cut into 1-inch cubes
Corn kernels cut from 1 cob corn
½ cup green beans, cut into 1-inch lengths and par-boiled until crisp-tender
2 medium tomatoes, diced
1 tablespoon chopped parsley
12 leaves Thai basil, torn

Clean the lobster mushrooms of any clinging earth by brushing lightly with a soft vegetable brush, then rinse them under running water. Lobster mushrooms are dense enough that a little water will not be readily absorbed, so long as they are not permitted to soak for an extended period of time. Slice the mushrooms into ¼-inch-thick slices.

Heat 2 tablespoons butter in a large skillet over a medium-high flame. Add all of the mushrooms and cook over high heat, stirring now and then, until any water that the mushrooms give off cooks away, and the mushroom slices *again begin to sizzle. Reduce the heat to medium and continue to cook the mushrooms for about 5 more minutes. Season the mushrooms with sea salt and freshly ground black pepper.*

*Meanwhile, heat the remaining 2 tablespoons butter in a large, shallow saucepot over a medium flame. Add the onion and cook until it has softened, about 3 minutes. Add the garlic and cook for another minute. Season with salt and pepper. Stir in the curry powder and fry the spice in the onion mixture until very fragrant, about 2 minutes. Add all of the mushrooms and stir gently to incorporate. If you are using the coconut milk and broth, add them to the mushroom mixture and bring the ingredients to a simmer. Simmer the mushrooms for 5 minutes. If you are not adding the sauce, reduce the heat to medium-low and continue cooking the mushrooms for 5 minutes.*

*Return the skillet used to cook the mushrooms to a high flame and pour in the olive oil. When the oil is quite hot (shimmering but not smoking), add all of the eggplant and quickly brown it on all sides. Season the eggplant with salt and pepper and remove it to a platter.*

*Stir the corn and beans into the mushroom mixture. Cook for a couple of minutes, until the corn kernels are tender and the beans are warmed through. Add the eggplant and tomato. When all the ingredients are hot, taste and adjust seasonings, then stir in the parsley and basil and serve, over cooked rice if desired.*

Courtesy of Kathryn Yoemen

# Red Velvet Cake

This is the best red velvet cake I have ever had, or baked. The food at Navarre is amazing, and the desserts are as good as the small and large plates. Keep this recipe forever; it will never let you down.

(Serves 8–10)

| | |
|---|---|
| 2¾ cups all-purpose flour | 1½ cups canola oil |
| 1¾ cups sugar | 1¼ cups buttermilk |
| 1 teaspoon baking soda | 2 teaspoons red food coloring |
| 2 teaspoons cocoa powder | 1 teaspoon vanilla |
| 2 large eggs, room temperature | 1 tablespoon white vinegar |

### For Frosting:

| | |
|---|---|
| 2 ounces butter, slightly softened | 16 ounces confectioners' sugar |
| 8 ounces cream cheese | |

Heat oven to 350°F.

To make cake: Put parchment on the bottom of three 8-inch pans. Mix all dry ingredients together. Beat eggs slightly and add all wet ingredients together. Mix wet into dry ingredients.

Pour into prepared pans. Bake for 25–35 minutes. When done, remove from oven, wait 5 minutes, then turn out on cooling racks.

To make frosting: Put butter in mixer and beat at high speed till soft. Slowly add cream cheese a few tablespoons at a time, stopping periodically to scrape bowl well.

Beat till light; slowly add sugar, waiting for it to completely get incorporated along with some air before adding more. When all the sugar is incorporated, beat a few minutes and frost cake immediately.

Courtesy of Navarre (p. 84)

# Pecan Shortbread

*The food at Screen Door is consistently delicious. These melt-in-your-mouth cookies are pretty easy to make and great with a cup of tea or coffee.*

*(Makes about 30 cookies)*

| | |
|---|---|
| 2 cups butter, softened | 4 cups all-purpose flour |
| 1 cup confectioners' sugar | 2 cups crushed, toasted pecans |
| 2 teaspoons vanilla paste | 3 dozen pecan halves, optional |
| ½ teaspoon salt | |

*In standing mixer with paddle attachment, cream butter, sugar, vanilla, and salt until smooth. Add flour all at once and mix on low speed just until incorporated. Add crushed pecans and fold in gently. Divide dough and place on parchment or waxed paper. Shape each piece into a log 2 inches in diameter and roll up tightly. Chill several hours or overnight until firm.*

*Preheat oven to 350°F. Slice cookies about ¼ inch thick, lay on parchment or Silpat-lined baking sheets. Press a pecan half on top of each cookie, if using. Bake 10–12 minutes until golden brown. Let cool. These also make a great crust when crushed, mixed with melted butter, and pressed into a pie tin.*

Courtesy of Screen Door (p. 62)

## SCREEN DOOR MINT JULEP

Sublime Screen Door cocktail.
(Serves 1)

    Fresh mint, muddled
    2 ounces (4 tablespoons) bourbon
    1 teaspoon simple syrup
    2 ounces (4 tablespoons) soda water

In a shaker combine the mint, bourbon, simple syrup, and ice. Shake and pour into a glass. Top with the splash of soda.

# Heirloom Tomato Salad

*The pizza at Dove Vivi has the most amazing crunchy crust and the toppings rock. The ingredients are always seasonally driven, as are the fantastic salads, which are excellent, different, and a perfect compliment to the 'za. This is one of my favorites.*

*(Serves 4)*

**Day-old crusty bread**
**Olive oil**
**Salt and pepper**

**4 fresh tomatoes**
**⅓ cup sheep's milk feta cheese, crumbled**

*Heat oven to 400°F.*

*Prepare bread crumbs. Place cubed day-old bread in bowl, then toss with a slight drizzle of olive oil, salt, and pepper.*

*Spread on cookie sheet and place in oven until toasty. Let cool, then pulse in food processor until crumbled.*

*Slice the tomatoes on a platter.*

*Ladle parsley malt vinaigrette dressing over them, and then top with crumbled feta cheese and bread crumbs.*

### Parsley Malt Vinaigrette:

**⅓ cup malt vinegar**
**¾ cup red wine vinegar**
**¼ cup olive oil**
**1 teaspoon kosher salt**

**1 tablespoon brown sugar**
**2 tablespoons chopped fresh parsley**

*Whisk to combine.*

Courtesy of Dove Vivi (p. 81)

# Butternut Squash & Parsnip Puree

*This side dish from Country Cat is the most wonderful marriage of creamy, smoky, and amazing. Easy to make, and everyone loves it.*

(Serves 4)

1 tablespoon unsalted butter

1 tablespoon olive oil

2 leeks, cut into coins and rinsed in cold water

4 cloves of garlic, peeled and sliced

1 cup white wine

1 cup water

3 medium parsnips, peeled and sliced into large coins

1 large butternut squash, peeled, seeded, and cut into a large dice

1 tablespoon herbes de Provence (no lavender)

1 tablespoon smoky paprika

Salt to taste

*In a large saucepan, heat butter and olive oil until butter has melted. Add the rinsed leeks and garlic and sauté until soft and translucent. Add the white wine, water, parsnips, squash, herbes de Provence, smoky paprika, and salt. Stir all the ingredients to combine, cover, and let simmer until squash and parsnips are very soft, about 30 minutes. Place vegetables in a food processor and puree to a smooth and silky consistency. Salt to taste. Serve warm.*

Courtesy of Country Cat (p. 44)

# Many Vegetable Frittata

My favorite is a frittata supper, served room temp, with a simple but well-dressed salad. And a frittata sandwich on a toasted roll is pretty sweet too.

*(Serves 2–4)*

Vegetable spray
2-3 tablespoons olive oil
1 cup chopped bell pepper
1 cup corn kernels, fresh or
    frozen
½ cup chopped green onion

6 large eggs
½ teaspoon salt
½ teaspoon black pepper
3 cups clean, fresh spinach
2 ounces goat cheese

*Heat oven to 400°F.*

*Spray a non-stick ovenproof pan with the vegetable spray. Add a tablespoon of olive oil. Sauté the peppers until tender, about 6-7 minutes. Add the corn and the green onion and sauté until cooked, 3-4 minutes.*

*In a medium bowl beat the eggs. Add the salt and pepper.*

*Place the pan with the vegetables back on the heat. Add the spinach and cook until wilted, 4-5 minutes. Pour the egg mixture into the pan; try to evenly distribute the vegetables. Place the goat cheese over the frittata, and place the pan in the oven. Cook until set and golden brown, about 10-12 minutes. Cut in wedges to serve.*

Courtesy of the author

# Spiced Nuts

(Makes 5 cups)

| | |
|---|---|
| 1 cup pecans | 2-3 tablespoons rosemary |
| 1 cup almonds | 1 tablespoon ground cumin |
| 1 cup cashews | 1 tablespoon brown sugar |
| 1 cup peanuts | 1-2 teaspoons cayenne |
| 1 cup hazelnuts | ½ teaspoon salt |
| 2 large egg whites | |

*Heat oven to 300°F.*

*In a large bowl combine the nuts. Beat the egg whites till soft and foamy. Toss with the nuts and herbs and bake for 20-25 minutes on a large baking sheet, stirring occasionally.*

Courtesy of the author

# Chunky Applesauce

*(Makes 4 cups)*

**4 pounds apples, mix of Granny Smith, McIntosh, Gala, and Braeburn, peeled and cored, cut in chunks or wedges**

**½ cup water**

**2 tablespoons apple cider concentrate**

**Dash salt**

**3-4 tablespoons honey**

**1 cup dried apricots, halved if large**

**½ cups cranberries, fresh or frozen**

**1 vanilla bean, cut in half lengthwise**

*Place the prepared apples in a medium pot that has a cover. Add water, cider concentrate, and the tiniest pinch or sprinkle of salt. Bring to a boil, turn heat down to low-med, add the honey, apricots, and cranberries, cover, and cook, 20-25 minutes, until apples are soft.*

*Turn the heat of, and, using a potato masher, give the apples a few mashes, until they are broken up and chunky. Taste, and if the applesauce is too tart for you, add 1 more tablespoon of honey, stirring until combined.*

Courtesy of the author

# Candied Lemon Tart

*The lemon curd is quick, easy, and foolproof. Using your microwave saves lots of time and attention, and it honestly is a good as the recipes that require frequent whisking and take three times as long. If you have leftover lemon curd it is wonderful on scones, pancakes, and fresh fruit. It's even good with just a spoon.*

*(Serves 12-14)*

1 cup white sugar

3 eggs

1 cup fresh lemon juice, about 6-8

3 lemons, zested

½ cup unsalted butter, melted

2 lemons, thinly sliced

1 ¼ cups sugar

1 ¼ cups water

Flour for dusting

1 package. frozen puff pastry, about 14 ounces, defrosted according to package. instructions

*In a microwave-safe bowl, whisk together the sugar and eggs until smooth. Stir in lemon juice, lemon zest, and butter. Cook in the microwave for 30-second intervals, stirring after each minute until the mixture is thick enough to coat the back of a metal spoon. It should be around 4-6 minutes, depending on your microwave. Be sure to scrape the sides of the bowl. Remove from the microwave, and pour into a jar or bowl and chill.*

*Place the lemon slices in a saucepan, cover with cold water, bring to the boil, then drain and repeat 4 times. Combine 1 cup sugar with 2 cups water in a separate saucepan, bring to a boil, and stir to dissolve sugar. Add the lemon slices, lower the heat, and cook until translucent (30 minutes). Allow to cool.*

*Gently roll out the defrosted pastry into a rectangle on a lightly floured surface. Heat the oven to the temperature on the package. Place the puff pastry on a piece of parchment paper on a baking sheet. Bake until golden brown. Allow to cool.*

*When the pastry has cooled and the lemon curd is cold, spread the curd on the cooked pastry. Place the candied lemon slices on the custard. Serve immediately or keep in the fridge till serving time, not longer than an hour or two.*

Courtesy of the author

# Whiskey by the Pitcher

*(Makes 1 pitcher)*

4 cups orange juice
½ cup fresh lemon juice
½ cup fresh lime juice
1 cup triple sec

2½ cups whiskey
Ice
Orange slices
Lime slices

*In a pitcher, combine orange juice, lemon juice, lime juice, triple sec, and whiskey. Serve over ice, topped with orange and lime slices.*

Courtesy of the author

# Prosecco Sangria by the Pitcher

*(Makes 1 pitcher)*

1 cup strawberries, sliced
1 cup peaches, sliced
1 cup raspberries
½ cup brandy

¼ cup St. Germain
   Elderflower Liqueur
1 bottle Prosecco

*In a pitcher place the fruit, brandy, and liqueur. Allow to chill for 30 minutes. Add the Prosecco, stir, and serve immediately.*

Courtesy of the author

# Pan-seared Salmon

*What a fabulous salmon recipe. Unexpected ingredients that make some magic on your plate.*

*(Serves 4)*

| | |
|---|---|
| 1 bunch beets, tops included | 1 bulb fennel |
| Kosher salt | 2 sprigs fresh sage |
| Fresh ground pepper | ½ pint blackberries |
| Extra-virgin olive oil | Unsalted butter |
| ½ cup water | 4 (7-ounce) salmon fillets |

*Heat oven to 375°F.*

*Cut beet greens from beets. Place beets in a baking dish, season with salt and pepper, drizzle with olive oil and ½ cup water and cover. Roast in oven until tender when pierced.*

*While the beets are roasting, bring a large saucepot filled with salted water to a boil. Have an ice bath ready. Plunge beet greens into the boiling water and cook 4 minutes. Remove and plunge into ice bath to stop cooking. When completely cooled, drain and set aside.*

*Slice fennel in half, remove the core, and slice into ¼-inch-thick slices. Pick sage leaves from the stems. Rinse blackberries and dry on paper towel. Peel beets and cut into ½-inch chunks.*

*Heat oven to 450°F.*

*Heat an ovenproof skillet with olive oil and 1 tablespoon of butter until the butter begins to brown. Season salmon with salt and pepper and add to hot pan flesh side down. Add the fennel and transfer to the oven. The salmon is best served medium rare, which should take about 5–6 minutes.*

Carefully return the pan to the stovetop, and remove the salmon to a serving platter. The fennel should be nicely caramelized. Add beets and beet greens and sauté until warm. Divide among 4 plates, and top with the salmon, seared side up. Return the pan to the stovetop. Over high heat, add 6 tablespoons of butter, sage leaves, blackberries and salt and pepper. Brown the butter, be careful of splatters. Drizzle the butter over the salmon, dividing berries and sage leaves equally.

Courtesy of Caffe Mingo (p. 98)

# Ahi Tuna Poke

*This is an elegant and beautiful dish. Tuna and avocado—perfect together.*

(*Serves 2*)

- 3 ounces ahi tuna belly, cut in ¼-inch dice
- 3 ounces avocado, cut in ¼-inch dice
- 2 teaspoons blood orange oil
- 1 teaspoon toasted sesame oil
- 2 teaspoons white shoyu soy sauce
- ½ teaspoon toasted black sesame seeds
- ½ teaspoon fresh grated ginger
- ¼ teaspoon finely diced red jalapeño
- 2 teaspoons fresh picked cilantro
- A few shiso leaves for garnish

Carefully *toss all ingredients in a bowl until well incorporated. Spoon onto plates, and garnish with small shiso leaves.*

Courtesy of Yakuza (p. 93)

# Yakuza Cocktails

Some amazing and unusual drinks from the happy bar at Yakuza.

### Beet Beat
 2 ounces (4 tablespoons) house infused beet tequila
 ¾ ounce (4½ teaspoons) simple syrup
 ¾ ounce (4½ teaspoons) fresh squeezed lime
Shaken, served on the rocks with a salted rim.

### Carrot Cool
 1½ ounces (3 tablespoons) juiced organic carrots (strained after juicing)
 2 ounces (4 tablespoons) Medoyeff vodka
 ¾ ounce (4½ teaspoons) thyme honey syrup (1:1 ratio of honey to hot water and thyme, strained)
 ¾ ounce (4½ teaspoons) fresh squeezed lime
Shaken and served on the rocks.

### Sugar Snap
 1½ ounces (3 tablespoons) organic sugar snap peas, juiced and strained
 2 ounces (4 tablespoons) Medoyeff vodka
 ¾ ounce (4½ teaspoons) simple syrup
 ¾ ounces (4½ teaspoons) fresh squeezed lime
Shaken and served up.

# Like a B.L.T. But Not.
## Roasted Asparagus, Bacon & Egg

*For the last few months I have been writing recipes for OPB. Recipes are seasonal and pretty simple. Here are some of my favorites.*

*(Serves 2)*

12 thin asparagus spears, bottoms trimmed

1 tablespoon olive oil

Coarse salt

6 tablespoons mayo

1–2 teaspoons sriracha sauce

2 (8-inch) pieces baguette cut horizontally and toasted

2 slices really good bacon, cooked and drained of excess grease

1 hard-boiled egg, chopped

Coarse salt

½ cup washed and dried baby arugula

*Heat oven to 425°F.*

*Place the asparagus on a baking tray with sides. Drizzle with the olive oil and sprinkle with the salt. Shake pan gently to distribute. Place in the oven and cook for about 5 minutes, until crisp tender.*

*In a small bowl combine the mayonnaise with the sriracha sauce. Generously spread the sauce over both insides of the bread.*

*Place a slice of bacon on each bottom slice of bread. Top with the roasted asparagus. Sprinkle with the chopped egg and salt. Divide the arugula between the two sandwiches. Cover with the tops, cut each 8-inch sandwich in half, and serve.*

Courtesy of the author

# Pork Cutlet Milanese

This recipe takes under 15 minutes to prepare. If you have never had the combination of fresh dressed greens atop a crunchy cutlet of chicken, veal, or pork, you are missing out. Great on a sandwich as well.

*(Serves 4)*

4 boneless pork cutlets,
   pounded thin
Salt and pepper
2 large eggs, lightly beaten
1–2 cups bread crumbs
Olive oil for frying
½ bunch watercress

½ bunch baby arugula
Handful fresh mint
½ cup cilantro
½ cup halved grape tomatoes
Good quality olive oil
Shaved Parmesan
Lemon wedges

Sprinkle the cutlets with the salt and pepper on both sides.

Place the beaten eggs in a pie tin and do the same with the bread crumbs. Dip the cutlets in the egg followed by the bread crumbs.

Heat the olive oil in a large skillet, about ⅛ of an inch of oil. When the oil is hot, add the cutlets and fry on both sides until golden brown, about 4–5 minutes per side. Place on a clean dishcloth to absorb the grease.

In a medium bowl, combine all the greens and tomato. Drizzle with olive oil. Place the greens over the cutlets, place some shaved Parmesan over the greens, and serve with lemon wedges.

Courtesy of the author

# Portland-style Peas & Rice

*This healthy seasonal comfort food can be served room temperature or warm. Between the pantry and your refrigerator you may have all the ingredients at home. Vary the cheese, or the rice; you really can't go wrong.*

*Serves 4*

**2 cups cooked peas**
**1 cup cooked short-grain brown rice**
**½ cup chopped fresh Italian parsley**
**¼ cup chopped scallion**

**Salt and pepper**
**4 tablespoons good quality olive oil**
**Juice 1 lemon**
**¼ cup crumbled goat cheese**

*In a medium bowl combine the peas, rice, parsley, scallion, salt and pepper to taste, and the olive oil. Toss to combine.*

*Squeeze the lemon over the salad, and top with the crumbled goat cheese.*

Courtesy of the author

# Steamed Spiced Salmon

*A foolproof way to prepare this super flavorful dish. Perfect every time. Feel free to change up the spice and the veg. Even the fish!*

*(Serves 4)*

4 (5-ounce) pieces skinless salmon

2 teaspoons chili powder

1 teaspoon coarse black pepper

½ teaspoon salt

2 cups fresh peas

1 cup grape tomatoes

1 cup thick shredded carrots

¼ cup chopped cilantro

8 thin lime slices

2 tablespoons lime juice

½ cup salsa, mild to hot

*Place the salmon pieces in a microwave-proof dish with sides. Top each piece of salmon with chili powder, pepper, salt, peas, tomatoes, carrots, cilantro, and two lime slices. Drizzle with the juice. Cook on high for 3–5 minutes. Allow to rest for a minute before opening the plastic wrap.*

*Discard the lime slices. Place on a plate and spoon the salsa over each portion.*

Courtesy of the author

# Egg-topped Garlic Asparagus

*Folks who are gluten free, give it up or leave out the bread crumbs! Simple and delicious, the tender egg contrasts perfectly with the crunch of the asparagus. If you are so inclined, lay a paper-thin slice of prosciutto or country ham over the asparagus before placing the egg on top.*

(Serves 2)

- 1–2 tablespoons good quality olive oil
- 20 thin asparagus spears, bottoms trimmed
- 1 clove minced garlic
- 2 large eggs
- Coarse salt
- Coarse black pepper
- 2 tablespoons shaved Parmesan
- 2 tablespoons bread crumbs, toasted (see Note)

*Place the olive oil in a large skillet and heat on medium. Add the asparagus and sauté for 3–4 minutes. Add the minced garlic and continue to cook for a minute or two. Divide the asparagus between two plates and keep warm.*

*With the heat on medium, place the two eggs in the same pan and cook until the white is no longer opaque and the yolk is set. While cooking, sprinkle with the salt and pepper.*

*Place an egg on top of each pile of asparagus and sprinkle with the shaved Parmesan and bread crumbs.*

*Note: Place the bread crumbs in a nonstick skillet over low to medium heat and stir for a minute or two till golden brown.*

Courtesy of the author

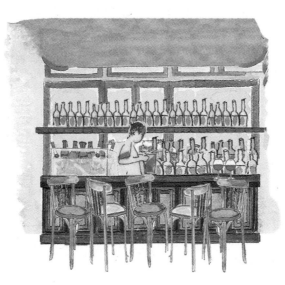

# Appendices

# Appendix A: Eateries by Cuisine

## American

Banning's Pie Shop, 161
Clyde Common, 20
Compote Cafe and Bakery, 44
Doug Fir Lounge, 46
Equinox, 118
Fat City Cafe, 21
Gilt Club, 103
Huber's, 27
Imperial, 27
Jamison, 105
Noble Rot, 57
Noisette, 108
Nora's Table, 149
Observatory, 58
Original, The, 58
Paragon, 110
Petisco, 86
Red Hills Market, 177
Roost, 61
Roseanne's Cafe, 136
Scratch, 156
Tasty n Alder, 32
Toast, 67

Trillium Cafe, 149
Verdict Bar and Grill, The, 159
Walnut City Kitchen, 177
Woodsman Tavern, 68

## Arabian

Levant, 53

## Argentinean

Ox, 85

## Asian

Baowry, 117
Boke Bowl, 39
Departures Restaurant, 20
Stickers, 63

## Asian Fusion

Saucebox, 31
Smallwares, 89

## Bakery

Crema, 45

## German
Gruner, 23
Spints, 89

## Greek
Mad Greek Deli, 55

## Hawaiian
Ate-oh-Ate, 37

## Healthy
Laughing Planet, 119
Proper Eats Market and Cafe, 125

## Hot Dogs/Sausages
Michael's Italian Beef & Sausage
   Co., 56

## Ice Cream
Prince Puckler's, 141

## Indian
Bollywood Theatre, 78
Swagat, 152

## Italian
A Cena, 36
Accanto, 35
Ava Genes, 37
Bar Mingo, 98
Cafe Allora, 100
Caffe Mingo, 98
Ciao Vito, 79

Coppia, 101
Decarli, 133
DOC, 80
Fulio's Pastaria, 135
Genoa, 49
Gilda's, 22
La Perla, 140
Luce, 55
Nel Centro, 29
Nostrana, 57
Piazza Italia, 111
Three Doors Down, 67

## Izakaya
Biwa, 39
Tanuki, 65
Yakuza, 93

## Japanese
Kaze, 148
Syun, 153
Yakuza, 93

## Korean
Nakwon, 133

## Lebanese
Ya Hala, 69

## Lunch
Lily Day Cafe, 54
Off the Waffle, 140

La Perla, 140
Lovely's Fifty Fifty, 120
Mean Street Pizza, 161
Mi Famiglia, 158
Mississippi Pizza, 121

## Polish
Bar Dobre, 38

## Polynesian
Trader Vic's, 114

## Pub Food
Fort George Brewery & Public
    House, 134
Fulton Pub, 22
Pause Kitchen and Bar, 124

## Sandwiches
Bunk Bar, 41
Bunk Sandwiches, 90
Lovejoy, 108
Meat Cheese Bread, 55
Monkey Subs, 133
Shut Up and Eat, 62

## Seafood
Bridgewater Bistro, 134
Chart House, 19
Eat An Oyster Bar, 118
Fishwife, 119
Jakes Famous Crawfish, 27

Parish, The, 110
Roe, 60
Salty's on the Columbia, 88
Silver Salmon Grille, 136

## Southern Soul
Irving Street Kitchen, 104
Papa's Soul Food Kitchen, 141

## Spanish
Ración, 31

## Speakeasy
Sapphire Hotel, The, 62

## Steak House
Daily Grill, 20
Huckleberry West, 152
Laurelhurst Market, 52
Ringside West, 112
Urban Farmer, 32

## Sushi
Masu Sushi, 29
Saburo, 61
Sushiville, 91
Yuzu, 137
Zilla Sake House, 94

## Swedish
Broder, 40

# Appendix B: Dishes, Specialty Stores & Producers

# Appendix C: Best of List

This is a quick look section to find the best of the most popular categories of PDX food favorites. I will list the best places to go for burgers, pizza, bakeries, brewpubs, brunch, happy hours, late night snacks, and ice cream and frozen yogurt. The list could be pages and pages; however, I am going to try to keep each category to around ten of each. Wish me luck!

## Bakeries

Where there is coffee there are baked goods. And where there is great coffee, there are great baked goods. I love that there are so many places to get a good croissant, muffins, cakes, pies—Portland has it all. Some homey, some fancy, some made with flour, some no flour at all. Many wonderful choices for every style and palate.

**Baker and Spice,** 6330 SW Capitol Hwy., Portland, OR 97239; (503) 244-7573; bakerandspicebakery.com

**Bakeshop,** 5351 NE Sandy Blvd., Portland, OR 97213; (503) 946-8884; bakeshoppdx.com

**Fleur De Lis,** 3930 NE Hancock St., Portland, OR 97212; (503) 459-4887; fleurdelisbakery.com

**Grand Central Bakery,** too many to list, look 'em up; grandcentralbakery.com

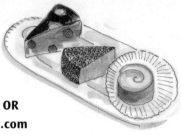

**Jade,** 7912 SE 13th Ave., Portland, OR 97202; (503) 477-8985; jadeportland.com

**Kens Artisan Bakery,** 338 NW 21st Ave., Portland, OR 97209; (503) 248-2202; kensartisan.com

**Little T American Baker,** 2600 SE Division St., Portland, OR 97202; (503) 238-3458; littletbaker.com

**Lovejoy Bakers,** 939 NW 10th Ave., Portland, OR 97209; (503) 208-3113; lovejoybakers.com

**Nuvrei,** 404 NW 10th Ave., Portland, OR 97209; (503) 972-1700; nuvrei.com

**Pearl Bakery,** 102 NW 9th Ave., Portland, OR 97209; (503) 827-0910; pearlbakery.com

**St. Honore,** 2335 NW Thurman St., Portland, OR 97210; (503) 445-4342; 315 1st St., Lake Oswego, OR 97034; (503) 445-1379; sainthonorebakery.com

# Best Late Night

It's always great to find places that are open late and have great food, drink, and service. All these spots are well visited by just regular folks, and often you will find a chef chilling out after a day behind the range.

**Bistro Montage,** 301 SE Morrison St., Portland, OR 97214; (503) 234-1324; montageportland.com

**Biwa,** 215 SE 9th St., Portland, OR 97214; (503) 239-8830; biwa restaurant.com

**Cartopia,** SE 12th and Hawthorne Blvd., Portland, OR 97214; facebook.com/pagesCartopia-Portlands-Food-Cart-Revolution/ 128371747213969

**Gilt Club,** 306 NW Broadway, Portland, OR 97209; (503) 222-4458; giltclub.com

**Le Happy,** 1011 NW 16th Ave., Portland, OR 97209; (503) 226-1258; lehappy.com

**Luc Lac Vietnamese,** 835 SW 2nd Ave., Portland, OR 97204; (503) 222-0047; luclackitchen.com

**Original Hot Cake House,** 1002 SE Powell Blvd., Portland, OR 97202; (503) 236-7402; hotcakehouse.com

**Rum Club,** 720 SE Sandy Blvd., Portland, OR 97214; (503) 467-2469; rumclubpdx.com

**Victory Bar,** 3652 SE Division St., Portland, OR 97202; (503) 236-8755; thevictorybar.com

I have never lived in a place that is so breakfast and brunch crazy. People wait on lines and seem happy to be there. There are lots of good choices, and it's hard to make a decision about where to go.

**Arleta,** 5513 SE 72nd Ave., Portland, OR 97206; arletalibrary.com

**Blue Hour,** 250 NW 13th Ave., Portland, OR 97210; (503) 226-3394; bluehouronline.com

**Fat City Cafe,** 7820 SW Capitol Hwy., Portland, OR 97219; (503) 245-5457; fatcitycafe.net

**Irving Street Kitchen,** 701 NW 13th St., Portland, OR 97209; (503) 343-9440; irvingstreetkitchen.com

**Mother's Bistro and Bar,** 212 SW Stark St., Portland, OR 97204; (503) 464-1122; mothersbistro.com

**Roost,** 1403 SE Belmont St., Portland, OR 97214; (971) 544-7136; roostpdx.com

**Salty's,** 3839 NE Marine Dr., Portland, OR 97211; (503) 288-4444; saltys.com/portland

**Screen Door,** 2337 SE Burnside St., Portland, OR 97214; (503) 542-0880; screendoorrestaurant .com

**Simpatica,** 828 SE Ash St., Portland, OR 97214; (503) 235-1600; simpaticapdx.com

**Tasty n Sons,** 3808 N. Williams Ave, Portland, OR 97212; (503) 621-1400; tastyntasty.com

# Brewpubs

I am not sure where the term beervana started, but it should end here. Just about everyone over the drinking age, and I am guessing a few younger, loves the pretty spectacular beer scene here in Portland. All kinds, although Portlanders seem to favor the hoppy IPA, you can drink beer with any meal and no one will bat an eye. So far there is only one beer for me, and that can be had at their tasting room in Hillsboro or in spots around town. Vertigo, vanilla porter. Mmm mmm good.

**Alameda,** 4765 NE Fremont St., Portland, OR 97213; (503) 460-9025; alamedabrewhouse.com

**Amnesia Brewing,** 832 N. Beech St., Portland, OR 97227; (503) 281-7708; amnesiabrews.com

**Breakside Brewery,** 820 NE Dekum St., Portland, OR 97211; 5821 SE International Way, Milwaukie, OR 97222; (503) 719-6475; breakside.com

**Burnside Brewing,** 701 SE Burnside St., Portland, OR 97214; (503) 946-815; burnsidebrewco.com

**Green Dragon,** 928 SE 9th Ave., Portland, OR 97214; (503) 517-0660; pdxgreendragon.com

**Horse Brass,** 4534 SE Belmont St., Portland, OR 97215; (503) 232-2202; horsebrass.com

 **Hub (Hopworks Urban Brewery),** 2944 SE Powell Blvd., Portland, OR 97202; (503) 232-4677; hopworksbeer.com

**Kells Brew Pub,** 210 NW 21st Ave., Portland, OR 97209; (503) 719-7175; kellsbrewpub.com

**Lucky Labrador Brewing Company,** 915 SE Hawthorne Blvd., Portland, OR 97214; (503) 236-3555; luckylab.com

**Lucky Labrador Tap Room,** 1700 N. Killingsworth St., Portland, OR 97217; (503) 505-9511; luckylab.com

**Saravesa Bottle Shop and Pasty Tavern,** 1004 N. Killingsworth St., Portland, OR 97217; (503) 206-4252; saravesa.com

**Victory Bar,** 3652 SE Division St., Portland, OR 97202; (503) 236-8755; thevictorybar.com

**Widmer Gasthaus,** 955 N. Russell St., Portland, OR 97227; (503) 281-3333; widmerbrothers.com

# Burgers

From "down and dirty" burgers to sophisticated, gourmet burgers, Portland runs the gamut. I love a griddled burger, old-fashioned and tasty, but never would pass up a burger that has been grilled, inside or out. I have come to like lots of things on my burger (unless I am in the car, where it needs to be easy to eat and not spill all over my clothing)—an egg, cheese, fried onion, raw onion, pork belly, and bacon, and am open to lots of sauces too. I love a burger. Too many burgers, so little time.

**Castagna Burger,** 1752 SE Hawthorne Blvd., Portland, OR 97214; (503) 231-7373; castagnarestaurant.com

**Foster Burger,** 5339 SE Foster Rd., Portland, OR 97206; (503) 775-2077; fosterburger.com

**Gruner,** 527 SW 12th Ave., Portland, OR 97205; (503) 241-7163; grunerpdx.com

**Killer Burger,** 4644 NE Sandy Blvd., Portland, OR 97213; (971) 544-7521; 8728 SE 17th, Portland, OR 97202; (503) 841-5906; killer burgerpdx.com

**Little Big Burger,** 122 NW 10th Ave., Portland, OR 97209; (503) 274-9008; 3747 N. Mississippi Ave., Portland, OR 97227; (503) 265-8781; 3810 SE Division St., Portland, OR 97202; (503) 841-6456; littlebigburger.com

**Little Bird,** 219 SW 6th Ave., Portland, OR 97204; (503) 688-5952; littlebirdbistro.com

**Roost,** 1403 SE Belmont St., Portland, OR 97214; (971) 544-7136; roostpdx.com

**Slow Bar,** 533 SE Grand Ave., Portland, OR 97214; (503) 230-7767; slowbar.net

**Stanich's,** 4915 NE Fremont St., Portland, OR 97213; (503) 281-2322; stanichs.com

**Sunshine Tavern Burger,** 3111 SE Division St., Portland, OR 97202; (503) 688-1750; sun shinepdx.com

**Tasty n Sons,** 3808 N. Williams Ave., Portland, OR 97212; (503) 621-1400; tastyntasty.com

**Yakuza,** 5411 NE 30th Ave., Portland, OR 97211; (503) 450-0893; yakuzalounge.com

## Coffee

A book about Portland without a coffee section is like a day without sunshine. Oops, Portland has lots of days without sunshine, which most probably is a reason for the vast array of great coffee and interesting coffee shops dotted, quite plentifully, around town. The impres-sive coffee shops are places to gather, to write, to read, and  to just watch. And on the wet, kind of dreary days, coffee shops and their talented baristas create taste and art and are just the jolt you need to keep on keeping on. Trust me, I know. These are the best of the best.

**Albina Press,** 4637 N Albina Ave., Portland, OR 97217; (503) 974-6584

**Barista,** 1725 NE Alberta St., Portland, OR 97211; 539 NW 13th Ave., Portland, OR 97217; baristapdx.com

**Case Study Coffee,** 5347 NE Sandy Blvd., Portland, OR 97213; (503) 477-8221; casestudycoffee.com

**Coava Coffee Roasters,** 1300 SE Grand Ave., Portland, OR 97214; (503) 894-8134; coavacoffee.com

**Courier Coffee Roasters,** 923 SW Oak St., Portland, OR 97205; (503) 545-6444; couriercoffeeroasters.com

**Extracto Coffeehouse,** 2921 NE Killingsworth St., Portland, OR 97211; extractocoffee.com

**Familia,** 811 NW 13th Ave., Portland, OR 97209; (503) 719-6605; familyroast.com

**Heart Coffee Roasters,** 2211 E. Burnside St., Portland, OR 97214; (503) 206-6602; heartroasters.com

**Ristretto Roasters,** 555 NE Couch St., Portland, OR 97232, (503) 284-6767; 2181 NW Nicolai St., in the Schoolhouse Electric Building, Portland, OR 97210, (503).227.2866; 3808 N Williams Ave., Portland, OR 97227, (503) 288-8667

**Singer Hill Cafe,** 623 7th St., Oregon City, OR 97045; (503) 656-5252; singerhill.com

**Stumptown,** 128 SW 3rd Ave., Portland, OR 97204, (503) 295-6144; 3356 SE Belmont St., Portland, OR 97214, (503) 232-8889; 1026 SW Stark St., Portland, OR 97205, (503) 224-9060; 4525 SE Division St, Portland, OR 97206, (503) 230-7702; 100 SE Salmon St., Portland, OR 97214, (503) 467-4123; stumptowncoffee.com

**Umbria,** 303 NW 12th Ave., Portland, OR 97209; (503) 241-5300; cafeumbria.com

**Water Avenue Coffee,** 1028 SE Water Ave., Portland, OR 97214; (503) 808-7083; wateravenuecoffee.com

**Woodlawn Coffee and Pastry,** 808 NE Dekum St., Portland, OR 97211; (503) 954-2412; woodlawncoffee.com

# Frozen Stuff

Even in the rain Portlanders wait in line to get some frozen goodness. Ice cream and seasonal are now a pair, so much so that in the fall one of the top shops had 6 apple flavors. I went for the chocolate, but that's just me. Both ice cream and frozen yogurt are hot, and new shops are opening all the time. And there is yummy soft serve at Sunshine Tavern.

**Cool Moon Ice Cream Co,** 1105 NW Johnson St., Portland, OR 97209; (503) 224-2021; coolmoonicecream.com

**Fifty Licks,** 4265 SE Belmont St., Portland, OR 97215; (954) 294-8868; fifty-licks.com

**Lovely's Fifty Fifty,** 4039 N. Mississippi Ave., Portland, OR 97227; (503) 281-4060; lovelysfiftyfifty.com

**Ruby Jewel,** 3713 N. Mississippi Ave., Portland, OR 97227; (503) 505-9314; 428 SW 12th Ave., Portland, OR 97205; (971) 271-8895; rubyjewel.net

**Salt & Straw,** 2035 NE Alberta St., Portland, OR 97211; (503) 208-3867; 836 NW 23rd Ave., Portland, OR 97210; (971) 271-8168; saltand straw.com

**Sunshine Tavern,** 3111 SE Division St., Portland, OR 97202; (503) 688-1750; sunshine pdx.com

**What's The Scoop?,** 3540 N. Williams Ave., Portland, OR 97227; (971) 266-178; whatsthescooppdx.com

Happy hour is a great way to try a restaurant without paying high prices. There are happy hours before and after regular dinner hours, and if you can make the times work it is an awesome way to go. See below for a cocktail recipe from one our top picks, Rum Club.

**Andina,** 1314 NW Glisan St., Portland, OR 97209; (503) 228-9535; andinarestaurant.com

**Clyde Common,** 1014 SW Stark St., Portland, OR 97205; (503) 228-3333; clydecommon.com

**The Observatory,** 8115 SE Stark St., Portland, OR 97215; (503) 445-6284; theobservatorypdx.com

**The Old Gold,** 2105 N. Killingsworth St., Portland, OR 97217; (503) 894-8937; theoldgoldpdx.com

## RUM CLUB DAIQUIRI

This is a strong and delicious drink. Do drink it, but don't drive. It's potent.

(Serves 1)
2 ounces aged rum (Bacardi 8)
¾ ounce lime juice
½ ounce (1 tablespoon) 2 to 1 Demerara syrup (unrefined sugar)
¼ ounce (1½ teaspoons) maraschino liquor
2 dashes angostura bitters
5 drops absinthe
Shake with ice and strain into a cup.

**Pints,** 412 NW 5th Ave., Portland, OR 97209; (503) 564-2739; pintsbrewing.com

**Rum Club,** 720 SE Sandy Blvd., Portland, OR 97214; (503) 467-2469; rumclubpdx.com

**Slow Bar,** 533 SE Grand Ave., Portland, OR 97214; (503) 230-7767; slowbar.net

**St. Jack,** 2039 SE. Clinton St., Portland, OR 97202; (503) 360-1281; stjackpdx.com

**Tasty n Sons,** 3808 N. Williams Ave., Portland, OR 97212; (503) 621-1400; tastyntasty.com

## Pizza

Pizzas you don't wanna miss. And pizza is big in PDX, from the thick, crunchy, and divine crust at Dove Vivi to the paper-thin crust at Ken's and Apizza Scholls, you can easily find excellent pizza in Portland.

**Apizza Scholls,** 4741 SE Hawthorne Blvd., Portland, OR 97215; (503) 233-1286; apizzascholls.com

**Caffe Mingo,** 807 NW 21st Ave., Portland, OR 97209; (503) 226-4646; caffemingonw.com

**Dove Vivi,** 2727 NE Glisan St., Portland, OR 97232; (503) 239-4444; dovevivipizza.com

**Escape from NY,** 622 NW 23rd Ave., Portland, OR 97210; (503) 227-5423; escapefromnewyorkpizza.com

**Firehouse,** 711 NE Dekum St., Portland, OR 97211; (503) 954-1702; firehousepdx.com

**Hot Lips,** visit hotlipspizza.com for locations

**Ken's Artisan,** 304 SE 28th Ave., Portland, OR 97214; (503) 517-9951; 338 NW 21st Ave., Portland, OR 97209; (503) 248-2202; kensartisan.com

**Nostrana,** 1401 SE Morrison St., Portland, OR 97214; (503) 234-2427; nostrana.com

**Pizza Depokos,** 2730 N. Killingsworth St., Portland, OR 97217; (503) 247-7499; pizza depokos.blogspot.com

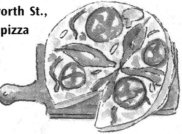

**Sunshine,** 3111 SE Division St., Portland, OR 97202; (503) 688-1750; sunshinepdx.com

# Appendix D:
# A Cooking Class
# at Ya Hala

For the last few months I have been writing recipes and covering food interest stories for Oregon Public Broadcasting, which has been a tremendous experience. Recently, I covered a cooking class that was fascinating to watch and added some terrific recipes to my repertoire. Here they are.

Mirna Attar is the chef and owner of the Montavilla neighborhood restaurant **Ya Hala** (see p. 69). Her menu offers Lebanese food that you might eat in someone's home, rather than the more standard fare. With the known health benefits of the Mediterranean diet, Attar is constantly being asked to teach a class on how to make some of her favorites—and I recently had the opportunity to check it out. The class was super fun. Attar and members of her family set up a classroom, and folks got to pitch in and then sit for a wonderful meal. Attar cooks and runs the kitchen, as well as oversees the prepared food at her family's other business, Barbur World Foods, a spectacular place to shop. Barbur has fresh almonds during the season; before the shells get too hard to eat, buy a pound and eat them, whole, dipped in coarse salt.

# Lamb Kabobs

*(Makes 8 skewers)*

2½ pounds boneless leg of
lamb, cut into 2-inch
cubes

½ cup vegetable oil

2 teaspoons 7-spice blend
(see Note 1)

1 teaspoon minced garlic

1 bunch fresh mint leaves
(1½ cups), finely chopped

1½ teaspoons salt

1 white onion cut into bite-size
chunks

1 red bell pepper cut into bite-
size chunks

*In a large bowl, combine the meat, oil, 7-spice blend, garlic, mint, and salt. Cover and refrigerate for at least 1 hour or up to 2 days.*

*Soak 8 bamboo skewers in cold water for 1 hour. Preheat grill to high (see Note 2). Thread the meat, onions, and peppers onto the skewers, making sure not to overcrowd the meat (if it is too tightly packed, the kebabs won't cook evenly).*

*Place skewers on the grill and cook until meat is medium-rare, about 4 minutes per side. Allow kebabs to rest for 5 to 10 minutes.*

*Note 1: Available in Mediterranean food stores.*

*Note 2: To check grill temperature, count the seconds you can hold your hand, palm side down, 2 to 3 inches above the rack, until it feels uncomfortable: 2 seconds for hot.*

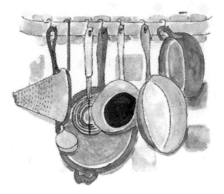

# Fattoush (Tomato and Pita Bread Salad)

(Serves 8)

2 rounds pita bread, split
   horizontally
3 tablespoons fresh lemon
   juice
¼ cup extra-virgin olive oil
1 red bell pepper, cut into ½-
   inch strips
1 small English (hothouse)
   cucumber, thinly sliced
4 radishes, thinly sliced

4 green onions, thinly sliced
2 large tomatoes, cored and
   cut into 1-inch wedges
1 cup chopped fresh Italian
   (flat-leaf) parsley
½ cup chopped fresh mint
1 teaspoon salt
1 tablespoon sumac
1 large bunch purslane, or ½
   head romaine lettuce

Preheat oven to 350°F. Place the pita bread on a baking sheet and toast until golden and crisp, 10–15 minutes. Set aside to cool. Break into 1-inch pieces and set aside.

In a large serving bowl, whisk the lemon juice and olive oil together until blended. To the bowl add the bell pepper, cucumber, radishes, green onions, tomatoes, parsley, mint, salt, and sumac and toss to combine. Immediately before serving, cut the purslane into bite-size pieces or cut the lettuce crosswise into thin ribbons.

Cut the ribbons into 2-inch pieces. Add the purslane or lettuce and pita pieces to the bowl, toss with the other ingredients, and serve immediately.

# Hummus

(Makes 2½ cups)

1 cup dry garbanzo beans
7 cups water (for cooking
   beans)
1 teaspoon baking soda
1½ teaspoons salt

½ teaspoon minced garlic
¼ cup tahini
½ cup fresh lemon juice
Olive oil

Rinse the garbanzo beans, drain, and cover with water to cover by 3 inches. Soak beans for 4–6 hours. Drain in a colander and rinse thoroughly.

In a large pot combine soaked beans, 7 cups water, and the baking soda. Bring to a boil, reduce heat, and simmer until the beans are falling apart, about 1 hour. Stir any foam that comes to the surface back into the beans while they cook. Pour beans and any remaining cooking liquid into a large bowl and cool to room temperature in the refrigerator.

Transfer beans and liquid to a food processor. Add the salt, garlic, tahini, and lemon juice and process until smooth. If the mixture is too thick (it should be the consistency of thick cream), add water 1 tablespoon at a time until the hummus is smooth. Transfer to a medium serving bowl. Drizzle with olive oil.

# Fatayer (Spinach Pies)

(Makes 25 pieces)

1 pound spinach leaves
1 cup finely diced onions
1 cup olive oil
1 teaspoon salt

¼ cup sumac
½ cup fresh squeezed lemon juice
3 pounds store-bought pizza dough

Preheat the oven to 450°F and mix all the ingredients (except the pizza dough) together.

Roll the pizza dough with a dough roller to ¼ inch thick. Use a round cookie cutter to cut the dough into circles of 6 inches in diameter.

Scoop 2½ tablespoons of the mixed ingredients into the middle of each circle and close it up in a triangle shape.

Oil a baking tray and place the spinach pies on it, leaving 2 inches between them.

Let them cool and serve at room temperature.

# Moujadra (Lentil Pilaf)

(Serves 6)

| | |
|---|---|
| 2 cups brown lentils | 1 cup corn oil |
| 8 cups water | 2 cups diced onions |
| 1 teaspoon salt | 2 teaspoons salt |
| 1 teaspoon cumin | 1½ cups basmati rice |
| ½ cup corn oil | 5 cups sliced onions |

Cook the brown lentils, water, salt, cumin, and ½ cup corn oil in a pot until lentils are tender but not smashed.

Heat the rest of the corn oil in a pan and add the onions and salt. Cook until the onions are golden, then add them to the lentils. Add the rice and cover and simmer for 20 minutes, then keep it covered with no heat for 10 minutes.

For garnish, deep-fry 5 cups of sliced onions until crispy and place them on top of the moujadra.

# Shaibeyet

(Serves 6–8)

### For the rose water syrup:

| | |
|---|---|
| 1 cup water | 2 tablespoons fresh-squeezed lemon juice |
| 2 cups sugar | 4 tablespoons rose syrup |

### For the cream:

| | |
|---|---|
| 2 cups heavy cream | ½ cup cornstarch |
| 2 cups whole milk | 4 tablespoons rose water syrup |
| ½ cup sugar | |

### For the dough:

| | |
|---|---|
| 1 package phyllo dough | 5 tablespoons ground pistachios |
| 3 sticks unsalted butter | |

**To make the syrup:** *In a medium saucepan, boil water, sugar, and fresh-squeezed lemon juice. Add the rose syrup.*

*Cook on medium until the mixture thickens and develops a yellow tint. Turn off heat.*

*Place in the refrigerator until it is very cold, approximately 2 hours.*

**To make the cream:** *Mix all the ingredients for the cream together until the starch is completely dissolved.*

*In a medium saucepan, cook the mixture on medium heat until the cream thickens.*

*Pour the mixture into a shallow bowl and cover with wax paper. Place it in the refrigerator for about 2 hours.*

*Heat the oven to 350°F.*

**To make the dough:** *Unroll the phyllo dough and lay flat on the table. Separate one layer of phyllo dough (a very thin piece) and lay it flat on the table. Fold it in half lengthwise, then fold it in half again.*

*Place ½ tablespoon of the cream centered, about 2 inches from the bottom of the dough. Fold the right corner over the cream and lay it flat on the opposite side. This should create a triangle shape. Take the remaining left corner and fold upward. The left corner should still be on the left side of the dough. Take the left corner again and fold it to the right. Continue this pattern until you reach the end of the dough.*

*Melt 3 sticks of butter and place in a medium size bowl. Dip each piece of the folded Shaibeyet into the melted butter. Place on a cookie sheet 2½ inches apart.*

*Bake on the middle rack of the preheated oven until golden brown, approximately 15–20 minutes.*

*Place directly onto your serving dish and drizzle the cold rose water syrup over it. Garnish with the ground pistachio nuts.*

# Index